Praise for #1 b

"We love a missing person suspense saga and *The Expat Wife* delivers. It's like a Switzerland vacation on the page. This riveting journey took us to Lucerne and had us glued to the page."
—Addison McKnight, author of *An Imperfect Plan*

"The story is filled with intrigue and nail-biting thrills. The twists and turns provided more than enough suspense to keep me on the edge of my seat...The characters were authentic and relatable. The story was superbly written and had me guessing until the end."
—Readers' Favorite

"An unputdownable psychological thriller that'll have you reading long into the night. I loved this book—the dynamics between the characters makes this an addictive read."
—BookGirlBrown_Reviews

Hargrove is a master at keeping us as confused and questioning as her protagonist...Then, when all became clear, it was most unexpected. Hargrove's clever use of dialogue is as skillful as her beautiful descriptions of settings and the creation of credible characters. Couple those style elements with her ability to keep us in suspense for over 300 pages, and you know why Courtney Hargrove is a number one best-selling author." **—Readers' Favorite**

THE EXPAT WIFE

Courtney Hargrove

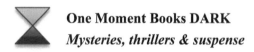

One Moment Books DARK
Mysteries, thrillers & suspense

For Lucerne. I'm glad I knew you.

CHAPTER
ONE

He did it. The posh Englishman with the cheeky grin killed his wife.

In the last gasp of the blue hour, minutes before sunrise, I can see enough in the pink light climbing the horizon to decide this is not a man broken by grief.

Peter Pewter-Browne is loose and relaxed as he sees his daughter off to school on the front stoop of his chalet. He slides a miniature backpack onto her shoulders with steady hands, and I catch a flash of white teeth as he smiles at something she's said.

The little girl shrugs to get the fit right, and Peter, still grinning, ruffles the top of her blonde head.

As if everything is normal. As if his wife, president of the Expat Social Club and stay-at-home-mom extraordinaire Jacqueline Pewter-Browne, didn't vanish two days ago.

Peter is immaculately turned out in pressed trousers and a salmon shirt, which is a red flag in itself and warrants a note scribbled clumsily with my gloved hand: *Why is he going to work today?*

A gust of wind kicks up a sheet of white from a snow bank next to my car, and it whooshes across my windshield like a dancing, curling ghost, obscuring my view. When the flakes settle, I get a fix on the pair again.

Peter would make a fetching WANTED poster. He is a modern-day incarnation of Hugh Grant in *Four Weddings and a Funeral,* a one-dimensional character with a full head of sandy brown hair and an adorable stutter at the right moments. Like Hugh, Peter has the charmingly crooked front teeth of a man raised with the relaxed ethos of British dentistry.

Here comes the sun. The dark blue sky has brightened in a matter of seconds, fading to gray and making way for pinks and oranges and yellows, and I can see the pair well enough in the new light.

A lock of sandy hair flops in Peter's eye as he crouches to kiss his daughter goodbye, then straightens up and waves her off to school, ever the proud father.

The husband is always the prime suspect for good reason: He probably did it. I figured this out early in my journalism career, right around the time I learned the value of trusting my instincts.

Instead of mourning his loss or god forbid *looking* for Jacqueline, Peter is embracing the festive season. The Pewter-Browne home, now one woman down, glows like a set in a gauzy Christmas movie.

Fresh powder lines the chalet like icing on a gingerbread house, windows twinkle with fairy lights, and a tasteful wooden reindeer reposes on the snow-covered lawn next to a pudgy snowman with twig arms and a carrot nose. Behind them, distant Alps lick the sky with whipped-cream peaks.

Jacqueline's burnt-orange Porsche SUV is still parked in the drive.

They say she disappeared without it. Or did she? What if she's still here? Is she in the house right now, taking a break from reality, never actually gone after all? What I wouldn't give for X-ray vision.

I can't rule anything out, not this early, not with the scant information I have.

I sit up taller, lean over the pleather-wrapped steering wheel.

A figure has appeared in the doorway behind Peter.

I'm too far away and now half-blinded by early morning rays shooting over Mount Pilatus to make out the shape of the person's features, but she's a woman—and she's not tall, willowy or dark-haired like Jacqueline.

A petite blonde with the long, flowing locks of a cartoon princess is inside Peter Pewter-Browne's home in the early hours. If I didn't know better, I'd say she's wearing men's boxer shorts.

I need binoculars. I have no idea where to buy *binoculars* in Lucerne. I don't know how to *say* binoculars in Swiss German, but if I did, and I bought a pair, Wesley would be onto me immediately: *You promised to let this go.*

It wouldn't do for Wesley Blackwood's wife to rise with the sun, leave him snoring in bed, slip out the door for a "hike," then park herself behind an SUV down the street from said husband's work colleague.

Peter's on the move. He throws one last pointless wave in his daughter's direction, turns away, and steps inside.

I hear a familiar call from above. I check the sky and see the raven is here again, circling, painting a dark smear on a cerulean canvas. He's been shadowing me as I track a murderer, which makes us both a cliché. I first noticed him after the snows came, when this calm Swiss canton grew uniformly, softly quiet as if the world was padded with cotton.

I'm about to press the ignition button when Peter steps outside again. I dive into the passenger's seat. Has he seen me?

Does it matter? Our car is as generic as it gets around here—a BMW in Charcoal Metallic. I'm puffed out in a down-alternative coat, fleece hat, and thick scarf. I could be anyone.

I jolt at the rapid *caw, caw* of the raven's angry calls, but I stay down. I know it couldn't be the same bird following me wherever I go, but it might as well be; they're all the same at a great height.

I was assigned to read Poe too young, in sixth grade, and the man's work made my skin crawl and my stomach lurch so violently that I had to be excused to go to the bathroom. *Nevermore* lived in my head for years, became a mantra squawked in my nightmares by various imaginary fiends. I never looked at ravens the same again.

I take a risk and slowly inch my way back up to a seated position. Peter and the woman are indoors now. The acid in my otherwise empty stomach rises in my throat, and I force it back down with one fierce swallow.

I'm afraid I'm responsible for all of this. Jacqueline came to me for help before she disappeared, and I listened, and I did nothing.

I make a note of the time and jot down my last observations, then drive away. I pass Peter's daughter, watch her meet up with her friends on the corner, none of them older than five or six, a slow-moving flock of innocents out in the open.

The first time I saw children walking alone in Lucerne I made a move to guard them until the cops could race to the scene. Where I'm from—Manhattan by way of Seagrass Cove, Massachusetts—the sight of tiny humans walking the streets unsupervised demands a frantic call to Child Protective Services.

But the handler assigned to Wesley by his new company, who was about to show us our new house, rolled her eyes at the hardened American from the crime-ridden dystopia.

Lucerne is the safest place on Earth. Every new expat freaks out when they see the children walking to school alone. Nothing bad ever happens here. Trust me.

Trust me. That is the reporter's siren call, a seductive song that draws us in and compels us to question every word the person says after *trust me.*

I check the time, then step on the gas. Wesley needs the car to get to work.

From our garage at street level, it's thirty-eight stairs to our front door and another eight from the foyer to the living room. Everything on our side of the valley is built into a hill, which I expect will be great for my glutes in the long run.

I bound up the concrete stairs, and by "bound" I mean haul my ass with great effort and burning lungs.

When I make it to the top, I catch a quick movement in my peripheral vision. I glance right to see a finger disappear and a calico curtain falling, its hem left swishing, betraying the spy behind it in the window.

Wesley and I share these thirty-eight stairs with people who live in an identical house across the stonework landing. On the hillside between us are slim concrete indentations built into the earth to aid with drainage during rainstorms, and the neighbors have chosen to use their side as a display case for an odd assortment of decorative plates.

They are painted, glazed or embossed with suns bearing human faces in various moods: gurning, grinning, angry, sweet. They come in colors from a garish yellow to dark blue to sparkling gold.

Today I notice some new designs, including a pentagram, a giant eye, and an upside-down triangle.

I don't usually spend time examining the plates for fear the neighbors will catch me. I don't know what they look like or how many of them there are. They never stopped by with a cobbler or a fondue or whatever Swiss people make to welcome new people, but then again, we didn't visit them with an apple pie.

The more I pass by this display the creepier it becomes. It's eerie, like clutter from a paranormal hoarding case.

I head into our house and lug myself up the last eight stairs.

"Hi," I call out at the top, my voice echoing in the double living room. The floor is laid with square cream tiles I loathed at first. I complained that they made the place look like a giant bathroom until I learned their purpose is to warm your feet in winter. All our floors are heated, and now I can never go back to cold tiles.

"In here," my husband calls from our en-suite at the far end of the home.

I pass our other two full baths to get to him, and peek in to see him shaving, towel around his waist, blond hair wet and slicked back so it appears brown.

"How was your hike?"

"Stunning, as always," I reply. "I'll never get sick of staring at Mount Pilatus. It's our very own Alp, and I adore it."

"Huh." He turns away from the mirror and raises his eyebrows. "That's interesting. I didn't think there were any hiking trails near the Pewter-Brownes's house."

CHAPTER

TWO

I don't want to know how my husband figured out what I've been up to this morning; every scenario annoys or sickens me. Him spying on me. Peter having caught me and reporting back. Wesley reading my mind.

"I don't have the faintest clue what you're talking about," I reply.

Wesley sighs and goes back to shaving. I watch him as the razor cuts a path through the cream, and I'm hit with the urge to lick it off him.

"That said, hypothetically speaking," I prod with a lightness that surprises even me, "how would you know where I was? You having me followed?"

He tilts his head and looks at the ceiling to sweep the last strokes on his neck.

I wait until he finishes, then hand him a towel.

"Swiss dealerships." He turns and faces me. "It's a GPS tracking app. They have everything. It came with the car."

He leans down and pecks me on the lips. "I know it doesn't jive with your feminist philosophy, but the stalking goes both ways. You'll always know where I am, too. We'll never be truly free as long as we share that car."

I smack him on the butt as he walks out, distracting myself so I don't scream that it's *jibe*, not *jive*, because it causes me physical pain when he screws up his vocabulary and his idioms. A three-hundred-grand Yale education with a minor in English and the guy still says "for all intensive purposes."

I wasn't aware of this before I moved in with him in New York two months ago; if I had, it might've been a deal breaker. I tried calling him out on his misuse of the English language, but after he accused me of being a pedant and a bore I abandoned all hope of educating him. There was a lot I didn't know about Wesley, even on the day we married in a small—miniscule, really—wedding at New York's City Hall last month.

He sidles past me and races off to dress. I watch him go and wonder as I often do what it would be like to be *that* objectively good-looking.

Wesley is an eleven on the hotness scale. If you take Westley from *The Princess Bride* and Paul Newman when he was young and throw in a dash of Chris Evans, you get my Wesley.

Our coupling was unnatural and against the order of things in the tradition of New York City dating. Him: ostensibly dull hedge funder, extremely attractive, family money, wears Armani, dates models, lives in a TriBeCa duplex. Me: prematurely pessimistic reporter making five figures, lives in Brooklyn with two roommates, no family or money to speak of, cuts own hair, wears H&M. When we met, he was wining and dining billionaires on Wall Street. I was getting spat on by a white supremacist at Rikers while reporting a news story.

I head back to the kitchen and set the French press for myself. Wesley likes to get his coffee in town. It's a whole new world after Manhattan's overpriced chains and darling craft coffee shops with long lines and brambly man-buns that always made me want to reach for the wasp spray. In Switzerland, the coffee is amazing everywhere: it's as good in the train station kiosks as in the finest Bäckerei-Konditorei.

I pull my notebook out of my waistband as I wait for the coffee to steep. The first few pages contain remnants of reporting on my last article before I quit my job at *Newsline*, scribblings about a mom fighting for clean water in the Bronx projects, but no one would listen to her, even after my investigation appeared in our pages. The story got buried under breaking news about a YouTube star's love triangle.

The next pages are blank, and then, hidden in the back, I locate my Jacqueline Pewter-Browne notes.

I've been fighting every instinct and desire to contact the *Polizei*. I have been told in the strongest terms that I mustn't butt in.

Let the community handle it their way, Wesley warned. *We're new. You don't know what you don't know.*

And how. I've never felt so hamstrung. I was born asking questions, and then it became a career, and now my husband is telling me to fade into the background and swim against my every instinct.

I lean on the counter and add today's events to the timeline: *Dec. 10: Jac's husband acting happy with very young woman (nanny?) early a.m.*

Wesley's Italian wingtips *click-clack* on the tiles as he strides down the hall toward the kitchen. I shove the notebook down my pants.

"What are you up to today?" He throws a glance to the coffee.

The question I predicted and dreaded before we left New York comes every day now. I'm "up to" being a stay-at-home TV watcher living off my husband, is the correct answer, and the shame of indolence engulfs me again.

"Studying," I say, same as I do every day. "I'm trying to come up with some freelance options back home, but no one's looking for a Lucerne correspondent who only speaks English."

"Hey." He comes close and takes me by the shoulders. "I know that look. Your B Permit doesn't *allow* you to work here legally. No one's holding that against you. Take all the time you need. Write that book you talked about. Sign up for those online private investigator classes. I make more than enough money to support us both."

The income chasm between us comes up frequently. I'm here following his dream, but somehow *I* feel like the lazy tagalong. He ripped me away from my job and my career and I'm the one apologizing.

"I'll take the car, yes?" He asks, shooting a meaningful frown at the Breitling his boss gave him when the ink dried on his contract with The Group.

That was the plan, but suddenly I don't want to be stuck alone on this hill without wheels.

"I need to pick up some things at Coop. I'll drive you."

When I pull up at The Group's glass-front office building on the banks of Lake Lucerne, Wesley leans over, kisses me, then opens the passenger door.

"What were you doing there?" he asks. "What were you hoping to find?"

A confession blurted into crisp winter air, a voluntary reckoning on a snowy lawn, a body carried out wrapped in a shag rug. I got none of that, because evil doesn't always announce itself.

"I…I needed to see Peter for myself," I reply. "See the house. Maybe I thought Jacqueline was still around, that she had come back. I don't know. I'm *worried* about her, Wesley."

"Do me a favor and stay out of the Pewter-Browne business. Let it go. For me."

He waits for me to assure him, so I give him my best version of the truth.

"I promised I'd stay under the radar and wouldn't ruffle any feathers, and I meant it."

The clichés roll off my tongue in a word soup of good intentions and platitudes I hope will calm him.

"I know you will," he assures me. "I'm only asking you to back off because I *honestly* believe Peter when he says his wife took off on her own. She does things like that."

He steps out of the car, and I've lost him to the work day ahead.

Maybe there's some wisdom in what he's saying. I just got here, I don't know these people or their ways or their history.

As Wesley reminded me the day I heard Jacqueline was missing after I asked who was calling the police, who was monitoring Swiss social media and who was putting up flyers, his company invested tens of thousands of francs in bringing us here, sorting our visas, paying his signing bonus. That comes with a price tag of its own: discretion and good behavior.

I pass two idling *Polizei* cars as I pull away. I want to flag them down and tell them everything. I want to go to the Lucerne Special Victims Unit and set them on the case.

I'm not *sure* Jacqueline's dead, but I'd bet the BMW on it. Still, if there's even a slight chance she's out there and needs rescuing, I won't be able to live with myself if I do nothing to try and get to her.

The guilt is gnawing at me. She was clearly unnerved when she came to me for help, but she resisted telling me the whole story and I chose not to push her. She was a new friend, my first in Lucerne, and I figured she would share everything in her own time. That was the wrong move, as it happened. There *was* no time.

I drive along the lakeside, distracted by the majesty of Lake Lucerne with its sharp bends and turns and cinematic backdrop, and I think how starkly it clashes with the ugliness of Jacqueline's disappearance.

This wasn't how it was supposed to go.

Wesley used the force of his charm, aided and abetted by food and alcohol, to lure me into the life of an expatriate.

I walked into the kitchen of our TriBeCa duplex after work, exhausted from another day of arguing with my editors, wanting only to tear my bra off and sink into the sofa, and before I could say hello Wesley was handing me a glass of Lafite Bordeaux blanc.

He kissed me on the cheek and took my bag.

I pulled out a stool and drank my wine while he went back to stirring his grandmother's secret sauce, and I watched it bubble like angry blood, releasing the occasional spray of hot liquefied tomato as he told me about the job offer.

That was the first time I'd seen him cook. In the one month we'd lived together I'd occasionally whip up a platter of my signature vegetarian tacos or a Caesar salad with homemade dressing, but most nights we'd order in or grab sushi and black cod at Nobu.

"Switzerland," Wesley said as he sprinkled in fresh oregano from the farmer's market we stopped at the weekend before, "is the Holy Grail for expats. It's the most beautiful, wealthy and well-ordered country you can be assigned to. This isn't *Dubai*. You can literally fly back here for the weekend anytime you want."

I swiveled ever so slightly, nervously, on his vintage stool at the granite island, and I thought about it for five seconds before I came up with my answer: *No.*

Switzerland, I thought in that moment, probably *is* perfection for my new live-in boyfriend, who is also beautiful, wealthy and "well-ordered."

"I can't leave New York for pastures and hills and yodeling. I'm claustrophobic just thinking about it," I said.

"Fear of open spaces isn't claustrophobia," he replied. "That's agoraphobia. You wouldn't have time to be afraid with how stunning it is there." Every once in a while he gets the big words right.

My father used to say the same thing about the Gloucester Bay and the Ipswich dunes and the Essex clam flats where he made a living. But Seagrass Cove and everything around it was too open, too desolate, a literal ocean of nothingness I could never grip onto or locate myself in. I would claw at the air and find nothing, and I always felt like I was in danger of disappearing like a wisp of cloud in an infinite sky.

New York woke me up. I could get lost and fade into the crowd in a way you can't in a small town, and I made a life for myself here. After graduating from the University of Massachusetts, I battled my way to a solid journalism career, first with an unpaid internship I couldn't afford and then a permalance gig with night shifts and no benefits.

It took five years to obtain a full-time reporting job with wild luxuries like dental insurance and sick leave, and I wasn't about to trade the media hub of the world for cows and remote mountain ranges.

"Switzerland is inconsequential. There's no culture or movement. I'll wilt," I said. "I'll fade away. I don't even ski. Did you know that about me? I don't ski."

I listened to his pitch as he served us linguine a la Wesley and poured more wine. He hammered home what I'd be gaining, and what a move abroad would do to enrich and expand my life.

After I'd spooned up my last drop of red sauce, he cleared the plates, washed his hands, and opened the briefcase on the far end of the island.

"Here's the offer," he said, setting a sheaf of papers next to my white wine. "You'd be free of those listicles and 'regurgitation pieces' you complain about."

It was a battle I fought every day. I demanded my editors let me investigate stories that could change the world for even one person, to let me help stop negligent landlords, unstick backlogged rape kits, highlight the need for foster families in New York.

And most days my bosses would remind me my salary was paid by the day's hashtags. *If it trends, it's your friend. Do the investigations on your own time.*

Wesley pressed harder. "No more walkups. No more galley kitchen or roaches. No more belching five a.m. garbage trucks."

I would've jumped at London or Paris, glamorous locales with flashy little cars and intriguing, trench-coat wearing people going cool places on the Tube and literati on the left bank sipping Aperol spritzes and absinthe. This quiet, landlocked country Wesley spoke of was not in the plan.

"The package is incredible," he said.

I scanned the contract, whose author had helpfully bolded the perks. This company, identified only as "The Group," was offering Wesley a salary in the high six figures plus bonuses, a company car, relocation costs, and a furniture allowance. The company would pay our rent as long as we lived there. For someone of my modest means, it was an over-the-top, revoltingly lavish package.

"Did it occur to you this could be too good to be true? I mean, who even are these people? *The Group?* It's not a name, it's a noun."

"Always the investigator," Wesley smiled. "One of these days I'm going to cure you of your cynicism. They call it TIG for short. It's un-Googleable. Try it—you'll see. I know who they are, and I assure you they're legit. They need people who do what I do. They need my particular set of skills."

I smiled along with him; it was funny because his skills were a dime a dozen where we lived. He managed risk, he invested rich people's money, he helped run a hedge fund. I didn't feel the need to dig too deep into what specific talent any of that actually required.

He still had his apron on. He knelt on the floor and gazed up at me. "Say yes. Say you'll come."

The writer in me wanted to remain employed, but the reporter in me wanted to experience life in a way I was never meant to. My mother always said, like a worn-out character in a bad movie, that I had zero chance of getting out of Seagrass Cove because I came out average and always would be.

I said it out loud before my mind was made up. "Yes. OK. I'll go."

"Thank god," Wesley breathed, and he was so genuinely relieved it made me believe, in a hot instant, that I was making the right decision.

Our story was unusual, and I loved us for that. This dramatic move after knowing each other for three months was one more leap we'd make together, damn what anyone else thought of how fast our relationship was progressing.

I told myself anyone can get a job at Buzzfeed or *Newsline*. How many people find themselves in the middle of an epic love story and get whisked to Europe for the adventure of a lifetime?

CHAPTER
THREE

Five days before the vanishing

I paw through my bare closet in search of a classy dress for tonight's gala. What do expatriated wives wear to a formal affair at a casino in the fifth-largest city in Switzerland?

I have three options. In my defense, we had two weeks to clear out of our Manhattan duplex, and I was allowed a grand total of two bags with which to launch my new life. The rest of our belongings are on a slow boat from New York.

I select a dress I know my husband will approve of, a black number that's not too short and shows no cleavage, but has a slim V dipping down far enough to show a teasing bit of breastbone. Sexy but classy.

My husband is guilty of being basic on certain topics. His philosophy is *Ogle my wife if you must, but treat her like a lady—or else.*

He's actually said that before, like he's Victorian nobility, not Westport new-ish banking money.

I dress quickly, then wobble out to the living room in the one pair of high heels I brought, scowling at my phone as I search the app store.

"I can't find it." I look up to see Wesley waiting at the top of the stairs that lead down to the front door. "There's no Uber or Lyft or *any* ride share. Think I have to search in Swiss German? Or French?"

Wesley jangles the BMW keys like a piece of jewelry, like he was born holding them. "I'll drive. My new colleagues will be there—I'm not going to overdo it on the cocktails. Neither should you."

I ignore that and keep searching. "No Uber? What's next— no Doordash? I'm going to want Swiss Uber at some point. Help me find it."

"There's no Uber in Lucerne, Rose. We're going to be late."

He cocks his head and inspects me.

"You look good," he says.

Good? I am stung. My gut is speaking to me the way it has since I was a child, communicating the most basic of warnings: *Something is rotten in the state of Denmark.*

Yes, my gut speaks Shakespeare, and it is telling me my new husband should be sprinkling more superlative terms on me like magic dust. *Beautiful, pretty* or even *hot* would've been nice, especially for a pair of newlyweds. Then again, I have no idea if that's how it works in real life. I've never seen a healthy marriage up close. One month into our union and I'm still guessing at what's normal.

He's checking me out. "Although…isn't that necklace a little chunky for that dress? I'm seeing something a bit more…delicate."

I'm seeing something more red, myself; maybe a scarlet slash across his cheek with the antique diamond on my ring finger. But I don't want to fight.

"I'll go change," I say.

"Hurry."

As Wesley guides the car around a bend on the shoreline, I catch sight of the casino, a white palace with grand columns and wide stairs taking up a stretch of precious lakefront real estate. We've landed in a fairytale by moving to Switzerland, though I've yet to discover if it's Grimm's or Mother Goose.

Moonlight dances on the surface of placid Lake Lucerne and rows of gingerbread houses, spires and steeples loom behind it in Old Town like ghostly guardians. The frontage screams Germanic roots, but the town itself is a mishmash of architectural styles.

"What's the history here, I wonder," I say, half to myself. "Is it baroque, renaissance, gothic?" I remember a few things from art history class in college.

Wesley pats my knee. "Fascinating question. Why not research it? It'll give you something to do this winter."

I say nothing. I have things to do, even if he doesn't want to hear about any of it. I let out a long, airy yawn that brings a glossy sheen to my eyes. No one talks about the jetlag when you move abroad. No one tells you your sleep will be so fitful, so uneven, it'll be like you've lost any sense of time. They don't warn you your body will betray you at three a.m. and won't let you fall into a slumber no matter how tired you are. That there is no such thing as catching up on sleep.

He pulls into the casino entrance behind four others waiting for valet service, and I notice our shiny BMW is a sporty, snazzy outcast in a line of Porsche SUVs.

Inside, everything is red and gold and chandeliers drip with crystals. The elevator deposits us directly into a cocktail reception humming with polite chatter and clinking glass, with many of the guests bellied up to a long, lit-up bar overlooking the casino floor below.

A man with floppy light-brown hair catches sight of us and cuts through the crowd like a surfboard through a wave, grinning, showing one crooked tooth and a deep dimple.

"Wesley, old chap! Good to see you, mate." The man backslaps my husband with one hand and holds out the other, and they shake.

"Great turnout," Wesley observes.

"Always is. This is the most important event on the Club's social calendar. Fundraising for refugees and sick kids and all that."

"Rose," Wesley turns to me. "This is Peter Pewter-Browne, a VP at The Group."

Peter eyes me up.

"So this is the missus," he says. "Pleasure to meet you. You're as lovely as Wesley and Jacqueline said."

He leans in. I go for the hug, twisting my neck and tilting my head toward his shoulder at the exact moment he attempts a light kiss on my cheek and hits my neck instead. I start to pull away, but he goes for a kiss on the second cheek. *Shit.* This is Europe. Two kisses—*always two kisses in Europe.*

I pull away, smiling, pretending it never happened. "It's great to—"

And then he plants the third kiss and I slam my head into his mouth.

It's a shit show. I can feel Wesley cringing beside me.

Peter lays two fingers on his lip, checks for blood, then pastes that grin back on.

"Everything's different in Switzerland. You'll catch on, darling," Peter says smoothly.

"It's three kisses," Wesley whispers in my ear.

I know. I keep forgetting.

"Everyone's here," Peter says to my husband. "You and I are off to put in some face time with Werner Fiat. Our CEO runs TIG from Monte Carlo and attends one social club event a year, so this is your chance to make sure he remembers who you are."

Peter makes a move to drag my husband toward a white-haired man holding court in the center of the party, but before he can, Jacqueline glides over to us.

"Rose, how lovely to see you," she purrs. "I'm so glad you're here. I want to introduce you to the others. They're going to adore you as much as I do." She leans in. *One, two, three.*

Her ankle-length jade dress fits her like couture, her hair rests in jet-black perfection to her shoulders, and her makeup is so flawless I can't tell if she's wearing any.

Jacqueline turns to my husband. "You must be Wesley. You're going to fit into the Club perfectly. We're going to have so much fun."

She turns to Peter. "Darling, excuse us, won't you?"

Jacqueline is my best friend in Switzerland, by virtue of being my only friend. Peter coaxed my new Swiss mobile number out of Wesley when he started work at TIG a week ago, and

Jacqueline called me the next day.

When the unfamiliar number lit up my phone, I was wandering around our sparsely furnished living room overthinking everything, panicking, checking the price of flights back home, running through a list of reasons I was going to fail at expat life. At wife life.

"This is Jacqueline Pewter-Browne. I'm your person," she announced when I answered, thinking it was my first Swiss spam call. "I'm going to show you everything and introduce you to everyone."

Jacqueline invited me for macchiatos by the river, and I learned she was born and raised in Hong Kong, has two young children, and is married to Peter, a posh, Cambridge-educated Englishman.

We wind through the party and land on a collision course with a tray of sparkling prosecco. Jacqueline selects two flutes from the tray and hands one to me. She takes a long swig, and I follow suit.

She swallows, then points to a group of women fifteen feet away. "Time for a crash course in your new best friends."

She lifts one arm, points, and then quickly lowers it. She rubs her shoulder, still holding the glass of bubbly. "*Ouch.*" She winces.

"You OK?"

"Oh, yes, of course." She reaches out to give my forearm a reassuring squeeze, and when she does, I see two finger-tip-sized bruises on the inside of her upper arm. "It's nothing."

It's not "nothing," and my first thought goes to her charming husband and what he might be like behind closed doors, but I stop myself from stewing on it and making assumptions. Jacqueline skis, plays tennis and has two presumably rambunctious young kids. She drinks. Any of the above can cause bruising on all sorts of body parts.

She uses her prosecco-holding arm to point to three women across the room.

"See the one with the natural blonde hair and an arse like she came off the Swedish bikini team? That's Nova Norton. She's married to Brett, a transplanted Texan."

I can see the woman's profile. She's shorter than the women she's with, is softly curvy, and she's rocking a silver dress.

"She actually *was* on the Swedish bikini team," Jacqueline giggles. "Well, the surfing team, actually, until she met Brett and gave it all up to move here."

I drain my prosecco in two more sips—the pours are stingy, in my defense—and look out for a server.

"The model type next to her is Seychelle von Verling, nee Windsor. She's English and South African—you'll find there are a lot of dual citizens around here. Terribly polite, terribly charming, terribly clever. If you let her, she'll pry your life story out of your cold dead hands and tell you absolutely *nothing* about herself. She's married to Kristoff, who's on the TIG board and is minor Liechtenstein royalty."

I'm unclear exactly where Liechtenstein is on the map, so I make a mental note to look it up later.

Seychelle is facing away from me, so my first glimpse of her is dark hair pulled back in one long braid that drips down her skin through a path left by her backless red dress.

Jacqueline points to the third woman, who has an athlete's build and bouncy brown curls. "The tall one in white is Heidi Mallick. She's American, from Ohio, has two young children, and is married to Raj, who's a senior VP at TIG."

I'll never remember all of that, but I try to at least lock in their first names.

"I know," Jacqueline smiles, laying a hand on my forearm. "It's a lot. But we're all going to be great friends, I promise."

Ding, ding, ding. The room echoes with the delicate tinkle of silverware tapping crystal.

"Distinguished guests," a man booms in a thick German accent, "please be seated. Dinner is served."

Jacqueline says, "I'll meet you at our table. I have to say goodnight to the children. I haven't missed a bedtime kiss yet, and I don't intend to start now."

She slips off to make the call, and I go looking for my place in a sea of white tables.

CHAPTER

FOUR

I find my place card between Seychelle and a ruddy-faced man in black tie with his jacket undone, showing the shirt underneath straining at the buttons.

Seychelle extends one bejeweled hand, drapes it on my shoulder, and leans in for some kissing. *One, two, three.*

"Seychelle von Verling. Pleased," she says as we pull apart.

I take my seat and mouth a hello to my husband seated across the table between Heidi and Nova. He winks back, then resumes chatting. Jacqueline returns and takes her seat.

Servers descend with bottles of red and white wine, and I choose the Fendant, a Swiss white I've never heard of. It's slightly sweet and comes with the slightest, almost imperceptible fizz that tickles my tongue.

When everyone has their drinks, Peter raises a glass and calls out over the din, "Friends, I'd like to welcome our newest potential members, Wesley and Rose Blackwood. Shall we proceed with introductions?"

One by one the eight of them reel off their names and their affiliations—Brett is the man next to me, the Texan married to

26

Nova, the Swede—and I absorb as many details as I can. The four men all work with Wesley at TIG.

A white-gloved server deposits an urn of creamy, steaming soup in front of me, then holds a grinder over it and shaves off some fresh nutmeg.

"Gruyere soup," Seychelle informs me. "I hope you like cheese. The Swiss put it in everything. They'd put it in coffee if they could."

"I don't know," I shrug. "A cheddar latte sounds refreshing."

I am rewarded with a throaty laugh that makes everyone look up from their first courses. It hits me that not one person at our table has their phone out. No one's texting, Tweeting, doomscrolling, or showing off photos of their cats or kids. Have I landed in utopia?

Brett turns to me. "Switzerland's a great place to raise kids. You'd better get on it, you two. What are you, mid-thirties? Tick tock," he bellows, then slurps some soup and winces.

I hope it burned his taste buds off.

Wesley hears this. His eyes have gone cold, but I don't know if others can see when he does this, or if it's only me, because I live with him, and I see all the changing moods that announce themselves in his hazel eyes.

I'm thirty-two. Not that it's Brett's business.

"I've got plenty to keep me busy," I say.

"Oh? What do you do?" Seychelle asks.

"I'm a journalist. I *was*. I worked for *Newsline*. It's fairly new in the States—"

"I love *Newsline*!" Heidi says. "I get all my updates from back home there. I'm addicted to the celebrity channel."

"Did I hear Wesley say you're studying, as well?" Kristoff,

who I recall is Seychelle's minor-royal husband, asks me.

"I'm looking into getting my private investigator's license," I reply. "I miss working, but I can at least start the process of becoming qualified online."

Brett narrows his eyes and leans back to regard me as if I've announced I'm one of the shape-shifting lizard people.

"Why would you want to *work*? It's illegal for a reason. Embrace it."

I must remember to congratulate Wesley. Not only did he fly us first class from New York, but he also performed the neat trick of time travel. Apparently we've landed in the 1950s.

Seychelle flits her hand as if to wave my aspirations away.

"You won't need those skills in this town," she says. "It's the safest place on the planet."

"Everyone has secrets," I say. "You'd be surprised."

Kristoff shakes his head. "You've come to the safest place there is," he says. "Nothing bad ever happens in Lucerne."

So I keep hearing.

Dinner is slow-roasted veal in a rich brown gravy, and since I don't eat baby animals, I'm forced to put in some time moving food around on my plate.

"You're going to love it here," Raj says between bites. "Skiing at Christmas, expat Thanksgivings—"

"The annual New Year's ski trip to Zermatt," Seychelle breathes. "*So* good for the soul."

"That's all fun, of course," Jacqueline takes over from her husband in a whispery voice that draws everyone's attention. "But *Fasnacht* will give you a real taste of Swiss culture. If you're still around in February, you're going to see something that will change you forever."

"Oh, don't," Seychelle frowns. "I loathe that time of year. It's positively ghastly."

"What *is* it?" Wesley asks.

Heidi says, "It's utter debauchery. It starts with a parade and turns into a carnival from your nightmares. It's about sacrifice, and about keeping the demons away. It's the chaos before Lent."

"Find someone to hold your hand at Fasnacht," Jacqueline warns.

"It's a night of unwanted pregnancies," Peter adds wryly. "The Swiss go on a shagging spree."

"The *masks*," Nova winces.

"The drums." Kristoff takes a bite of veal.

"The marching and the *robes*," Heidi says.

Seychelle shivers. "It's very loud."

"You will be truly alive for the first time. You will have electricity coursing through your veins in a way you've never felt before. If you make it to February, you're in for a life-changing experience," Brett confirms.

"*If* we make it to February?" I prod. He's the second person to say that tonight.

Everyone at the table is staring at their meat or exchanging glances.

"You know expats," Brett replies after a moment. "Notoriously transient. Never in one place for long."

"Look at Lars and Lara," Heidi gestures with her wine glass. "They up and left after less than a year. Just *vamoosed* one day with the kids. Said it wasn't for them."

Brett's face flashes with anger so fast you'd miss it if you weren't trying to read him, weren't already examining his every expression. I flit my eyes over to his wife, and sure enough Nova sends Brett a "calm down or else" glare.

"Switzerland's not for everyone," he says lightly, stabbing a chunk of baby cow with his fork. "Sometimes people just up and disappear if it's not a good fit."

"And thank god for that," Seychelle says, raising a glass. "Self-selection means this place will always belong to the ones who appreciate it. We wouldn't want everyone knowing about our secret utopia."

"To our Eden," everyone agrees, and we clink glasses across the table.

I make a bathroom run before dessert, and Heidi joins me. As I wash my hands, swipe on some lip gloss and check my teeth, Heidi frowns at her reflection and scrunches her chestnut curls with both hands.

I jump when a stall door flies open and smacks into the wall with a sharp bang and a woman bursts out.

"Rose, right?" She inquires as she joins us at the sinks, her voice bouncing off the tiles. "Get out while you can. If you let the Real Housewives of Lucerne suck you in, you'll never get away. They won't let you."

She washes her hands with a furious lather, up her palms and past her wrists as if preparing for surgery.

The woman has short lilac-colored hair and is wearing an embroidered maxi-dress and multiple earrings on each ear. She tears off a towel and dries off.

Heidi turns away from her reflection and rolls her eyes at the woman. "Oh, Teresa. Don't be dramatic. You're in the club too. Just because you—"

"Because I what? I don't bow to the great Jacqueline, or I have an actual job and earn my own money, or I don't fit in with your high school clique? Or because I see through all of you?"

"*Teresa.*" Heidi's eyes are wide, blinking fast. "You're embarrassing yourself in front of our newest member."

Teresa throws me a knowing look—*I see you. You're not one of them either*—and that makes me shiver in a way her purposely melodramatic warning did not.

"*Potential* member," she says to Heidi, then turns to me. "You still have a chance to save yourself. Don't say you weren't warned."

Teresa does a Groucho with her eyebrows and exits.

"Ignore her. She's a glorified secretary at TIG. You'll rarely run into her," Heidi advises me. "She has to *work*."

She grabs the door handle. "Trust me, Rose. You will never have a better friend than an expat friend. We take care of our own."

After dessert and coffee, there is dancing and more drinking, at which point Wesley and I discover we're objects of fascination to many of the Expat Social Club members. Everyone seems to know who we are, and we field inquiries throughout the final hours of the gala.

I learn the Club is fifty years old and has about 150 members from twelve countries, though all of them address us in English. Everyone lives in the Canton of Lucerne, but many members commute to work in Zug or Zurich, and most of those appear to work for banks, consulting firms or pharmaceutical companies.

My mouth goes dry answering all their questions, and by night's end my face hurts from smiling.

The odd encounter with Teresa in the bathroom is soon relegated to a blip, a joke, an easily forgotten aside during an otherwise joyful evening.

When we arrive home, Wesley takes the stairs two at a time while I lag behind, dragging myself up, drunk, exhausted, in pain from shoe straps digging into my heels.

When I reach the top, he is examining the assortment of plates, metal and ceramic, covering the neighbors' side of the hill.

"These people are so fucking odd," he says when he hears me behind him. He stares at the plates as if he wants to wipe them away like a stain. "I wonder if there's anything we can do. Someone we can complain to."

I catch my breath and say through huffing and puffing, "It's their country. We should embrace their customs."

He sighs, shrugs, and heads to our front door. We step inside and trudge up the last eight stairs to the living room, at which point he swings a left into the kitchen and drops the car keys on the counter.

"One for the road?"

Wesley pulls out the last half-bottle of white from the fridge, grabs two glasses, and heads for the glass doors in the living room. He steps out onto the grand stone balcony that stretches far over the land below, like an outdoor living room.

A blast of frigid air roars in.

"A bit cold out there for a drink, isn't it?" I shiver.

"I want to do it outside," he says in that voice, with that look.

I follow him out, wincing in the cold, bracing for my bare skin to be exposed to the elements. I can't say no to Wesley.

CHAPTER

FIVE

Two days after the winter gala, I'm gathering up clothes to toss into the washer when I hear a series of progressive knocks: light, moderate, then hard.

I skitter down the warm tile stairs and press my ear against the door. I don't have a peephole. Furthermore, I do not have a chain lock, nor do I have a landline for the Swiss authorities to rapidly locate me should this be a brazen Swiss day burglar.

I start when another loud knock punches my ear.

I can't remember a Swiss hello, so I go with, "Hello?"

"*Grüezi*," comes a quiet female voice.

"Yes?"

"Rose, it's Jacqueline."

"Jacqueline!" *Ugh.* I'm in no state for guests.

I still don't know her well, her husband is senior to mine, and I'm in saggy flannel bottoms with flyaway hair and splotchy skin. My hands fly to my head and I swiftly re-do my disheveled topknot. I wrestle with the lock and the L-shaped handle on our heavy front door.

I fling it open to see Jacqueline holding her purse in front of her like a designer shield. Her light-blue factory distressed jeans fit like they were stitched on, and her laced black boots would make my New York friends jealous. Her pale pink silk top reveals a triangle of creamy skin at the neckline.

"I was just doing laundry," I say, smoothing down my plaid flannel bottoms with a splotch of yesterday's yogurt on the thigh. "I'm a bit underdressed for guests."

I don't think she even notices.

The three times I've met Jacqueline she's been confident, happy, brisk. Now I see fear in her eyes, and when I recall her stiff shoulder and bruised arm at the gala, I get a bad feeling.

"Hi, Jacqueline. I—"

"I'm sorry to drop by like this," she interrupts. "I was just in the neighborhood…"

No, she wasn't. There's nothing up on this hill for Jacqueline Pewter-Browne: no stores, no Club members, no restaurants. Just me. I'm now intrigued as well as embarrassed.

"Please—come in."

I lead her up to the living room, cold and barren with only a loveseat, a flimsy dining table and two stiff chairs TIG gave us in our expat starter kit. Jacqueline settles on the blue velour seat, and I angle a chair off to the side so it doesn't feel like I'm psychoanalyzing or interviewing her for a job.

"I'm surprised you don't have an elevator." She remains delicately breathless from our endless stairs.

An elevator? I don't have dental floss. I don't have *tampons.*

"I…" I didn't realize that was a thing. "I guess…we like the exercise."

Her eyes flit about some more to our airy, open, double-sized

35

living room waiting to be beautifully furnished, then land on our smaller kitchen around the corner.

"Our real furniture arrives in few weeks," I say. "Can I get you anything? Coffee? Water? Fanta?"

I don't have any Fanta, but I blurt things when I'm nervous.

"Thanks. I'll have a macchiato. Your espresso machine should have a setting for that."

"I…we don't have our espresso machine yet." Note to self: Buy an espresso machine.

"Oh. Tap water is fine."

"I don't have a filter…"

"It's Switzerland," she says. "The water's safe. No ice."

Good, because I don't have ice, either. Jacqueline is tightly wound, knees up, bag still protecting her, though from what I'm not sure.

I bring us two tap waters and take my seat. Finding no end table, Jacqueline uses her handbag as a tray and grips the glass like a talisman.

"Your place has an incredible view," she says. "How are you and Wesley doing with all these big changes? I remember being a newlywed. They tell you you're supposed to be in the honeymoon phase, but it's never *truly* easy, is it?"

I smile and nod, but take it as a rhetorical question and wait for her to tell me why she's here.

She glances out at the valley. The get-to-know-you small talk we engaged in by the river, at lunch, at the gala—it's all been dispensed with. She clearly has a secret, but something in her won't let her share it with me. The good news for both of us is I'm trained to pull answers out of people who don't want to talk.

"Jacqueline…is there something I can help you with?"

She meets my eyes. "Have you ever thought about what kind of person you are, Rose? I mean, *really* analyzed your character. Faced the things you've done and felt something, anything, about the people you've wronged?"

I am taken aback by her blunt questions, and I'm nowhere near able to answer them right now. I know I should respond in a way that won't get my husband in trouble.

Before I can say a word, she asks, "Do you want children soon? TIG loves it when you have kids. You get extra perks."

Wait, what? I try to imagine what the "perks" are for procreating on Swiss soil, but I don't ask. Part of me doesn't want to know.

"I'm not sure I want kids," I hedge.

I might adopt, someday, I hope. We'll see how the world turns. What Wesley thinks. We dated for only three months before tying the knot, and it never came up beyond idle, nebulous big-picture chit-chat.

Him: *We'd have adorable children.*

Me. *We would.* Hypothetically.

To her credit, Jacqueline does everything possible to hide her shock and horror at my ambivalence, but I see it in her face.

She clears her throat, then takes a sip of her room-temperature flat water in a mostly clean glass.

"I think someone's watching me," she says, sighing loudly as if she'd been holding her breath the whole time.

"Oh?"

Ideas tumble through my mind like clothes in a dryer: Watching her on the street? Watching her right now? Watching her when she sleeps?

"I feel eyes on me. I hear things…"

"You mean, like, someone is following you around town?" I prompt.

She shakes her head, holds out her glass as if looking for a place to set it, and I stand and take it, then set it down on the floor by my feet and face her again.

"It's in my house," she says, setting her hand free for a moment to gesture at me as if offering a gift. "I know it sounds ridiculous, but when I'm home I feel eyes on me even when no one's around."

"You don't mean *Peter*? Are we talking about hidden cameras, or…?"

"No, no, no," she shakes her head fast, as if I'm simply not getting it. I'm not, to be fair.

"Well…" I start gently. "I'd say the first step is to figure out who's regularly in the house. Who lives there, who has a key and the alarm code, who comes and goes without restriction?"

Jacqueline holds out her hand and counts out on four slender fingers: "Two live-in help, two children, and of course Peter. It's none of them, I'm sure of it."

"How can you be certain?"

"Because we've been in the same room when I hear it. It's a scratching sound sometimes, and occasionally a *thump*. It's not loud, mind you—at times it's subtle enough to make you feel like you're imagining things."

"Maybe it is mice. Or other animals burrowing in for winter," I suggest.

"With no droppings ever, no hair, no moving through the walls? With no smell? With no way in? The Swiss demand perfection. When they build into a hill, they use concrete. There is no room for holes or mistakes with them. They'd rather die than do it wrong."

She's holding something back. Maybe she's seeing ghosts. I wonder if there's something bigger going on, like a stalker, or if she fears a Swiss serial killer I haven't heard about.

"Have you mentioned it to Peter? Has he heard anything himself?"

"I…I did ask him about it, if he was hearing it too, but he told me I was overtired and imagining things. What he doesn't get is that I'm only overtired *because* of the noises. That's why I'm hoping you can look into it. I figured with your investigative experience…and after what happened to you when you first got here…maybe you have some insights."

I'm certain my face betrays my surprise and discomfort. How does she know what happened to me? And what does that have to do with her fear of being watched?

She seems to misread my confusion as reticence.

"I can pay you," she offers.

One hand crawls into her purse. I see knuckles imprinting in leather and then receding, and then she is still. Her hand remains in the bag.

Accepting money from my husband's boss's wife is a hard no.

"Oh, don't worry about that. Please." I wave her away. "I can poke around under the radar."

But no; she changes her mind in a flash. Something spooked her. I'm thinking it was the words "poke" and "radar."

"Oh, um…you know what? On second thought, forget I said anything. I was silly for telling you all this. I'm sure it's nothing."

She stands, and I follow suit. Her hand is still in her purse. After a few moments, her hand slides out slowly, and I see something hard and dark in her grip. It's a small book the size of an airport paperback, though slimmer. She stares at the cover, then extends a hand.

"Take it," she says. "We usually give it to expecting Club women, but I thought you should have a chance to see it. In case."

She doesn't trail off. *In case* is a full statement.

I take the book. I *am* expecting, anyway. I'm expecting my new life in Switzerland to continue to get weirder.

I run the pads of my fingers over the soft leather cover, feeling the grooves of gold-embossed calligraphy and noting the loosening binding. It has the aura and weathering of a personal diary, but it is a published book, an antique how-to titled *The Expatriate's Guide to the Secret Life of the Swiss*.

Not a very concise title, but what it lacks in brevity it makes up for in clarity.

"Thank you. I'll take good care of it."

"It's not urgent," Jacqueline says. "When you're curious, flip through it. It's been passed down to Club members since after the war. The early fifties, I think. It's a bit dense, but you might find it interesting. Careful with the binding, you know, since it's so old. And…maybe don't mention to the others I gave it to you just yet."

She gazes out the picture windows. "I should go."

"Of course. I'll see you out."

I lead her downstairs, open the door for her, raise my arm to wave her goodbye. She steps out, then turns back.

"The reason I came," she says, putting on a shaky smile, "was to invite you to a girls' night tomorrow at Nova's place. Bring your favorite wine. Seven-thirty."

"Sounds fun," I reply. "I'll be there."

"Remember," Jacqueline says again, "I came to tell you about girls' night." The wind blows dead leaves around her feet in a perfect circle. "Or maybe I didn't come here at all."

I make direct eye contact and nod to let her know I get it.

I close the door behind her and carry the book upstairs, almost afraid to open it.

I wonder if she realizes she shook me. *How did she know what happened when we first arrived here?*

CHAPTER
SIX

Wesley and I landed in Zurich on Thanksgiving Day. TIG sent a driver who took us straight to the Lucerne home the company had selected for us, where the BMW Wesley had ordered before we left New York was already in the garage.

We had a three-day honeymoon exploring Lucerne, kicking leaves along the cobblestones, inhaling autumn in a new place, Wesley hugging me to him when I shivered.

We regressed in tandem as we immersed ourselves in the culture and the language, taking turns pointing out dirty sounding German words like *Abfahrt* on bus stops; some version of *fahrt* was everywhere. Our instant favorite was *Kunstmuseum*. We circled the grand KKL center on Lake Lucerne's shoreline, saw the sign, and agreed to visit before the year was out.

I told Wesley I'd remind him every week until we actually went: *Have a good day at work, dear. Don't forget our upcoming visit to the Kunstmuseum.*

On the night before Wesley started work, we crossed the River Ruess over an ancient bridge, the famous *Kappelbruke*, landed at a waterside restaurant, and ate fondue with white wine and a kirsch digestif to untie the knot of cheese the waiter told us would clog up our insides if we didn't.

We wandered out after dinner, full and pleasantly tired, and came upon a plaza glowing with holiday lights hung on lampposts, in windows, on storefront archways. A violinist was rocking a tune that stole all the oxygen in the square. Locals and tourists alike surrounded her, drawn in.

Wesley was mesmerized. I lost him as I zipped up my coat; when I reached for him to warm my hands, he was gone.

I couldn't place the piece she was playing, but I think Wesley could. He walked like a zombie toward her, seeming to forget I was there.

I didn't realize I'd backed up to a darkened alley while avoiding the throng, and as I stood apart from the rest, I saw a figure moving toward me. They fast-walked around the arc of people, almost as if they were coming *at* me. I assumed they would swerve because I was well away from the crowd and there was room to move, but instead they barreled into my shoulder, pushing me down, grunting as they passed, a faceless and uncaring vessel with an oversized hood and a purposeful stride as they kept walking as if nothing had happened.

No one noticed me in the alley, on the ground, wincing, rubbing my elbow and checking my wrists where I'd broken my fall.

"Asshole!" I'd screamed out, the New Yorker in me revealing itself like a magician's rabbit springing out of a hat. I gingerly clambered to my feet. I scanned the crowd to see if Wesley was near, but I couldn't see him.

I turned back to the dark alley. The person must have heard my screaming expletives, because they were now barreling back toward me.

I opened my mouth to scream, but nothing came out, or maybe it did, but I couldn't hear it over the amplified violinist who was rocking out at full volume, and then my husband was suddenly, thankfully there, blocking me from danger, standing firm and tall.

Wesley faced the assailant down, and they stopped short, turned, and took off down the alley.

"That's right! Run, you coward!"

He turned to me, checking my face, my hands, my limbs.

"What the hell was that? You OK? Check your pockets. That's a thing in Europe, you know. They use distraction to make it easier to pick your pockets."

He squeezed me and held me to his chest. I felt tears welling up from the shock and the sting of my scraped hands. I didn't think the encounter was about stealing; it felt more like an attack meant to hurt. Someone wanted to be violent that night, and I was there.

Man, woman, monster, thief. I didn't know, and I didn't care. I wanted to forget it as soon as possible. We stopped for a quiet drink at Seebar by the lake, and soon, I did forget. I stuffed the memory of it down and buried it deep.

After Jacqueline leaves, I sit on the bed and examine the book. It's bound in a soft leather cover, and the edges of the pages are gold-tipped.

I flip through to find whatever she wanted me to see. She's

not wrong about its density. It's packed with walls of text in tiny type, printed, I presume, in the olden days for fresh-eyed readers who never spent hours staring at screens. It is full of abstruse language more likely to bore than inform, such as:

Should a person of excellent character and standing wish to confabulate inside the sacred domicile of a neighboring personage, they are advised prepare a small feast, a single pot of the finest offerings easily transported and shared. Ex: charcuterie or berry tart. Furthermore, a visitor shall don a habiliment worthy of such a visit, and appear scrubbed and trimmed without odor or foul breath.

Translation: if you want to visit your neighbor, brush your teeth and bring some food. I continue flipping but uncover no hidden messages. I fan the pages gently with the book upside-down, but no secret missives flutter out.

I read the table of contents. By far the most interesting section is Chapter Three, eerily titled *Understanding the Mess of Witches, Monsters and Folklore in the Swiss Culture.*

I also skim through Chapter Four, *A History of the Alps,* and find wordy descriptions of explorers and the strange formations and deep valleys they encountered, of gigantic boulders and impassible routes.

I consider the possibility I have read too much into Jacqueline loaning me the book.

I stash it in my closet, and as I get dressed to go grocery shopping, I think about how, in four years living and working in New York City, I had never once been assaulted or run down by a violent stranger.

Safest place on earth, indeed.

CHAPTER

SEVEN

Nova's house is a mile away from our place. When I arrive for girls' night, I'm surprised to find the wife of a bigwig at TIG has such a modest home, a modern ranch with lightly tinted picture windows.

I cradle a bottle of wine in the crook of my arm and ring the bell. Ten seconds later a young woman wearing no makeup, her brown hair drawn into a tight bun, opens the door.

"Grüezi."

"Grüezi," I smile. She doesn't. She gestures for me to come in, and I follow her to the kitchen.

Nova is wiping down a spotless countertop, her lips pursed with concentration and what appears to be some annoyance. "Ah, Rose. You're early. I'm almost done."

"Gorgeous granite," I say, trying to speak the language of the wealthy.

"Quartz. It's all *quartz* now." She fixes her eyes on me expectantly, as if she's waiting for me to start taking notes on Swiss interior design.

Nova runs her cloth over an invisible crumb, then reluctantly impales the fabric, moist and ghostly, on a platinum hook sticking out of her windowsill. She turns on the faucet and washes her hands, wipes them on a clean cloth and applies lavender moisturizing cream.

"Irina, would you set out the prosecco and the wines? I think three bottles of each will do for a start."

I didn't realize bun lady was still in the kitchen with us. She is standing in a corner, hands folded neatly above her crotch.

"Yes, Miss Nova."

"And can you get us both glasses of Fendant."

"Of course, ma'am," Irina replies, reaching around an aloe plant set against the backsplash to grab a smudged wine glass. "I'll get you a fresh one."

Nova opens a dishwasher and adds one lone, clean-looking coffee cup from the sink.

She clicks the door shut, reaches over, and opens another door.

"Is that a second dishwasher?" I'm realizing now how huge the kitchen is. How long this "ranch" is. The kitchen is ultra-modern, immaculate, and lined with matching chrome appliances.

Nova's face relaxes, and I can tell I am speaking her language; she's about to share the homemaking tip of a lifetime.

"Oh, yes. It was the best advice I ever got. Everyone said it during the design phase: 'Trust me, Nova, you're going to want two dishwashers.' I honestly don't know how I survived with *one* before we built this home."

"I can't imagine." *Act like this is normal, Rose.*

A cold glass of white wine appears in my hand. "Thank you," I call after Irina, who is already walking away.

I take a sip and instantly recognize that gorgeous, slightly fizzy wine from the gala, so I take another.

"It's a Fendant—a local wine." Nova notes my enthusiastic drinking. "You can get really good bottles for under ten francs. Don't be fooled. The price doesn't reflect the quality."

Nova moves us on, and I discover how naive I was to think this was a "modest ranch." It's a Tardis. I entered at the tip of the iceberg, with only the ground floor visible from the street. It is, like everything seems to be here, built into a hill, and the front of the house faces out to the valley with glass walls I imagine let sunlight flood in by day.

The overarching color scheme is dark, with walls painted with charcoal, gray and scarlet. Technology runs the home. I can see sensors and buttons blending in with the slate gray and dark charcoal walls and baseboards, and I get the distinct impression the house is watching and listening to me.

Nova leads me to the front of the home, away from the street, to a grand living room with a glass wall facing Pilatus. I stop and peek over, and I can see several floors below—it appears they have an infinity deck *and* an infinity pool.

"It's four floors," Nova informs me. "If you'd like the tour, I can take you down in the elevator later…"

She moves on and I follow her to the left wing on the street-level floor. She stops at a dark grey wall, raises her hand, and touches it with one delicate index finger.

"This," she says, "is our oasis. No children allowed."

The wall whirs as it slides open to reveal another gigantic living room that looks like an upmarket nightclub with grand picture windows.

There are deep velvet scoop chairs I could get lost in, a low sectional sofa, two love seats and scattered suede ottomans. Irina has laid out glasses on a long bar with underlighting, but I see no wine. Nova turns to me.

"You need a refill," she says.

She sits on one of the love seats and presses a button on the ottoman in front of her. The top slides off, revealing a built-in refrigerator filled with chilled wine bottles and a wine opener.

"There are two others, so anyone we're entertaining can reach a fresh bottle at any time. If Irina is otherwise occupied, of course," Nova says, gesturing around the room like we're on *Wheel of Fortune*.

She freezes, tilts her head to listen. "Here they come," she smiles, and puts on her hostess face while I take a long sip of my second drink.

I hang back as Nova, composed and relaxed, accepts three kisses and bottles of wine from a stream of guests, all of whom remember me.

"Hi, Rose."

"Rose! It's so great to see you again. We didn't get to talk much at the gala, but I'm Lisa." Or Julie. Or Emma. I think I might like it here.

There is a choreography of settling in. Platters of crudités and a charcuterie appear, someone unveils her homemade artichoke dip, and the sound of prosecco corks popping and wine pouring into glasses overtakes the room.

When the chatter reduces to a low roar and everyone has a seat, Nova and Heidi stand in front of us.

"Welcome, everyone! Put your magazines on the table and grab some scissors and glue sticks," Nova orders. "Everyone's sharing. A few of us collected some glossies in London last month, so we have all the best fashion and gossip mags, not to mention a few of you made a trip to Italy and brought back some *sumptuous* fashion books."

Irina, bun so tight it stretches the skin around her eyes, enters with a stack of unwieldy white cardboard.

Heidi clears her throat. "Irina is handing out your poster boards. Remember: If you can dream it, you can have it. You manifest what happens to you. *You're* in control."

Nova takes a board from Irina. "Can I manifest Brett being better in bed?"

There are a few hoots and giggles from the crowd, and Heidi winks. "You can," Heidi tells her. "If you ask the universe every single day. If you want it bad enough, you'll conjur it into existence."

"Oh, I want it bad," Nova insists. "He's barely touched me since Midas was born eighteen months ago."

"What *is* it about having kids that fucks up your sex life so badly?" Heidi shakes her head.

"Shush," Nova warns quietly, throwing a glance over my way.

"Oh, don't worry," I shrug. "Wesley and I aren't even trying yet."

Nova frowns at me with the fire of a thousand suns and makes the tiniest twitch of her head toward Seychelle, who's standing next to me. *Oops.*

"I'm *fine*," Seychelle says, dragging out *fiiiiine* so I know we've ventured into a sensitive area. "Kristoff and I have only been trying for eight months. It'll happen."

Heidi bites her lip as if all is lost. I don't get it. Eight months doesn't sound that long.

All is forgotten as the women grab scissors and glue sticks and find places to lay their poster boards, and I think seriously about bolting. After a minute, though, I accept my fate. In for a penny with the Real Expat Housewives of Lucerne, in for a pound.

I picture Vi's face when I tell my best friend back home that I went to a Vision Board Party, that my time-travel journey continues, and that this time I've walked into the year 2007. I fear they'll pull out a Ouija board next.

CHAPTER
EIGHT

I settle on the floor next to Seychelle and flip through a magazine.

"Is everyone here a member of the Expat Social Club?" I ask her.

"They are," she nods. "About a third of our members are affiliated with The Group in some way. Thank god for expats. The Club builds a real sense of community in a place that can be lonely for an outsider. You've probably already been Swissed."

Seychelle tears a page out of an Italian *Vogue*.

"It's certainly possible," I smile. "They've been quite welcoming, but I *have* had a few locals wag their fingers at me. One yelled at me in the Coop parking lot, but—"

"—but you have no idea what you did wrong," Nova pipes up from the next sofa. "You probably parked crooked. Were your wheels touching the line? They don't like that."

"And here I thought Switzerland was the nicest country in the world," I laugh.

Seychelle and Nova exchange glances so quick I would've missed it if it wasn't my literal job to notice everything. Or used to be my job.

"Has your stuff arrived yet?" Heidi scrunches up her face in concern.

I shake my head and swallow some Fendant, its subtle fizz tickling my throat.

"I didn't bring nearly enough for fall and winter," I confess. "I'm desperate for some cozy pants to bum around in. I saw some at the Bahnhof and I keep meaning to pop in and try them."

Heidi gazes with scorn upon my new friend Jacqueline.

"Have you taught her nothing?" She turns to me. "You go to Milan for clothes. *Milan*. Not the *Bahnhof*. Not the *train station*."

"And when it's time to get your hair done," Nova throws in, "you go to London for cut and color. There's a girl on Bond Street. She might take you if you call in advance. Call now."

"Yes," Heidi nods. "Call *now* for an appointment next month."

First of all, what the hell is wrong with my hair that they're so concerned about me getting an appointment immediately? And second: *London*?

I focus on my magazine and snip its crinkling pages, cutting out a woman's torso with rippled abs, a fat baby in a diaper, and a handsome couple holding hands. There you go, expats. Here's your dream, on paper, laid out by my own hand. I get it. I'm in.

Later, I try to find a bathroom, and wander far down the hallway in the opposite end of the house. I find nothing resembling a bathroom, so I make a guess on a slate-gray door. I feel along the wall for a button or a spring, then touch the door itself.

It slides open.

I let out a quick, sharp, involuntary scream when I see a face staring back at me.

It takes me a moment to realize the figure standing three inches from me is Irina, posture ramrod straight, staring ahead with blank eyes like a giant doll.

"Grüezi," she says.

"S-sorry," I mumble, and the door closes on its own.

I skitter away, now needing the bathroom more than ever and wondering what the hell kind of place I've walked into if Irina, a living, breathing human being, is kept in a cupboard.

I find a bathroom at the end of the hall. As I'm washing my hands and checking my teeth in the mirror, I'm trying to shake the image of Irina stuffed in a closet.

Everything's fine. I saw something normal and interpreted it incorrectly.

But did I? Irina, who'd been handing out wine not long ago, was stock-still in a space the size of a broom cupboard. My mind races to come up with possible explanations: was this a closet where she waits for orders? Is she kept out of sight while guests are around? What the hell is going on in this town?

Back in the living room, I survey my posterboard masterpiece, and hear Vi's voice in my head: *Get out while you can. Rip up that poster and LEAVE.*

A bunch of the women have finished, and they're starting to mix and mingle, relaxing on the sofas or congregating in Nova's futuristic kitchen.

I chat with Heidi over her famous artichoke dip, and when I've finished my latest glass of wine, I admit to myself I *have* to go find Irina. The curiosity is pecking at me like an angry bird.

Is Irina free to move about? Is she crated, like a dog? Is she a robot? Seriously: is she a robot? Everything else in this house is automated.

"This wine is going right through me," I say to Heidi. "Excuse me."

I set off in search of an elevator but find the stairs first, dark and hidden at the end of the first-floor hallway. I tiptoe down, worrying I'll run into the nanny or wake up the boys, because I have no viable reason to be here.

I make it safely down to the pool level on -4, where I am guessing the help lives.

I step lightly down the hallway lit with soft nightlights along the ceiling, and while I do not find Irina's cage, I freeze mid-stride when I hear voices. They are quiet, fast, urgent.

I tiptoe a few steps further, then stop again. I don't see anyone, but I hear tense, angry voices. I creep along, figuring if I get caught I'll say I got lost on the way to the bathroom.

I stop when I can distinguish the voices, which appear to be coming from a room a few doors down from me. Irina and Jacqueline are arguing, but I can't make out much of what they're saying because it's all in German. I hear *nein* several times. I listen for other familiar terms, but I don't know the language well enough to understand much.

I hear one phrase sprinkled throughout the heated conversation: *das Geheimnis.*

The voices grow louder until Irina snaps in English, "I know. *I know everything.*"

I hear a hand fumbling on a wall, I assume to push one of the well-disguised door-opening buttons, so I dash back down the hall and make it safely to the stairwell. It occurs to me that a house like this probably has an intricate surveillance system, and there's every chance my snooping has been caught on camera.

I don't see any lenses, but then again everything around here seems to be buried just beneath the surface.

If I was seen, and if someone points out my side trip to Nova or Brett or Wesley, I can plead Fendant intoxication. I'm three glasses in, and it's perfectly reasonable even for a sober person to get lost in this multi-floor labyrinth.

I keep that one curious phrase I heard in mind so I can remember to translate it later: *das Geheimnis*.

I return to the living room to find the women gathering up their things, the party ending as quickly as it began, and somehow Irina has beaten me here and is already clearing up empty glasses.

Many cheek-kisses later, most everyone has filtered out, the last women are maneuvering out the front door with a vision board tucked under their armpits, and I make a move to grab my coat and say my goodbyes.

I see Seychelle chatting in the foyer with Heidi and Nova, and I'm about to thank Nova and say goodbye when someone grabs my arm from behind.

I whirl to see Jacqueline, her face pale, her brow furrowed, clearly upset. It looks to me like her fear has ratcheted up since her visit to my home.

"I have to tell you something," she whispers. "It's important."

"Let's take a walk." I nod toward the front door.

"Not here," she shakes her head. "Tomorrow. I'll call you."

She pastes on a smile as Nova, Heidi and Seychelle join us. I open my mouth to say my final goodbyes, but before I can, Nova clears her throat.

"Before you go, Rose," she says, "we've been meaning to talk to you about your social media."

Heidi takes over. "We strongly recommend you shut down your QuickChat account and phase out Facebook," she tells me. "We—well, the company, really—*TIG* recommends that wives stick to Instagram only, and that you set it to private and leave your real name out of it entirely."

I'm blinking too fast, trying to take this in while suppressing my natural instinct to laugh at this suggestion.

"I-I don't think there's anything to worry about," I hedge, taken aback by this attempt at controlling how I communicate with the world. "I don't post much as it is."

My Facebook page exists only to spy on Seagrass Cove high school classmates, and occasionally to search for my mother's current location. I mostly used my QuickChat feed to promote the articles I wrote and trawl for story ideas and sources.

"We did notice a Facebook post with some pictures of Old Town," Nova says coolly. "We think it's best if you shut those down. We don't want to draw attention to our unique community."

"Why? What do we have to hide?" I ask with a nervous giggle. *Ha, ha.*

"Oh, bloody hell, you two," Seychelle waves a hand at Nova and Heidi. "You're scaring the poor girl. It's not a rule or anything, love. Until you get the lay of the land and Wesley is established at TIG, it's best to keep a low profile. You're a TWAG now, after all."

"A what?"

"TWAG. TIG Wives and Girlfriends. You know, like WAGS in soccer, but we're *TWAGS*," Seychelle explains.

Heidi adds, "Some people are jealous, and they'll take anything you post and twist it, like that bitter Teresa you met at the gala. Even seemingly innocent posts can trigger people. One girl posted a photo of her and her husband getting on a private jet in Rome, and it put TIG in a real position. Made them look like they were paying executives too much. Which doesn't please clients. You see what we're saying?"

"I understand," I assure them, though I don't.

Seychelle smiles. "Good. The bottom line is that TIG is a discretion-based company, and if our husbands want to work there, we all have to follow the rules. They say it's fifty-thousand times harder to get into TIG than it is to be accepted to Harvard. You can't apply—you can only be recruited. Once you're in, you don't mess it up." She squints at me.

They're all four too close to me, too still.

They want me to promise. "I get it," I say. "I'll take care of it."

I drive the mile home and take the stairs slowly, checking my translator app as I trudge up in the dark. I have to try several spellings, but I eventually manage to put the right letters together and get a hit on the English translation of *das Geheimnis*.

The robot says it out loud in the silence: *The secret.*

At midnight on the hill, there is no other sound.

The robot voice is like maple syrup pouring on a waffle. *The secret*, she coos again. *Das Geheimnis. The secret.*

I step faster and fumble at the door with my key, suddenly

needing to be inside, to be warm, to be close to another human being who knows me.

I slip as quietly as I can into bed, but Wesley stirs, yawning and snuggling up to me. "How'd it go? Any friend material?"

It's so dark in our room at night with the metal shutters down that I can't see even a glint of his pale skin. I speak to a wall of blackness. If not for his scent and his voice, he could be anyone.

"I think so," I reply. "They've welcomed me into their circle. I think I might like it here."

He kisses my cheek and I feel the tension from the evening seeping away, and then I fall into a slumber.

I sleep well until I'm jolted awake at two a.m. I try to quiet my mind, but still it whirs, and the persistent jetlag I can't shake, can't cycle off no matter how many tricks and tips I try, owns me. The last time I look at the clock it's five a.m.

After that night the snows come, and my autumn in Lucerne is over.

Wesley takes the car to work the next day. I spend the morning poking around for online private investigator classes, and the more I research the profession, the more I realize the life of a reporter and writer looks far more interesting than stakeouts for cheating husbands or insurance fraud.

I've started taking three walks a day to keep myself busy and clear my head. On my first hike of the day, I head up the steep path to Sonnenberg, and I fast-walk past the cows, their bells clanging behind electrified fences, and wonder how they get to the grass buried six inches below. The landscape is snow upon snow, white upon white.

Beauty surrounds me like a crown. Miles of white hills are backed by snowcapped mountains, jagged, towering, out-of-focus promises of great adventures beyond. We have two local Alps: Pilatus, said to be inhabited with dragons, touches the sky across the valley and keeps watch over the sweeter, more petite Rigi a hair further away.

When I've worked up a light sweat under my coat, I pivot and head down. The man is there again, coming up the hill toward me. He's bundled up much like I am, but unlike me he uses a walking stick as he ascends, staring all the while with those small, hooded, wrinkled eyes.

"Grüezi," he grunts as we grow closer. I force myself to meet his gaze. The Swiss, with their insistence on full-eye-contact greetings, will beat the closed-off Manhattanite out of me yet.

It doesn't matter what time I take my walks. The man is always there with his stick, locking on to me, making sure to say hello, waiting for me to reciprocate before continuing on.

I feel eyes on me here, all the time. I should accept it, but I can't yet, because it clashes with decades of Americanness, a particular way of life where mom always said, *Don't stare, Rose! It's rude.*

In Switzerland, staring is a national sport.

But no, I remind myself, I can't lump the cantons into one unified culture, much like a visitor to the United States can't get a taste of southern living by visiting New Hampshire. This is the German side. I have yet to visit the French, Italian or Romansh parts.

Before Wesley and I left New York, I studied up on Switzerland as much as I could while wrapping things up at work, and learned my new country is a *Willensnation*, which loosely translated means "nation of the will." It's technically a federation, though, not a nation.

Back at home, I check my phone, then my email, but there's no word from Jacqueline. I resist texting her. It's not a good look for the new executive's wife to start stalking the spouse of a TIG vice president, even though I *know* something's wrong, even if I only want to help, no matter how worried I am about her.

The night stretches out before me, empty and still. I'm on my own. Wesley is at his first poker night with his new colleagues and I have no concept of how late it will go.

With no comfy sofa to curl up on, I head to bed after a sandwich and a salad and sink into a cloud of pillows, cruising social media for any sign of Jacqueline. All four of the TWAGs found my locked-down Instagram and put in follow requests, and I accept each one.

I cruise all their accounts, starting with Jacqueline's. Her most recent photos provide a vivid record of a girls' night out, with fresh images of a bunch of the women I met last night posing with beer steins and cocktails in Old Town. I scroll through a series of posts, one after the other, peeking in on my new friends drinking, smiling, partying, posing. My stomach lurches.

They're all there: Nova and Jacqueline. Nova, Heidi, and Jacqueline, Jacqueline and two women I don't know.

I cruise the other women's accounts. Nova, Jacqueline and Heidi are all posting from the same location, and I see a few other women I recognize from the gala and the vision board night in the background.

The silence of this neighborhood is so aggressive it has

become like noise. I feel locked in by four o'clock every afternoon when the sun sets. I thought New England had short winter days, but I can't get used to the darkness here, of not seeing any sun at all until after eight a.m.

I'm beginning to feel catastrophically lonely and cut off, wondering if Jacqueline, who looks healthy and happy compared to last night, has been messing with me with her claims of being uneasy, of being watched.

And then a DM pops up.

CHAPTER

NINE

The message is from *Fashionistafriendabroad*.

Ro! You up for a night out? Get ready. I'll see you in 30.

It's Seychelle, and no, I'm not up for it. I'm in my PJs, and I'm annoyed to be asked last minute.

I write back, *I'm in. What are we doing?*

She replies, *See you in 30!*

I can't afford to be lazy when I'm still trying to make new friends in this small expat community. I throw on some makeup, jeans and a sweater, ready for a casual night in Old Town.

Seychelle picks me up in an ice-grey metallic Porsche Boxster.

"Where are we going?" I ask as I strap myself in. "Are the rest of them out in town, or—"

"Oh *god* no," Seychelle revs the engine and we take off down the hill. "We're not meeting exhausted mums to talk about mashed peas. We're going clubbing, darling."

"I didn't hear anything about tonight," I say, trying not to pout. "I assumed I wasn't invited."

"Neither of us were invited to tonight's festivities," she glances over at me. "We're not in the mums' group."

"Wait…the *mums'* group?"

She wiggles her eyebrows.

"Ah."

"Oh, don't fret." Seychelle takes a hairpin curve like a Bond girl chasing 007, and I'm thrown against the passenger door. "We can do things mums can't. We don't have to be up in the morning. We don't even have to be *home* in the morning if we don't want to. We have to go crazy while we can!"

Once we're flying down the motorway, Seychelle side-eyes me. "So, tell me. How did you and that hunky man of yours meet? I adore these stories. Tell me *everything*."

"I'm surprised you have to ask," I reply wryly, intending to avoid the question for now. "People around here seem to know things about me *I* haven't even learned yet."

She rewards me with one of her throaty laughs. Out of all of them, even Jacqueline, I feel the strongest connection to Seychelle. She gets my humor, she's edgy but kind to me, and, let's face it, neither of us are mums.

"The usual," I shrug. "We met over the buffet at a summer party in Connecticut, he drove me home, and that's all she wrote."

"You're leaving out the best parts," she chides me.

"I thought you didn't know a thing about it," I reply, giving her my own side-eye.

"Everyone knows you two had a whirlwind romance. I think more than a few of us are jealous of your passionate love story. I think Heidi had to wait like three years for Raj to propose. Don't mention it, though. She's pretty sensitive on that topic."

Seychelle navigates off the motorway and races the car up to a row of warehouses somewhere in Zurich. A valet appears from nowhere and takes her keys.

My new friend is in second-skin white suede pants and a silver halter top, and I'm in jeans and an unremarkable green sweater.

She gets us past the doormen with some languid German and a casual wave, and we step into an undulating mass of noise, bodies, sweat and pheromones, all of it lit up by a pulsating rainbow of strobe lights.

"I'll get the first round," I yell. "What are you having?"

"Whatever you're having," Seychelle replies, scanning the pulsating room.

I work my way to the bar and buy forty francs worth of vodka sodas with shriveled lime slices and two stingy pieces of ice. This has been a problem since I got to Europe. Ice machines don't seem to be a thing, as they do not value cold drinks in this country.

I carry two high-ball glasses through the crowd, miraculously not spilling any liquid. I find Seychelle surrounded by four men.

"Hey! Guys, this is Rose. Rose, these are the guys."

"Hi, guys," I say, handing her a drink. "These taste like crap."

"Doesn't matter. It's just to wash down these babies."

She holds up a tiny blue pill between a thumb and index finger, tosses it in her mouth and chases it with a mediocre vodka tonic.

"OK," she says. "Your turn."

I take the pill she holds out. Drugs have never worked for me. I'm the daughter of an addict and anything stronger than alcohol sends me off the rails, but I know better than to waste time arguing in situations like these.

I palm the pill and throw back a drink. She wouldn't have noticed, in the dark, with the distractions, if I'd shoved it up my left nostril or tossed it into the crowd.

Seychelle sees someone she knows. Two someones. She turns away from me.

"Pierre! *Mon chéri.*" They commence a series of cheek kisses, and Seychelle chats with the man in rapid French before deftly switching to German to greet his girlfriend.

"How many languages do you speak?" I yell over the music.

She flails her arms. "Oh, I don't know. Four? Five?"

Now it's back to English.

"Celine! That necklace is *divine.*"

Seychelle makes a half-hearted attempt to drag me onto the dance floor with her, but I resist, she gives up, and I slip away.

I sink into a velvet sofa and think about ordering a shot, but I'm not ready to face a pressing crowd again, so I kill time checking the mums' Instagram accounts.

There are a few newer photos. They're all still seated at a bar, but now there are only five mums left.

Jacqueline was in the images from earlier in the night, but nothing later. It's midnight.

I text Wesley to let him know I'm with Seychelle in Zurich and won't be home until morning, but I get no read receipt and hear nothing back. It's another reason I felt safe marrying him; he's the anti control freak, the anti-jealous type.

A figure plops down next to me, too close, almost touching my thigh, and I instinctively flinch and jerk away, sliding a few inches down the sofa. I turn for a quick look, and it takes me a moment to realize I know the person. The colorful maxi-dress is back. The lilac hair. The sharp eyes.

"Hi," Teresa says, an impish grin covering her face. "Seychelle couldn't coax you to the dance floor?"

"I've never been a fan of clubbing," I reply.

"Don't worry about the mums' night thing," she says into my ear. She's way too close, and I can smell the liquor on her breath. "It's like, we *get* it, you procreated."

She whips her head around as if she's seen a ghost. "Anyway, I'm heading out. Good seeing you," she says. "Before I do… lemme see your phone."

"What?" I can barely hear anything above the chaos of sound.

"Your phone! For when you need me. Because you will. I'm gonna give you my number." She shouts and enunciates so I can't help but hear her.

I unlock the phone and lay it in her palm. She punches a bunch of buttons and returns it to me.

"When you're ready," she says, "call me. Those bitches *will* turn on you, and when they do, you're gonna want some real friends."

I have no answer for her.

"*You'll see*," she trills in a sing-song voice, smiling a goodbye as she bounces up off the sofa, dancing away toward the exit.

Now I really need a shot of alcohol. I give up my place on the sofa and head for the bar.

CHAPTER

TEN

I open my eyes to a solid wall of blackness, and I bolt upright with a gasp. Everything is wrong.

Where am I?

I wake with a stinging throat, dry lips, stabbing headache, and the heavy fog of too much sleep, but also the exhaustion of not enough. I scramble to find my bearings and realize I'm at home.

Tiny pinpricks of light bleeding through the shutters let me know I'm in my bedroom. Not in New York. In Switzerland. I lay a hand on Wesley's side of the bed and hit mattress.

I feel for my phone, then use it as a flashlight to find the button on the wall that opens the shutters.

It's 12:30 p.m., and I have two missed calls and two texts from my husband. Before I reply, I need food to settle my stomach and medicine to numb the pain in my head, so I slouch to the kitchen and find the butt of yesterday's loaf, pop it in the toaster, and shake out a few of the remaining ibuprofen I brought from New York. I'm going through them like M&Ms.

I choke down some buttered toast and call Wesley.

I can hear his smile through the phone. "You're alive. How hung over are you on a scale of one to ten?"

"I…I shouldn't be," I say, my head throbbing. "I think I only had one drink…maybe two…"

"One or *two*? You stumbled in at six in the morning the most jolly I've ever seen you. You said you loved Seychelle, wanted to marry her, and never danced so much in your life. You weren't two-drinks drunk. You were gone-to-a-rave, drank the house out, and got high as the proverbial kite wasted."

"I don't do drugs," I snap.

I fight to remember what happened to the pill after I palmed it. Did it go in my pocket? Or on the floor?

"Hey, no judgment!" Wesley is contrite. "I didn't mean anything, honey. I'm thrilled you're fitting in here. What did I tell you? This is where we were meant to be, right?"

"Right," I say, just to get him off the phone. I need to throw up.

I am stepping out of the shower, dripping wet, the warm floor radiating through the bathmat, when I hear my phone beep. Then again. And again.

The third time makes it sound frantic.

Wesley.

I quickly dry off, wrap my wet hair in a towel turban, and grab my phone off the sink.

The first message is from Heidi to me, Seychelle and Nova:

911! Pickwick's 30 mins

Nova: *I'll save us a booth*

Seychelle: *Ima be a few minutes late.*

Me: *I'll be there*

No word from Jacqueline.

Guesses about what this could be about rattle around my brain as I moisturize my winter-dry legs: Someone's husband cheated. Someone's kid is getting bullied at school. Someone's Porsche has a ding.

I'm relieved I'll have a chance to talk to Seychelle. I need to know what happened to me last night, how I went from sipping a weak vodka tonic to blacked out. I need her to fill in the blanks so I my imagination doesn't spin its own dark narrative. It's already offered up some ugly suggestions I've had to swat away.

I choose something appropriate to wear to this Pickwick's place, which sounds like an upmarket hotel restaurant or tea and crumpets type of venue.

It doesn't hit me until I'm dressed and ready that I don't have a car. I go to grab my phone to text the four and ask for a ride, but I see the BMW keys on the kitchen counter.

I grab them, not thinking too much about how Wesley got to work, nor letting myself wonder if he ever came home at all.

I park at the Bahnhof and fast-walk across the plaza and the bridge, bumping into people as I go because I can't walk in a straight line while gawping at the crystal-clear reflection of the snow-capped mountains on Lake Lucerne.

I hang a left and stride down the cobblestoned riverwalk past restaurants and touristy cafes. I stop in front of the door of a faux-British pub and look up at the sign.

This is Pickwick's?

The sign is charmingly literal, with a headshot of a man holding a beer stein who is presumably Mr. Pickwick himself:

Mr. Pickwick Pub

The place where people meet.

I walk in and immediately catch sight of Heidi and Nova huddled in a back booth, hands wrapped around their pint glasses.

I weave my way through tables of people guzzling beer and munching on mayonnaise-tipped fries. The place smells of stale beer and recycled grease.

Heidi catches sight of me. "Oh, Rose, good. It's *so awful.* Get yourself a drink. You're going to need it."

"I'll wait for the server," I say, pulling out a chair, ready to slide in.

"It's English style," Nova tells me. She is stuffed up and her eyes are red-rimmed. "You order at the bar."

I point to their pints. "What are you drinking?"

"Cider and black," Heidi replies. I make a confused face. "Cider with a squirt of Ribena."

I don't know from "Ribena," but I head to the bar and order this strange brew, and when I taste it, I immediately see the appeal. It's calming and sweet and there's an entire pint of it to nurse.

I turn to head back to the table and notice Seychelle ahead of me, racing through the crowd to get to the other two.

Seychelle halts at the edge of their table. "Does she know?"

Nova's eyes go wide. "Hey, Rose! Have a seat. We'll fill you in."

Seychelle swivels, sees me, and pastes on a melancholic smile.

"Oh, you're here, darling. Brilliant. So much to talk about."

After we're both seated, Seychelle swivels her neck and takes in the packed bar. "Could you have picked a more crowded place for this?"

"It's better this way," Nova leans in. "No one pays attention in crowds. It's harder to hear what we're saying over the din."

"It's not like we can do this at any of our *houses*," Heidi stage-whispers. "And we know TIG bigwigs won't be lurking around here."

"Will Jacqueline be joining us?" I ask, scanning a laminated menu someone left on the table. Everyone freezes. "I—well, I hope it's not something too terrible." I laugh nervously. "Is it?"

"It *is* terrible," Heidi informs me. "And we asked you here because it involves you. We need answers."

CHAPTER

ELEVEN

"Something that involves *me*? What's going on?"

I'm on the defensive, unsure what's coming. I remain off-kilter in my new role as a representative of my husband. I still can't be *me* in this social circle. Not entirely, anyway. For now I'm still Rose, Wesley Blackwood's Wife.

"Jacqueline is gone," Heidi says flatly.

"What do you mean, *gone*?" I clutch my pint with two hands.

"Fucked off. Left town. Bounced," Seychelle assists, crossing one long leg over the other.

"To visit family? For a vacation?" *What does Jacqueline leaving have to do with me?*

Heidi's eyes well up with tears as she plays with a paper straw sleeve. "We all met in town last night for mums' night out."

She meets my eyes. "We do it a couple times a year so we can let loose and commiserate about the challenges stay-at-home mums face. Anyway. She seemed fine. She was having a great time! We had a few drinks, but nothing too crazy, and then she left a bit early. I didn't think anything of it..." Heidi sniffles.

"But Peter called the guys this morning and said Jacqueline

didn't get up for the kids!" Nova cries. "I can't *believe* she did this."

"Peter goes to check on her when she doesn't get up for the kids, and she's not there," Heidi continues.

"Wait. Why would he have to look for her? Don't they sleep together?" I blurt.

"Fair question," Seychelle says. She lifts her palm off the shiny finished wooden table and gets half-stuck. She grimaces and grabs a paper napkin to scrub the sticky remnants of a past customer's meal off her fingers.

"When one of them comes in late, that person sleeps in a guest room to avoid waking the other. I mean, I assume that's what they do," Heidi shrugs. "Raj and I have done that on late nights before."

"Regardless," Nova says to me, "when he checked the guest room she wasn't there. He searched the whole house. Her keys, wallet, passport and phone were all gone."

"Wait a minute." My blood is running cold. Everything about this discussion is wrong—the delivery, the facts, the victim-blaming. "Hasn't anyone called police? If she walked out of the bar last night and disappeared, she could be in terrible danger, or even—"

"No, no, no," Nova shakes her head. "I *saw* her get into her car. I followed her to confirm the kids' play dates this week. I watched her get in and drive away."

"You talked to her?" I ask. "Did she seem OK? If she was planning play dates with you, it doesn't track that she'd take off and leave the kids behind."

Nova and Heidi exchange glances I translate loosely as, *The new girl has no idea what she's talking about.*

Nova is shaking her head again. "I called her name, but she didn't answer. She didn't hear me. She got in and took off. I know she made it safely from the bar to her car. For *sure*. I figured we'd talk about it in the morning after the kids left for school."

Her voice cracks, and Seychelle lays a hand on her shoulder.

I'm trying to read between the lines to determine what's going on here. From what I gather, a new friend of mine might be missing, in danger, in pain, dead. And her longtime friends are acting like it's her own fault.

"What's Peter saying?" I ask.

Inside I'm screaming, *Call the police. Get up and report her missing.* My conscience is saying what these women won't. I glug some sweet cider.

Heidi takes over. "That's where you come in," she says, swiveling on her chair to half-face me next to her.

Seychelle scrapes her chair away from the table, rises, and announces, "I'm going to the bar. You're all almost empty. I'm getting wine. I suppose you want more of that sickly sweet concoction?"

I'm realizing she's right. Two-thirds drained, the drink feels heavy and gassy. "I'd love a glass of white," I raise one finger. "Anything's fine."

It's not—I detest Chardonnay and Pinot Grigio, to name two—but I figure it's not the time to get picky about my grapes. I make a show of fishing out my wallet, but Seychelle waves me away and heads to the bar.

"As I was saying," Heidi starts again. "We don't believe this is an issue for the police. Or the authorities, or the Chinese embassy. We believe Peter when he tells us Jacqueline has been unhappy. That she, well…" Heidi's voice cracks, and she clears her throat. "He told Raj this wasn't the life she wanted. That she'd been pulling away for weeks and inventing reasons to start fights, sleeping too late to get the kids off in the mornings, drinking too much wine…"

Nova asks me, "Did she ever mention anything to you about wanting to get out of Lucerne? Or leave Peter?"

"*Me?*" I shake my head. "I only met her a couple of times. We were nowhere near the stage where we'd share intimate details like that."

Lie.

"What about you?" I flip it back on them. "You're her best friends. Surely she would have shown signs if she was that unhappy…"

Seychelle returns balancing four drinks. "Don't worry, ladies! I've got this. Really—don't bother yourselves."

I hop up and take two full glasses from her.

My wine is alarmingly yellow and not cold.

"Aren't you worried?" I press them all once Seychelle is seated. "I mean, isn't it worth reporting to police to be on the safe side? What if she's been taken? What if she had a breakdown and got lost in the Alps somewhere?"

Seychelle leans in. "This is why we're asking questions. We need to know if Peter told Wesley anything about Jacqueline wanting to leave. I mean, we're her friends, but you know how it is. It can be tough around here to be honest about your failings if your relationship isn't…"

Nova stares down into her almost-empty glass, rings of foam

clinging to the insides, and lowers her voice.

"Maybe she felt like she couldn't share her marriage troubles. It's not easy around here if you don't have a husband."

Not easy? More like impossible, from what I've seen. They don't seem to have many single friends, if any.

"What can I do?" I ask them.

Heidi lowers her tone. "As you know, Wesley and Peter are becoming quite close, and ..."

No, I didn't know.

"...so we're wondering if Peter confided in Wesley, and maybe Wesley mentioned something to you about Jacqueline's frame of mind?"

I take a moment to measure my words. "I think Wesley would have kept Peter's confidence if that were the case. I can ask him, but in the meantime, I assume someone's reported her missing. Surely Peter has called the police?"

"The *police*? Shush, Rose!" Nova is horrified. "She's not... she's not *kidnapped* or anything. She left him. She even wrote a note."

A *note*? Why didn't they lead with this information?

I'm profoundly missing my gang back in New York, my fellow cynics and writers who spent so much time at happy hours after work together that we formed our own society. The Dead Newspapers Club is made up of five friends who came of age when newspapers still mattered. We know they're at death's door—thus the name—but we celebrate them anyway, like coal or the Dinagat bushy-tailed cloud rat, which scientists believe is *probably* extinct but hedge their bets in declaring it so.

TDNC members never stop questioning, and they'd never

put up with this kind of group delusion.

"We don't have all the details yet," Heidi assures me, "but apparently the note was left on the computer. Peter opened her laptop and there it was."

"This is third-hand information," Seychelle throws in.

"She left without her laptop?" No one reacts. "What did the note say?"

The three of them shrug in unison.

"If there *was* something left on her screen, anyone could have written it," I remind them. "There would be no handwriting, no signature, nothing to show who put it there."

Heidi sighs. "You have to trust us. Do us a favor and talk to Wesley, OK? If there is something there, we want to know about it. I think you'll find, though," she says, leaning in and whispering, "that Jacqueline went back to Hong Kong to rejoin her old life and get away from Peter and his…let's just say, his *challenges*."

I take a sip of my wine and almost spit it out. It's hot, thick, and cheap. I need a walk. I need some space before these three drag me into normalizing a friend's disappearance.

"Anyone want anything?"

They shake their heads, and I meander to the bar. I don't need another drink, but I want to get away. I wish I could run out of the pub. I give myself time to think while waiting in line behind two scruffy backpackers.

"Cider and black, bitte," I say absently when it's my turn.

"You got it."

I forgot I was in a faux-British pub. I'm relieved I don't have to worry about trying to speak German for a few moments. I came to Switzerland planning to blend and learn, but I'm craving familiarity and a feeling of being understood. Even if it's talk of booze and the weather.

The bartender pulls the pint and turns to grab the container of red currant syrup. "You new here?"

He's young, maybe twenty-five, and he has an English accent.

"I am," I say. "How'd you know I wasn't a tourist?"

"Welp, I've seen the Four over in their favorite booth for the two years I've been here. I've never seen a fifth with them."

I glance over at the three of them chatting furiously, leaning in close.

"It's still only four, though," I point out.

"Oh, yes. We'll have to get used to the Five, then. All the expats in Lucerne know the Four. Glamorous and that. Where *is* Jacs today? She loves her cider and black."

"She…well…" What do I say? "She's left Lucerne, as far as I know."

I have no idea what to say to this bloke, this stranger who seems to know my new friends.

"Oh? Odd she didn't say goodbye. I just served her last night."

CHAPTER

TWELVE

The boy bartender squirts a rivulet of scarlet into my foaming cider, and it spreads in a blood-like bloom, overtaking the pint. He sets it on the bar until it drips over, cold and foamy. I pick it up and chug.

"You must be mistaken," I say after the sweetness goes down.

He's got his dates mixed up. The mum's group was at the *Schnitzel Scheune* restaurant last night based on their Instagram location tags.

As I weigh whether to argue further or not, a throng of rowdy young men crowd the bar and shout for lager, so I move away and gulp down more cider.

I set down the half-drained glass and bolt out of the pub, damn the consequences of leaving my new friends without a farewell. I need to see Wesley *right now*.

I check my phone, but there is nothing from my loving husband, nothing about Jacqueline, no sign of worry or concern. I send the three women a quick note: *Something came up. I'll explain later, I promise! xo*

Wesley must have known Jacqueline was gone when we

talked earlier this afternoon, when he was joking about how wasted I was when I stumbled into the house.

I text him: *I'll be outside TIG in 10. Need to talk.*

I don't want to fight. I walk slowly back to the Bahnhof, remind myself he must have his reasons. *Hear him out. Don't go in hot.*

I make it to TIG and wait outside, pacing and staring up at the windows, for five minutes before Wesley walks out in his suit and his Italian shoes and his perfect sun-streaked hair.

He sees me, smiles, waves, then frowns down at his phone as he walks toward me. He looks up when he's in front of me.

He kisses me like nothing is wrong. I pull away.

"Why didn't you tell me about Jacqueline? She's been missing since last night and you knew, and you didn't tell me?"

"I'm fine," he says. "How's *your* day going?"

"Seriously, Wesley! Jacqueline vanished and everyone's acting like it's no big deal and they haven't called the police and she's already been gone for—"

He takes me gently by the shoulders, tries to envelope me in a hug, but I don't let him. He drops his arms.

"I didn't tell you because I knew you'd react like this. Calm down, Rose."

"*Don't* tell me to calm down. That's Husband 101. No, scratch that—it's *Person* 101."

"We're not going to get anywhere if you're worked up like this," he says flatly. "Let's go to Seebar. I can take a quick break. Come on."

He rubs my back, which is nice, but he thinks I don't notice that he's adding extra pressure to push me along, to get me away from the TIG parking lot.

It's less than five minutes to the glass-fronted, elegant bar I loved so when we first arrived. I thought this would be our place. It's dim and intimate when the sun is setting over the lake, and flooded with light through its walls of glass by day.

We secure ourselves a velvet sofa with a view, and Wesley orders us two glasses of Sancerre.

"First of all," he begins when the server walks away, "I have *not* been lying to you. I'm new here too. I'm trying to figure out who my friends are, just like you are. Don't think I'm not aware that you and I have a new dynamic as a couple because our expat friend group is completely incestuous. I know you're feeling it too."

He reaches out and massages the back of my neck.

I start to deflate. It's his calming touch, but also his reasoning. The wine arrives, and I'm glad for once it's a stingy pour, because I had enough at Pickwick's.

The first time I ever ordered by the glass in Lucerne I thought, *huh, nine francs for a nice white Bordeaux? What a steal!* Wines by the glass all have a measure listed next to them, and 1dl sounded great to me. Then I found out what 1dl is. One deciliter, as it happens, is a Smurf's portion of wine. I once ordered a 5-dl glass and the bartenders both looked at me like they'd never seen such brazen intemperance.

Wesley spins the stem of his glass. "There are some things I haven't told you," he admits. "Little things."

"This isn't little."

He tips back his wine glass, takes a slow sip, gazes out at the mountains. "I wasn't going to tell you about Jacqueline on the phone. I can't risk someone at work hearing that conversation and thinking I'm the office gossip."

"We're supposed to trust each other, Wesley." With that, the rest of my 1dl of wine slides down my gullet.

"This has nothing to do with trust," he argues. "It's about our new friends. My colleagues. TIG is all about discretion, and when I hear chatter at work, I always want to tell you. But I have to consider what you'll tell your friends. Even if you don't mean to be indiscreet by sharing stories or anecdotes, even if they seem harmless, we might be ruffling feathers. We just don't know."

He's talking in muddled circles. "Such as?"

He gazes out at the water. "Peter and I have started to form a sort of alliance. Brett is a big personality. At work he's a bulldozer, and clients really respect and listen to him. And Kristoff....well, that guy is a wolf in sheep's clothing. I can see it already."

"Kristoff? But he seems so unassuming," I say.

Seychelle's husband has a close-shaved ginger beard and wavy, dark-auburn hair, and I remember him well because I was expecting Liechtensteinian royalty to be snobby, but he was nice and didn't ask obnoxious questions about my age and my uterus like Brett did.

Kristoff inquired about my career and asked where he could find my work online. He loved that I covered what he called "gritty" things like cops, social issues, disability law and activists.

Wesley finishes his wine, holds up a finger, and summons the server.

"That remains to be seen," he continues. "These people don't get where they are by being nice and 'unassuming.'" He makes air quotes. "It's very political at TIG. You have to watch your step. When there's that much money involved, people get funny."

I decide not to share what I'm thinking about his wordy confessional: *What does any of this have to do with Jacqueline going missing?*

"I wish you would tell me these things," I say to him. "I'm sorry I got so worked up. I'm worried sick about her, Wesley. Something's not right."

Again, his eyes leave me for the lake view.

"If Peter says she left him, I have to believe that."

"Do you think the president of the Expat Social Club, who has two small children she adores, would leave an unsigned note on a computer screen, disappear without her car, and not say goodbye to anyone? You know that sounds absurd, don't you, Wesley? Tell me you know that sounds batshit bananas."

"Things are different here," he offers. "We just met these people. Maybe this is normal for them."

"That's just it," I say, lowering my voice. "None of this is normal. I gotta be honest, babe. I'm getting some cult-like vibes from your company. First it's Brett talking about how it's so great 'the wives' can't work, then it's the women telling me to stay off social media because TIG 'frowns on it,' and now it's nobody will call the police because they don't want to call attention to the company or its executives. Oh, and did you know TIG gives out extra *perks* when you have kids?"

"Keep your voice down," Wesley hisses. "This is the go-to place for TIG happy hours and client cocktail meetings. You never know who's listening."

I bite my tongue. This fence-sitter is not the man I thought I knew. If Switzerland Wesley is going to be a recurring character in our marriage, I'm afraid our first real fight might be on the horizon.

Anyone with sense knows Jacqueline could have been taken or killed, and no amount of gaslighting from anyone is going to make me pretend otherwise.

"What do you think happened to her?" I ask him.

He finishes his wine and checks his watch.

"Honestly?" He leans in and kisses me smack on the lips. For the first time in our relationship, I think he knows exactly what he's doing. Making my knees weak so my mind won't be strong. It's semi-working. "I think we should mind our business. There are a lot of people circling this thing, and if Peter believes she left him, she probably did. He's all broken up, Rose. He's humiliated."

"So he says."

"Here's the thing," Wesley leans in. "There's no way he *could* have done anything to Jacqueline. I was with Peter all day at work yesterday, and then we went to poker night together. Eight of us were at Brett and Nova's until one in the morning. The guy was acting perfectly fine and frankly, I feel terribly for him."

"That leaves at least five hours when he could've done something," I point out. I can't muster any sympathy for Peter right now.

My husband checks his watch again.

"We'll talk more tonight, I promise." He gets up and extends a hand to help me up, and I take it, though I'm perfectly capable of standing on my own.

"You'll be home for dinner?"

"Of course."

"Good. I'll cook."

"Can't wait." He waves, and off he goes, and I realize no one's paid the bill, so I pull out my credit card and take care of it.

CHAPTER

THIRTEEN

'll cook…what? What was I thinking promising to whip up a glorious repast? It's all veal and cheese in this town. The grocery stores shut by five.

Switzerland, being a landlocked country, is not great on seafood judging from the stores I've been to around here, so for an easy meal tonight I'm left with vegetables or pizza.

I slow the car and hang a right into the convenience store parking lot a half-mile from our house. It's a last resort. I notice a truck parked off to the side, no sign on it and no line. But there is a window.

I wander over and peek inside. A man in an apron and Swedish-chef style hat is skewering whole chickens while other birds spin on rotisseries lining the back of the truck.

"Hello," he says, and I'm thrown that he knows I'm an English speaker. "They are not ready yet."

"What? Uh…*bitte*?"

"Chickens!" Now he is frowning. "You want chicken? Come back at five. I will reserve one for you."

And with that kind offer I realize I know him: He is grouchy walking-stick man.

"Danke," I reply, smiling back at him.

I promised Wesley dinner, and dinner he shall have.

I pop into the convenience store, pick up some root vegetables, a loaf of fresh bread, and a few bottles of ten-franc Fendant, then head up the hill back home.

Precisely at five p.m., I return to chicken man. The lot is almost full and the line is ten deep.

I case the situation, walk around it, approach the window from the side.

The person at the front of the line takes his chicken and leaves. The next guy steps up, but he is summarily dismissed by my grouchy truck friend. The angry customer taps his watch. Chicken man shrugs.

He pokes his head out of the window and beckons me over.

He turns back to his rotisserie, removes a browned bird covered with blackened spices, and sets it on the chopping block between us.

"Zwei Abendessen?"

"Entschuldigung?" When in doubt, employ the German word for "excuse me" or "sorry," which I always think sounds like a cold-war era European game show. *Step right up—it's time for the Entschuldigung lightning round!*

"Two dinners?"

I nod.

"Genau." *OK, right.* He slams a cleaver down and the bird is cut in two.

He wraps it in a foil bag for me so I can keep it warm and tender for the next half hour, when Wesley is due home. In

Europe, they don't like to work late.

The line behind me is growing. Chicken man says something in slow Swiss German. I pick out *Deutch*.

"Entschuldigung?"

"Come every Thursday. We will practice our English and German together. Deal?"

"Deal. Genau." A very bad deal for him. His English is excellent. My German is woeful.

"I am other places other days. I am here every Thursday." He pauses. "Most weeks. Sometimes not."

Got it. He'll either be here or he won't. I smile as I walk away, swatting away disgruntled glares from cold people in the line, happy to have my first Swiss friend. My first friend here who doesn't know my husband, that is.

I trudge up the stairs, chicken in foil in hand, and as I prepare to mount the final ten steps I realize there's someone on the landing at the top.

I stop and listen, then tiptoe up two more stairs.

I'm hyper-aware of the smell of the hot, seasoned bird in my hand, and of the hard edges of the foil bag scraping my thigh.

I flinch at the sudden, loud, cackling call of a raven above, and I look up to see a bird circling, screaming, its noise covering up my own movement. A dead bird in my hand, an angry one above.

Two more steps and I see a woman in a yellow coat, shoulder-length blue-grey hair tucked behind her ears, rearranging her plates on the hillside so they will be visible even in the snow.

I continue walking up, watching, hearing her mumble to herself in Swiss German.

When I hit the landing she hears or senses me, and she freezes in place with a yellow plate in her hand.

She turns slowly, slowly, until her eyes meet mine.

"Grüezi," she says.

"Grüezi," I reply.

These are the times when it gets awkward for expats. Addressing a local in our native tongue is too American, too gauche, but mangling their language feels futile and disrespectful. I opt for the latter and try some German.

"Guten aben. Mit name es Rose."

She stares. I said it wrong. I give up before I say something absurd or offensive.

I smile, wave and keep going, then struggle to open my front door with the chicken in hand, suddenly desperate to get indoors. That blasted crow has alighted on the ledge again, and I swear he's watching me.

I set the table and set candles I suspect are vanilla, based on what looks like a vanilla bean on the label.

Wesley clomps up the stairs right on time, and when we are seated over a dinner of roasted vegetables and rotisserie chicken, we dig in and he proceeds to pretend everything is normal.

"I could get used to this," he smiles. "What did you do to this chicken? It's positively succulent."

"I have a guy," I tell him, though I wish I had the disposition to lie and claim I toiled over a hot rotisserie all afternoon.

"Wesley," I say. "What do you actually *do* at your job?"

His mouth is full. When he washes the food down with wine, he says, "You don't want to hear it. Trust me. *I* barely want to hear it."

"I do, though. Try me."

His fork freezes in mid-air, leaving a sliver of white meat jiggling on its tines.

"I've been here less than two weeks," he replies wearily. "I'm still finding my place. At TIG we build relationships, we make introductions, we manage reputations. It's kept vague to outsiders for a reason—our business is about discretion. It's in my contract that I don't reveal company secrets."

He takes the bite, chews, then adds, "I'm there to help calculate the cost and reward ratio. I analyze what each client will bring to us and how much energy and resources they might require…but it's so much more than that. When I know more, I'll share more."

He reaches out to cover my hand with his. "Tell you what. Let's watch a movie tonight on the big screen," he says, deftly changing the subject. "Your choice. It's about time I set up that TV."

He eyes the massive box against a wall, the 72-incher we ordered along with the king-sized bed before we arrived and never opened.

I pick an oldie, and as we curl up in bed and watch *Smilla's Sense of Snow*, I ask casually during a lull, "Oh, by the way, any word about Jacqueline since I left you at Seebar?"

He looks me dead in the eye, blinks innocently, and replies, "Nope."

I realize in that moment I've been asking the wrong question.

The one no one has even bothered to address the right one: Why was Peter at work on the day his wife went missing and his two small children lost their mother?

I'm up half the night again. Falling asleep is easy; staying asleep is impossible.

At first it was pure jetlag causing the insomnia, but I've added racing thoughts and nagging doubts, first about Jacqueline, and now about my young marriage. I'm legally bound to a man I've known for four months, and moving here has shone a harsh light on the fact we barely know each other.

I thought we knew enough. I thought we *got* each other, that we were the perfectly impossible match.

I should never have been at the party where I met Wesley. Violet conned me into going, begged me to be her cynical sidekick in a sea of wealthy white people.

"It won't kill you to go to Connecticut for half a day," she'd said when we were both living in Brooklyn. "You owe me."

I didn't owe her, but I went anyway. I threw on my trusty black H&M dress, spruced it up with silver dangly earrings bought off eBay, slipped on my comfy wedges, and worked up a sticky sweat schlepping from Brooklyn to Grand Central and on to Dullsville, Connecticut on a hot July morning.

"You promised me Dom Perignon," I reminded my so-called best friend as we entered Ye Olde Rustic Inn of Westport and found the party room. I halted at the threshold. "Oh, dear god."

We froze at the sight of the glorified tea party, then stepped gingerly into the dead zone, I in wrinkled black linen, Vi in a pencil skirt and tank top, and everyone else in pastel Ann Taylor or Chico as far as the eye could see, like a gigantic bowl of Jordan almonds come to life.

I whispered to Violet, "Do you think any of these people ever get tired of being a cliché?"

"I doubt it," she replied. "Don't hate me, but I see my boss. I'd better go say hi. You OK alone for a bit?"

"No."

"Cool. Back in a few."

I'd glanced around, caught no one's eye, and observed small groups of people talking quietly and munching canapes like it was a funeral.

No one spoke to me or even seemed to know I was there, so I hung at the fringes drinking champagne and eavesdropping. Within minutes I learned there were at least two Olivias, one Olive and two Emmas in the room.

I moseyed over to the buffet and was instantly entranced by the deviled eggs. When I was young they were the party food of American trash. My mother would bring a tray of them, fuzzy filling piled high in gelatinous white boats, covered in smoked paprika to cover up the slapdash effort she'd made filling the scooped-out egg-white halves, to every seaside summer picnic.

But here, the upper-class twist of deep frying and sprinkling them with bits of organic smoked bacon made them not just deviled eggs, but *artisan* deviled eggs.

"Disgusting, aren't they?" A deep voice next to me asked.

"Are they?" I pointed to an egg that looked like it was covered with red ants. "I think they're charmingly retro."

I glanced over to see who was talking to me. It was a stunning man whose gaze was currently fixed on me, and only me.

"I'm looking for the ambrosia salad," he deadpanned. "Have you seen it?"

His eyes twinkled, and somehow I managed a quick comeback. "I think it's over by the spam croquettes."

He laughed and pointed to the eggs.

"How long do you think these have been sitting out?"

"At least six hours," I replied.

"Enough time for the mayo to ripen nicely."

"You *know* there's a microscopic bacteria party going on before our eyes."

I should've been nervous speaking to this gorgeous, charismatic specimen with the swoop of sun-streaked hair, but I was so over this Stepfordian event that my bad attitude canceled out any jitters and I felt free to insert bacteria humor into my party chatter.

"I'm Wesley," he smiled, holding out one strong, tanned, manicured hand.

I grasped it and gave him a too-strong handshake; to this day I swear I saw him wince.

"Ah. Like *The Princess Bride*."

"Common mistake. He's *Westley*. I've got no T."

"How embarrassing." I was only half-kidding. "I've only seen the movie twenty times."

He picked up two chartreuse-heaped eggs and held one out for me.

"Tell you what," he said. "I will if you will."

I took one and held it like it was nuclear waste. He popped the whole thing into his mouth. I followed suit. We chewed the warm mush and kept our eyes locked until we'd both swallowed.

"Now," he said, licking his teeth, "we're bonded for life."

I was smacking my lips quietly as I could and trying to suck the grit out of every crack and crevice.

"I need some champagne." I winced and licked my teeth. "*Right now.*"

He turned on his heel and disappeared. I used my tongue to cleanse the pasty residue from my palate and waited for him to return, calculating there was about a seventy-percent chance he would.

Two minutes later he broke through the crowd holding two drinks.

"Let's never speak of this again," he said in my ear, and we clinked glasses and tossed back the bubbly.

Vi ditched me for a hot bartender, which was fine because now she owed me. At sunset, Wesley dangled car keys in front of me and drove me to the beach in his BMW convertible, and we made out on the dinner jacket he laid out for us in the sand.

We fooled around for a while, keeping everything at a non-threatening PG-13 level. We sat up after an hour or so, me squeezed between his legs and leaning back on him as he played with my hair, as the first blur of pink announced the sunrise. He said, "'My soul is full of longing for the secrets of the sea.'"

I inhaled the ocean air, then let it out slowly.

"Profound," I replied.

"Not me. Those are Longfellow's words."

"I thought you were a finance guy?"

"I'm a 'finance guy' by trade," he said, "but I have the heart of a littérateur. I minored in English."

I knew it would be over by morning, even when he made the obligatory overture for my phone number, so I made a point of enjoying every second.

Minutes before the sun came up he ordered a town car to take me back to New York, then called me on the way home to tell me he missed my lips.

I told him he was delirious from salmonella poisoning, and he laughed so hard he choked on his own saliva.

CHAPTER

FOURTEEN

One day after I conducted my dawn stakeout at the home of Peter-the not-so-grieving husband, it's clear I didn't learn enough on that early morning mission.

Jacqueline has been missing for three days now, so I decide to get inside the house somehow, and do it in a way that Wesley can't freak out about if he happens to find out.

A casserole will not do for a wealthy, refined Englishman like Peter Pewter-Browne, so after I drop Wesley at TIG I head into town. I buy chocolate animals for the kids, wine for Peter, a ready-made fondue kit, a fresh loaf of bread, and a basket to put it all in.

I drive to their home for the second time in two days, but this time I park in front.

Jacqueline's Porsche Cayenne remains in the driveway, dead, static, orange. I carry my gift basket to the door and knock with my free hand.

The door swings open a minute later. A petite woman in the same grey uniform and tight bun as the staff at Nova's house opens the door and frowns at me. I am starting to understand these are their neutral expressions. It's as if I've entered the official country of Resting Bitch Face.

"Grüezi?"

"Grüezi. Ich heisse Rose Blackwood—"

"Yes."

I extend my offering. "I brought this for Peter and the kids. It's heavy…please, let me." I take a step closer to the door.

She doesn't move. There is a brief standoff, and then she gestures for me to come in. She closes the door and latches it behind me.

"I didn't catch your name," I say when we're in the kitchen and I've set the gift basket down on the soapstone island.

"Helena."

"Helena. I'm happy to meet you. I hear you've been a godsend since Jacqueline left. Those poor children. And poor Peter!"

Helena gives away nothing: no smile, no emotion.

Face to face with her, observing the way she stands, the color of her slicked-back platinum hair and the small build, I am certain she is the same smiling, languid, blonde-locks-flowing-in-the-breeze young woman I saw with Peter yesterday.

This explains why a pretty young woman is in his home at odd hours, but what explains her wearing his boxer shorts?

I must tread carefully. If Helena is sharing pillow talk with my top suspect, everything will get back to Peter. Every move I make, every word I say. More to the point, he'll believe her.

"Well," I say, wiping away one squeezed-out tear with a careful swipe of my index finger, "I hope they can use this basket. Wine for him, chocolate for the children, some dinner. I hope…I hope it makes the nights easier."

I'm babbling. I've been thrown off course by this woman who appears to have dual personas. There's one important question on my mind now: *What would Peter want to hear?*

I sink down on a kitchen stool and put my head in my hands.

"Wesley—my husband, he's a colleague of Peter's—Wesley and I are horrified by all of this. I thought Jacqueline and I were becoming friends. I thought she loved it here, you know? I can't *believe* she did this. I'm so glad you're here to comfort him and the children."

It's in her eyes; I see it. Suspicion, nerves, and smugness collide. I can read her face and her mind: *I'll be the woman of the house...soon.*

It occurs to me Helena might have had something to do with Jacqueline's disappearance.

I hear footfall. I stand and walk to the door of the kitchen.

"Oh! Is someone else home?" I ask.

"The Pewter-Browne family is fully staffed," she replies in perfect English with an Eastern European accent I am not worldly enough to place precisely. "That is the cleaner."

I begin sniffling loudly from my fake crying, then smile regretfully. "May I use the restroom?"

"Of course," she says, almost warming up, as much as a frozen side of beef would if left out for five minutes. "I will show you—"

"Please...no need. I remember how to get here from when I was here last week. I'll be right back."

I don't actually know where I'm going and I've never been inside, but these people seem to have bathrooms on every floor. I locate a stairway and wager the marital bedroom is at the top where the best views are. I am not wrong.

I make it to the main bedroom and stop at the threshold, listening for footsteps, whirring elevator parts, or breathing. Problem is, I think the staff are trained to tread lightly, to pad around and be invisible and soundless. I step inside.

The bedroom is huge, as expected. The en suite has Jack and Jill sinks, a deep Jacuzzi tub, and a walk-in a rainforest shower with a selection of nozzles on the wall.

I move silently to the closet.

Jacqueline has—or *had*—her own. Clothes and hangers are strewn on the floor and much of what's left on the racks is askew. I examine what remains.

Some women separate their wardrobes by color, some by size, some by occasion. Jacqueline categorized hers by season. Two things jump out at me: Only the winter and fall seasons have been raided. The other wardrobes have been mussed, but spring and summer appear fully intact.

Second, the winter wardrobe is entirely gone; how could she flee on her own with such a heavy load? I wonder if Peter has answers ready to address this. I pause, listen out, hear nothing, then sit on the edge of the bed and open her nightstand drawer.

When I see what's in there, I'm positive Peter isn't expecting anyone to do much searching for his wayward wife.

He made the basic gestures, sure, but his attempts were haphazard.

That much is clear to me because, right there in the nightstand drawer, is a familiar rectangular booklet.

It's blue, like mine, though a darker shade, and BRITISH PASSPORT is emblazoned at the top.

How does a woman flee without her passport? I close the drawer and stand up.

I turn to see Helena standing in the doorway, but this time her expression isn't blank.

It's pure venom.

Thankfully, I have something in my back pocket.

I hoped I wouldn't be caught, but I planned on it.

I pull out a mauve silk scarf and lay it carefully on the bed.

"I...I thought Peter should have this," I say in my most pathetic voice. I am not thrown by this woman's death stare, because I'm getting used to it—from everyone in this town. "Jacqueline left it at my house and I wanted to give it back."

She didn't, but she loves accessories, and I've seen her wear scarves and pashminas in various shades of purple.

I collapse on the edge of the bed and put my head in my hands.

"You shouldn't be here." Helena moves two paces toward me.

"I didn't mean to go out of bounds...I passed by on my way to the bathroom, and I just...I had to see for myself. Jacqueline was my best friend here. I feel so betrayed, you know?"

I stand and look her dead in the eye. "If you and Peter need *anything,* you let me know."

Crap. I might have gone too far. She narrows her eyes; I'm not supposed to know they're together, if they actually are.

"I want you *all* to know that if you need anything, Wesley and I are here. Babysitting, dinners, a listening ear, whatever."

Helena relaxes some, and seems to relish my insistence on using language that levels her up with Peter. That's the trick: validate them as a couple. Treat her like the woman of the house, not the help, not a homewrecker.

A hint of a smile flickers at the corners of her mouth. I see the confidence in the eyes. The ownership.

Or, I'm reading too much into all of it. Not for the first time, I consider the help in this town might be victims themselves. They're all young and dressed like dystopian servants, and they cater to their wealthy bosses silently, without complaint or personality.

I stand and let Helena lead me out. She'll tell Peter I was out of bounds, of course, but the spin will be in my favor. The sympathy will be with me.

If I've done this right, she'll be beholden to me. I'm a way in. If Helena *is* having an affair with Peter, she'll need someone like me to help smooth things over with the TWAGs if she ever wants to be introduced into expat society.

CHAPTER

FIFTEEN

I swing back to Old Town for a shopping excursion I've been putting off. I try Manor, one of two department stores I've found in town, and discover they have a decent selection of espresso machines.

I glance at the fancy chrome ones, the kind you see in coffee shops, then pass them by. There's a smaller box on a lower shelf. I crouch and see it's a cute one that appears to have a macchiato setting. I check the price tag: CHF 2,300.

Are they kidding? I could buy a car for that back in Seagrass Cove.

I skid along the row, examining every machine they have in stock. There is nothing under 800 Swiss francs, and the cheapest one looks like it's made of plastic. Worse, you'd have to foam your own milk separately.

I'm in no position to buy any of it. My financial situation is tenuous at best, and I've been avoiding any mention of money. I've been waiting for Wesley to wake up and make me a partner in this marriage, but he's forced my hand. It's time to have the talk I've been dreading.

The laptop balances on my lap on our stiff loveseat as I check my latest credit card statement. I bite my lip hard, preferring the pain of the flesh to the sting of my dwindling bank account.

The rainbow wheel turns, the page transitions through a fog, and then the numbers relay my situation in dire clarity. Seeing the math hits me like something that happened *to* me, not something I did.

My credit card balance is astronomically higher than I imagined. I've been keeping track of my spending in my head since I arrived in Zurich: 110 francs for groceries; 122 on wine and bread at the bakery-slash-convenience store down the road; 22 francs on weird new shampoo; and many macchiatos and pastries in town.

When I'm with Wesley, he pays. When he's at work, it's all on me.

I click on the latest statement, my anxiety blossoming like a time-lapse garden, so fast I can't squelch it.

Bäckerei Konditorei: 7.10 chf

Fee: 0.31

That was the first day I drove Wesley to work, when I dropped him, left the car outside TIG's offices, and wandered back through the Bahnhof where I discovered *Schoggigipfel,* which could be called croissants but are actually ethereal, buttery clouds oozing with warm chocolate-hazelnut filling that no New York bakery could come close to replicating.

Coop: 231 chf.

I forgot about that first grocery haul. I'd meant to spent less than a grand of my savings before mingling my financial life with my husband's, and with that one swipe went a fifth of it.

Fee: 10 USD.

Every purchase is followed by a charge I never authorized.

Fee.

Fee.

Fee.

I've been paying an additional five percent with every charge. A quick Google search reveals this credit card—many credit cards, apparently—charge for "foreign" transactions.

We're well into the twenty-first century and banks are pretending we're not a global community now? Worse, I've made more purchases than I entered into my mental spreadsheet. My spending here was always meant to be a stopgap.

The childhood triggers engage as if no time has passed. I shut the laptop and close my eyes. The sting of *not enough* hits me like a sack of steel balls to the kidney, even in this home, right now, even with a wealthy husband due home in a few hours.

If it's not in my hand, if I can't see it, if it doesn't have my name on it, it doesn't exist.

There was never enough growing up. When I was eight, I was told I couldn't go on the school field trip to the museum in Boston followed by lunch at McDonald's because we didn't have the money.

We don't have it, Rosie. My father had gestured around the shabby living room where my mother would spend the day once she got her fix. *There's nothing here.*

He'd turned away when I began to cry. *Cold*, I thought even so young. *My father doesn't care.*

I didn't know until years later that he turned away because he was crying, too. The next day he told me I was going on the field trip, but he never talked about where the money came from. *I've made arrangements. You're staying at Vi's for the rest of the week,* he told me.

Sometimes when my mother was in a bad stretch, my father would send me to grandma Mixie's house inland, a cottage that smelled of powdered sugar and decaying books, and she'd teach me about men and money. She explained to me how my mother chose well, but my father didn't.

"Most men aren't like your father. Or Violet's, for that matter. They will promise you everything and once you wear their ring, they can do whatever they want. Only you can make your dreams come true," she'd say.

"What about Princess Di?" I'd seen her on TV and splashed over endless covers on the *People* magazines my mother stole from her hairdresser.

"Perfect example," Mixie would say as she brought me a tray of her famous pecan cookies splayed out like flattened molasses mountains. "She's trapped—for now. Charles and his family control her. But she has a way out. Watch. She has her own resources. She has something about her, that one."

I wasn't sure Princess Di would ever get away from Charles, but I knew I didn't ever want to depend on another person for my survival. I thought I might like to get married someday, though. Violet's parents seemed happy, and they laughed, and her mother was always awake during the day.

"What are we supposed to do if we meet our prince?" I'd asked Grandma Mixie when I was ten. "Don't fall in love, don't take a chance, don't quit your job even if it means giving up love and adventure?"

"Of course not." She'd sat next to me on her sagging sofa and taken my cheeks between her warm, papery hands. "You get married if you love him. And you keep a sock drawer full of cash he doesn't know about, and you never give up your power.

"Take the leap," she'd said. "Bring your parachute."

I have Grandma Mixie cash in my sock drawer in Lucerne. Two grand in hundred-dollar bills. I know now that I should've brought more, but I believed Wesley when he stood in our kitchen in Manhattan and swore he understood that I was terrified to go to a place in which I'd be legally prevented from earning my own living.

That he grasped what he was asking me to give up. When TIG sponsored Wesley's work permit, I grew hot with panic when I read the part about the B permit, which stipulates I am legally prohibited from securing a paying job in Switzerland.

Wesley and TIG take care of all the big bills, so I avoided pushing him about giving me access to our accounts. I assumed he would step up and invite me into our marital finances.

I have told myself he is too busy, too distracted, too used to having all his needs met to understand my torment. He stood in that kitchen in TriBeCa and said, *No wife of mine is going to be wanting for anything.* Then he'd kissed me and reached under my nightgown and the conversation was over.

After I pay this credit card bill I will be left with fifty-one U.S. dollars with which to keep my New York bank account open. I didn't plan well. My sock drawer money is all I have to my name.

Wesley texted earlier to say Brett was dropping him home, so I sit alone and wait.

He walks in the door as I'm rifling through the cabinets for something to whip up for dinner. Why didn't I suggest a night out? This is a conversation best had in public.

"You up for a pre-made Swiss pizza? I bought it the other day at Coop. It doesn't look too dreadful."

"Sure," he calls from the living room. "I had a big lunch with the boys anyway."

I flip the oven to bake and paste on a smile.

He kisses me hello, and as we pull apart, I remark, "Speaking of food, you won't believe how expensive groceries are in this town. I discovered my American credit card has the *most* obnoxious fees. Should we stop by Suisse International Bank this week and open an account?"

He strides over to the dining room table.

"Here." He opens his briefcase and removes a fat envelope. "They gave me cash for my moving bonus the other day. Should be around five grand. Take it all."

He hands it to me like I'm a sex worker he just rolled off.

"*Wesley.*" It's heavy in my hand, but no matter what's in there, it won't last long enough. "Come on. I'm not going shopping in Old Town with five grand in my pocket."

"Why not?"

I stare him down.

"OK, OK. I'm sorry. I'm unorganized."

He sits on the love seat and exhales in an overly loud sigh.

"I know it's early, but this job...they don't mess around at TIG. Now I see why it's so competitive to get in. You have *no* idea how hard it is. I'm all over the place."

I perch next to him and rub his knee slowly, gently. "Where

is your paycheck going?"

He side-eyes me. Money, I can see, is an issue for both of us. In New York I never had to deal with it. I had an income, he spent his own money, and no one had to talk about it.

"It's going into a bank account TIG set up for me, I think. I don't know. It's all automatic."

I tilt my head. "You can't set up bank account without presenting an ID, I'm sure…"

"It's different here," he yawns. "Or…oh, yeah—wait. I remember, I did get my passport out at one point. Maybe there's a TIG credit union or something?"

He rubs his eyes.

"We can figure that out later," I say nonchalantly. "I'll need a credit card though. Sooner rather than later."

"It's not that easy, Rose," he snaps. "We have no credit history here. TIG gave me a company card we can always use until I have time to deal with all of this."

"Great! I assume there's an additional one for me?"

"It. Doesn't. Work. Like. That. Give me a break, will you?" He springs up and stalks to the bathroom. I hear the shaking of pills in a plastic bottle.

I knew better. I predicted this outcome, but I didn't prepare for it. I skated along with the promises he made, and now I'm in this place, begging for money to eat.

I shuffle over the warm tiles to the kitchen and slide the pizza into the oven. Wesley returns a few minutes later, his face more relaxed, his demeanor telling me he's ready to move on and pretend this never happened.

"By the way," he says lightly, "our things arrive tomorrow."

"Hallelujah," I say, trying to let the credit card argument go for now. "I really need some clothes. And the sectional."

There *is* one more thing we need immediately, and I know how to get it without a fight.

"By the way," I say brightly, "I was at Manor today and tried to buy an espresso machine, but they cost a fortune."

He looks at me.

"A half-decent machine costs at least two grand. It's the same one Nova and Brett have, but I can just get the cheaper one for eight hundred…"

He snaps to attention. "*What?* No. Get the best one. Not at the department store. Let's go pick one out online after dinner."

"Perfect," I smile, and we both relax, and he grabs some wine out of the fridge while I set out the plates.

Everything's fine. I take the envelope of cash and put it in my handbag.

Later, in a locked bathroom, I pull the wad out and count 5,500 Swiss francs. I peel off eight hundred, an amount I figure won't be missed, and tuck the bills into my sock drawer.

CHAPTER

SIXTEEN

I lurch upright in bed as a thunder crack and a flash of light penetrating microscopic holes in our blackout shutters jolts me awake.

I register the pounding rain coming down in sheets. I don't hear Wesley stir, so I rise and tiptoe out of the bedroom, heading to the living room and the glass wall overlooking the balcony.

The valley has morphed from marshmallow white to drab gray in a matter of hours, thanks to the pelting rain dissolving the snow and ice. I thought winter was here for good, and I barely noticed the warming yesterday as clouds rolled in. I should be more aware of my new climate, but I gave up checking local forecasts because they're all in German.

The wind howls and blows more snow away, carrying the remaining ice with it over the edge of our balcony. I'm cold, jittery, on edge. And then I hear screams. They are not distant, through-the-valley yells. They are loud and close.

I open the door and step outside, wincing as my feet hit the wet, icy stones as I walk to the ledge. I peek over, and I see something that makes my knees wobble.

A woman. My neighbor.

She lights up under a bolt of white lighting that illuminates her face like a spotlight. She senses me, and she swivels.

Her arms are held in a V, raised up to the sky, her head thrown back as she screams at the rain.

I am about to run back to bed when the flood comes. I hear it first, and then I look up and see the river rushing down our hill right toward her, as if a small dam has burst.

I race back inside and run through the living room, down the stairs, unlock the front door and wrestle it open, and dash, barefoot, into the waterfall. The snow that built up on our steep hill has turned to a muddy mess, and as the water pounds down, I can see the heavy load loosening.

The rain instantly soaks me, my hair, my nightgown.

The woman turns to face the hill and the river rushing toward her. She protects her head with her arms as the worst of it pours over her, and thankfully it soon becomes a slower, though still voluminous, rush.

My neighbor stands in the face of it and begins taking down her plates, one by one, in a futile rescue mission.

I look up the hill when I hear a great roar. The earlier deluge was the starter flood. The big one is coming now.

I scream into the storm. "Stop! Please! You must go inside. It's too dangerous!"

But it's as if my voice doesn't work; it is swallowed up by the sound of water pounding on stone. I scream again, and as I do, someone grabs my shoulder.

"Get inside, Rose!" Wesley yells at me. "What are you doing? Come on!"

I turn back to the woman.

"Wesley! We have to help her!" I kick my way through two inches of water on the landing at the top of the cement stairs.

"Rose—no!"

He's right. We *all* need to get out of this immediately. Fresh, fat rivulets of water are sluicing down the hillside. We're in danger of a mudslide or a flash flood.

Thunder cracks. Lightning follows, lighting up our hill and the valley like a flash on god's camera. All at once, as if choreographed in advance, two hands reach out: one long arm emerges from the neighbor's door and yanks her inside, and Wesley takes my arm and pulls me to him.

I hear another crash and look back to see ice, rocks, water, mud roaring down the hill. Wesley drags me inside me like I'm a rag doll.

"*Never* do that again," he scowls, rubbing water out of his eyes, smoothing his hair down. "You could've been killed."

A part of me knows he's right.

Another part of me, perhaps a bigger part, can't help but acknowledge the nagging feeling that I don't know this person, this man who had a choice and didn't help a human being in danger, didn't want to try, and is angry that I did.

The next morning, Wesley rises early to get ready for work. I'm half asleep when he shuffles back into the bedroom with a towel around his waist and toothbrush in hand.

"I checked out the damage," he says. "It's not too bad. These people really know how to build to the environment."

"Should we call someone?"

"Nah. It's a little mud and some twigs and leaves and stuff. Whatever drainage system they use worked brilliantly. You'll see when you get up. If you want, I can help you clean it up when I get home tonight."

"I don't even know if we have a broom or anything to clean it with," I yawn.

"You'll figure it out," he says.

I reach around and hit the button to raise the shutters. The sun pours in, and Pilatus comes into view across the valley, snow tipped as always but now presiding over a land returned to its natural brown and green state.

"That old woman creeps me out," Wesley says, and then flips his toothbrush on and pads back into the bathroom. "We should keep our distance."

I don't bother replying. I'm not sure if our neighbor is interesting or threatening, or if she's not well, or if she despises us, because she hasn't spoken more than one word to me.

After coffee and toast, I venture outside to assess the damage. Will I be scrubbing concrete for the next four hours? Will I have to instruct Wesley to buy a shovel?

It's nothing like he described.

The walkway between our two homes is immaculate, slicked wet but clean, with little trace of detritus or fallen mud. The dirt is cleaned up, but the collectibles, the strange plates now in pieces, are not.

I see my neighbor alone by the hill, grimly picking up her collection outside her front door. I approach gingerly.

She turns her head slowly, her blue-grey hair, that striking, pretty color, curled under her ears again. I gesture to her plates with two hands. I try to speak with my body language: *Can I help?*

She nods and keeps working. I stand next to her and begin the slow bend and rise of picking up pieces of shattered ceramic and dented metal, setting them in the bag she's using to collect scraps.

We work silently until they're cleared away and the broken ones are separated from the intact. I make eye contact to let her know I'm going back inside.

"Watch out," she says in a sharp, croaky German accent. "*Look.* Take care."

I should walk away.

"Watch out for what?" I ask. She points to my front door.

"Of them," she says. "Take care of *them.*"

CHAPTER

SEVENTEEN

Take care.

Surely my neighbor doesn't mean "take care" of them—she means *be careful.* Her English is coarse but her delivery is crystal clear.

The only people who have been in our home since we moved here are Wesley, Jacqueline, Heidi, our TIG handlers on the first day we moved in, and me. Wesley's at work every day, and I'm always home.

Almost always.

Walk away, Rose.

"*Who*?" I ask again. "My husband? You've met my husband, Wesley?"

"No, no, *no*," she says, shaking her head. She seems to be in some distress now.

Jacqueline mentioned to me early on that older-generation Swiss aren't always fluent in English, partly because many don't practice it once school ends. I guess her age to be between seventy and eighty. For all I know she's saying to take care of the little animals I sometimes hear skittering around hidden places in our home.

I check the time. The movers arrive in an hour, and I want to be ready for the poor souls who have to lug our life's possessions up fifty stairs.

"Entschuldigung," I say as a goodbye, because *Auf Wiedersehen* feels a bit aggressive, given she's trying to help me.

She watches me go, and I know it's time I took my German lessons seriously, because I'd really like to know what she's trying to tell me.

The movers arrive a few hours later and I worry someone's going to have a heart attack as they strap boxes to their backs and hunch up the steep stairs, but they manage without collapsing, and when the last box is carried up and they're back in their truck, I peel off some fifties from the cash Wesley gave me.

I'm left alone with endless stacks of boxes. I start on my closet, then make a dent in the kitchen, then take a break and wait for Wesley to come home and help.

Wesley doesn't come home. Not until I'm reading in bed at nine, angry, fuming, worried.

"I waited for you," I say when he strides into the bedroom like nothing's wrong. "I texted you. Nothing. I was worried sick. How hard is it to send a text?"

I grew more furious than concerned as time passed with no response from him. I slurped down yogurt and munched on toasted two-day-old peasant bread for dinner, then felt overwhelmed unpacking boxes one at a time.

I pictured him with the boys at Seebar, losing track of time, not wanting to be the guy who has to ask his wife's permission to party.

"We had a last-minute client to entertain," he says as he unbuttons his cuffs. "My phone ran out of power, and, you know…"

He clears his throat. I give him nothing.

"Come on, Rose—it's not *done* here. You don't pull out your phone in social situations. It's considered extremely rude."

"Yeah? Well, in this house it's considered extremely deadly to leave your wife hanging."

"Point taken," he half-grins. We're both irritated, I can tell, but he tries to brush it off.

I am still suspicious. The phone-ran-out-of-power routine is not a viable excuse at our age.

"I made some decent headway on the unpacking," I inform him. "But we're far from the cozy nest we deserve."

"I'm sure you'll finish it tomorrow," he says, stepping to the bed and bopping me on the nose with two light fingers. "Not to worry."

I'll finish it. Not a chance.

"I'll wait for you before I start on the living room," I say, setting my book aside, ready to sleep. "I can handle the kitchen, and I'll start on the bathrooms while you're at work."

I'm not organizing your closet, either. We're a team.

He's headed to the bathroom, and I'm treated to a noncommittal "Mm hmm."

Later, when he slips into bed, I lean over to kiss him and take the chance to smell him from his neck to his wrists to his ears.

There are no alarm bells. He's not freshly showered, nor does he emit any unknown perfume or *eau de cute intern* scent that I can detect.

Before this moment, I never worried about him cheating on me. I can't predict what will happen in ten years, but right now our sex life is on point, we have fun together, and he's never gone off the grid before. He always comes home.

After our first "date" on a Connecticut beach, Wesley surprised me at every turn, starting with calling me while I was still in the car, and then again the next day.

I didn't answer the second, third or fourth times.

That year alone, I'd been ghosted after the fourth date by Jim The Accountant and dumped via text by Richard The Broke Poet. I knew this guy with the dimple and sparkling eyes would dump me for a model before you could say Soho House. I'd rather skip straight to the breakup.

On the fourth call, I hit *cancel*, and within two minutes Wesley sent a text.

I'll be at Grande Tavern at 8. Look for the guy with the eager eyes and the pink carnation.

I smiled in spite of myself and wrote back too quickly.

I'm not a carnation kind of date. I see a carnation, I run.

Ha. Smart girl.

In the end I decided I had nothing to lose. I went in eyes wide open. Free dinners, maybe some amazing sex if it got that far, and fountains of champagne I couldn't afford on a writer's salary.

"Come to my college friend's party this weekend at the beach," he said at the end of our Grande Tavern dinner date, at which he ordered the mushroom risotto after I told him I was trying to stop eating animals. "I'll pick you up at eleven."

"I'll think about it," I said.

He picked me up downtown.

In a helicopter.

I have permanent jetlag, so it doesn't take much to wake me. The night after the big storm, an alarming sound penetrates the whir of the white noise app we sleep with. I blink in the darkness and try to hear past the static.

There it is. Rustling. Close enough for me to hear it from our bedroom.

I throw off the covers and pad out to the living room. The open-plan space is fortified by a frozen army of shadowy stacked boxes, and my adrenaline kicks up. Too many places for an intruder to hide.

I stand motionless at the top of the stairs and wait for the burglar to announce himself with a footstep, a bang, or maybe an involuntary bout of heavy breathing after climbing our endless stairs.

I flip on the lights in the living room, dining room and kitchen, then freeze in place again. I hear nothing but the distant static of white noise from our bedroom.

I tiptoe down to the laundry room, poke my head in, then turn on the light. There's nowhere to hide, and nothing there but a basket, ironing board and two appliances. I do a recon in the small storage room across the foyer, but it's all clear.

The windows at the back and side of the house are narrow and open outward, leaving a space where nothing bigger than a squirrel could fit through, and none of them appear to have been broken or forced open.

I head back upstairs and stop in the kitchen for a glass of

water. Just as I hear the sucking of the seal when I pull open the fridge, the foreign noises kick in again: *Rustle, rustle, click.* My heart pounds so hard I can hear blood rushing in my ears.

Something's off, my gut says.

The noises are the unfamiliar sounds of a new place, my head retorts.

It's nothing sinister, nothing like what Jacqueline was experiencing in her house. I bring my water back to bed and lie awake for another two hours while I try to quiet my mind so I can sleep. I fail.

But as I stare into the dark and listen to the sound of my husband's breathing, the answer to two of my problems comes to me.

I'm up at eight making coffee while stepping around stacks of boxes, and when Wesley wanders out in underwear and a T-shirt, I hold out a mug from my kitchen fort.

"Thanks," he says, and leans over a box for a quick kiss. "How'd you sleep?"

I pause. I decide not to tell him about the noise. It was nothing.

"Like a rock. You?"

"Not too bad. I'm a bit hung over. The client was Russian. The vodka was flowing."

He shuts his eyes hard for a few beats as if to flex them, stretch them.

"You should take the car," I tell him. "Can you bring something home for dinner? I don't see myself cooking tonight. There's nothing here to make, anyway."

"Affirmative."

"Oh. One more thing before you go." I add sugar to my mug and step out to meet him in the living room, where he's drinking coffee and gazing at the mountains.

I stand next to him. "You're aware all the TIG wives have hired help? Maids, butlers…"

"And nannies, yep," he says.

"And nannies." I choose not to read anything into that addition to my list. "You're busy at work, and this unpacking job is a lot for one person, so I thought I could get someone in to help set up our home. Nova suggested we request our staff sooner rather than later, so don't you think—"

"Absolutely," he says, turning to me. "Sooner. I'll get you the agency's number."

"No need." I'm already texting Heidi with my free hand.

He drains his coffee.

The agency everyone uses is Happy Helpers, Heidi writes back.

Happy Helpers? Seriously?

Ha ha. It's a translation thing. U will see a lot of that here.

"Off to shower. I'll leave it to you," Wesley says, smacking my butt as he leaves.

My Spidey sense has been tingling about Happy Helpers ever since I saw Irina in Nova's cupboard and heard her arguing with Jacqueline about *secrets*, so this is the perfect chance to dig deeper. If the expats' household staff are being exploited by a sketchy agency, if the workers aren't treated right, or if something illegal is going on, it could be linked to Jacqueline's disappearance.

CHAPTER
EIGHTEEN

After Wesley leaves for work, I tuck my laptop under my arm and stride to the bedroom to begin my search. The Happy Helpers website pops up right away.

Potential clients can choose from various combinations of help: cleaners, cooks, nannies, all-in-ones, live-in, live-out, full time and weekly.

Under each category there are two large silver buttons:

ENERGY! EXPERIENCE!

I click on **ENERGY!**

I'm directed to a page with rows of headshots of young women, none of them smiling, all of them sporting severe buns like mugshots from a Robert Palmer music video gone wrong.

I click back to the homepage and hit the **EXPERIENCE!** button.

I can't believe what comes up. More rows of women with severe buns and neutral expressions—but these women are all older, appearing to be fifty, sixty, seventy.

I count six countries of origin on one page alone, then catch sight of a sidebar where you can search for your preferred Happy Helper by country.

Seeing it laid out this way, like a restaurant menu, pings my radar. This is not a search by skills or qualifications. It's something else.

There's no phone number listed, so I click a "chat" bubble at the bottom of the screen and explain what I need to the virtual agent.

You are with TIG? Of course, madam, how can we help? If you are flexible on the category you receive, we can send someone for you right away, if you wish.

Whoever is available is fine.

Except that's not true. I quickly add, *Today's work will include some lifting and unloading of moving boxes.*

She will arrive by noon. Let us know if she is even one minute late.

The bell rings right on time, and I open the front door to see a clone of Irina and Helena. My Happy Helper has the same pale skin, bun tied back so tight the skin around her hairline appears uncomfortably stretched, and the same dead, neutral expression.

"I am Maira," the young woman says.

"Welcome," I say. "Please, come in."

I lead her upstairs and weave my way into the kitchen. "Can I get you a drink, water, soda, coffee…?"

"Which room shall I start?" She doesn't smile. None of them do. It must be a rule. I can't place her accent, but it sounds similar to Irina's.

"Follow me," I say. I lead her down the hall to Wesley's closet, and she eyes up the towering boxes crowding the space. "If you could unpack these and organize his closet however you think is best, that would be great. Let me know if you need help with anything."

She is already using her fingernails to pull the tape off a box with the focus of a surgeon.

With her setting the pace, we unpack everything in the house before dinnertime. I'm sweating and filthy at the end of it, but Maira doesn't have a hair out of place.

Just before six I approach her as she's sliding the last book onto the shelf in my office.

"Great job," I smile. "Thank you for your hard work."

"Of course." She bows her head.

"I'll see you out," I tell her, leading the way toward the stairs. I stop at the top.

"Oh, I almost forgot. Is cash OK for a tip?"

The red fifty-franc bill is in my hand, folded over.

"*Entschuldigung.* Sorry. No tips. We work on salary."

Her English is perfect. It occurs to me that Irina could have been playing down her grasp of the language that night at Nova's house. I had a strong suspicion she understood everything we were saying.

"Oh? Do they pay well?" I ask.

"I'm sorry?" Maira is looking at the floor.

Too blunt. Even if my probing might help discover what happened to Jacqueline, this is a clunky way to go about it.

"No, *I'm* sorry," I assure her. "I should never have asked such personal questions. It's just, well…I want to be sure the company is a good one to use. Back in America there are some places that don't treat their workers well."

That's too much information. I don't know how else to do this. She is trying to politely leave without enraging the client, who is me.

She's staring past me to the stairs, which I'm blocking. I move aside.

"Maira," I blurt. "Do you feel safe?"

She hurries past me. "Thank you, ma'am. Have a nice day. It has been a pleasure."

I hear the door slam shut behind her.

Wesley brings home a pizza not long after Maira leaves, and after he sets the box on the counter he makes a slow three-sixty turn to take in the warm, bright, settled home. Candles flicker on the dining-room table and a cozy rug warms the tiled floor between the fireplace and our plush sectional sofa.

"This," he says, turning slowly to me, "is a place I can *live*. You're amazing, you know that?"

He grabs me and draws me in, and I didn't realize until this second how much I've missed our closeness. Two weeks of scrambling to start a new life and a new job have pulled us apart physically and emotionally.

We're comfortably quiet as we plow through the pizza and chase it with Fendant. When we've finished, we take our wine over to the sofa.

"Oh, how I've missed you," Wesley says to the couch as he sinks into his favorite spot in the corner.

I sit perpendicular to him, stretching my legs out and leaning on his shoulder.

"How was work?"

"Not too bad, actually," he replies, stroking my hair. "I'm getting the hang of it."

"Someday you'll have to tell me what you actually *do*."

"When I know, you'll know." He points to the wall in front of us. "It's a crime we haven't used the fireplace yet."

"It's tough to enjoy dancing flames without something to sit on," I point out. "Can you ask around at work tomorrow about where to get firewood? I wouldn't know where to start."

Our breathing synchs as we relax, sip, and rest. After a few minutes, I ask him, "How's Peter doing? The kids must be traumatized."

"Not great," Wesley says. I feel him tensing up. He's not stupid.

"Has he told you what was in her goodbye note?"

He drains his glass and faces me.

"If I tell you, will you drop it? And you can't tell the other wives. Promise me you won't."

"Cross my heart and hope to die. I won't tell the other wives."

But I probably won't drop it. And I'll definitely tell Vi, if I can ever get ahold of her. It's been impossible with her schedule and the six-hour time difference.

Wesley shrugs with great effort, as if a heavy weight is pressing down on him. "Jacqueline told Peter she wanted a clean break. She said he'd been pulling away, that she needed space, and she was going home."

I'm going to play Peter's game and pretend that is a viable explanation for why a woman who left a gala to say goodnight to her children would then abandon them without so much as a hug goodbye.

"Wow," I say. "That's rough. Isn't it odd, though, that she never said anything to me, and even her closest friends thought everything was fine? She was president of the club. That's a commitment. And I can't get past her leaving the kids."

"They're *step* kids," he tells me. "They have a mother."

I sit up straight. Jacqueline never told me that. It shouldn't change things, not really, but it does add a new layer.

"Where's their birth mother?"

"Back in England, I think," he shrugs. "I heard something about how she has a new family so she gave Peter custody. I really think Jacqueline took off, Rose. Around here, things aren't always what they seem."

I've figured that out. I didn't know *he* noticed it.

"Apparently, she left open the possibility of coming back," he adds. "But I don't advise her trying it."

He yawns, a great, slow, loud, Cowardly Lion gawp.

"Oh?"

"Peter's moved on," Wesley says. "He's totally shut down. The thing about men is, Rose, once you screw us over, we're done. You'll never get us back again."

"Good to know."

"Oh, by the way, we're going to need some good boots before Saturday," he says. "The Club's meeting for a family hike now the mud's dried up, before the winter snows come back for good."

CHAPTER

NINETEEN

A few dozen club members, including a gaggle of chirping children, pile into cable cars up to the Mount Rigi *Panoramaweg* on a frigid Saturday morning.

On the way up in the swaying pod, Wesley is glued to the window. I shrink back. The incline is steep and the drop to earth from this bouncing, razor-thin wire is too far for my liking.

When we make it to the top, Wesley and I fall in with the chattering, excited crowd that would make an outsider think nothing was amiss. You'd never know their president, their friend, their fellow mom, had disappeared without a trace.

Someone's small child races past us as we hike, knocking Wesley in the knee so he almost buckles. "Ouch!" my husband calls out as he catches himself. "Hey! You better run, kid. I'm coming for you!"

The boy turns and sees my husband charging at him, growling, arms out, pretending to be a monster with a twinkle in his eye, and the child shrieks with delight and sprints ahead.

I hang back, soaking in the splendor around us and observing my potential fellow Club members. No one is talking about

Jacqueline. No one pats Peter on the back and says, *There, there.* Perhaps that's because his demeanor doesn't call for such treatment.

He jokes and laughs with the rest of them, wielding dark English humor to charm whomever he's talking to, ambling along the path in his Tom Brady pom-pom hat, checking in with various members with a tap on the arm, a quick rub on the lower back, a cheeky wink.

The path here is wide, and at the start it is all downhill, though I was assured we will be subjected to a steep upward slog before long.

Teresa, whose lilac hair is poking out from under her hood, passes me, waving and throwing me a knowing glance. She's with two women who offer *Grüezis* in unison. I don't recognize them, and I doubt they were at the vision board party, but I could have met them at the gala.

I see Heidi trailing behind Raj, who stays with their two kids as the trail grows narrower and steeper. Then Heidi stops. I'm near the back of the pack, save for a harried family with a pregnant mom and a dad pushing a stroller, and it takes me a moment to catch up with Heidi.

"Hey," she says when I do. "I didn't want to ask you down in the parking lot in front of everyone, but what happened to you at Pickwick's the other day?"

"Wesley called while I was at the bar," I say as we start walking again. "He had a break at work and I wanted to ask him about the Peter thing. Turns out there's nothing to tell. They're friendly at work, but Wesley doesn't know any more than the rest of us."

Heidi nods and turns to me. Her natural eyelashes are like spiders' legs, long and make-up free, framing huge, light-brown eyes. Her auburn curls bounce under a soft white hat.

"I'm glad that's all it was," she says. "I thought you might've left because you were upset we weren't out searching for our friend. I know it's hard, Rose. I do."

Her breath curls out into the cold in clouds of white smoke. "You're a newlywed, so things are probably amazing and perfect. But Jacqueline and Peter…well, they've had their troubles over the years. We'll talk more over cocktails, but I can tell you it wasn't all rainbows and unicorns in their house."

No shit. "Of course I believe you. I'm sorry if I was too pushy," I apologize, despite a New Year's resolution to stop apologizing so much. "It's fine—really."

I want to run and meet up with Wesley, but he is deep in conversation with Brett, and I decide not to bother him while he's got the ear of a TIG senior vice president.

"Good." Heidi reaches around my shoulders and gives me a quick squeeze. "Because we're happy you're here. I'd hate for you to think we're terrible people. Oh—and I'm not sure if Jacqueline told you before she…I mean, um, did anyone tell you the next London trip is Thursday?"

I shake my head and try to hide my distaste. Their good friend has vanished, and they're planning a fancy vacation? If *my* best friend went missing, if Violet disappeared without a trace, I couldn't conceive of flouncing off on a girls' trip to get my hair done. It's surreal.

"I'll text you all the details," Heidi smiles. "It's all about pampering ourselves. Hair appointments, Christmas shopping, and divine restaurants, of course."

Something catches her eye and she lets go of me. I follow her gaze, but the only action I note is Seychelle and Kristoff walking stiffly, and notably far apart. When he strays her way, she strides forward and joins a conversation with Nova and another woman.

"Oh, no. Raj! Silas, no spitting!" Heidi breaks into a run, because Raj is deep in conversation with someone and not paying attention to Silas the spitter.

And then, out of nowhere, interrupting my quietude, Peter appears next to me. I'm startled, but I manage to avoid giving him the satisfaction of yelping in surprise.

I hadn't noticed how far Heidi and I had lagged behind the others. I walk faster.

He stays in lockstep with me and every ten feet or so he "accidentally" bumps lightly into me as we walk. He's too close. Every time I move, he shadows me.

"Don't like heights?" *Bump.*

"I'm sorry?" *Shuffle.*

"I saw you cowering in the gondola. You know what they say about phobias."

I walk faster.

"The best treatment for irrational fear is immersion." The others are almost out of sight around a bend. "Oh, darling. Don't be offended. I'm *joking*, love."

He laughs and wraps an arm around my waist. I squirm, but he pulls me tighter. "You'll get used to British humor."

The trail has narrowed, and I'm not going to accept being grabbed by a man reeking of faux charm. I wrench myself away and race ahead.

"I understand sarcasm better than you think," I snap back.

An understatement. Sarcasm is my love language. *His* brand of banter, a barely concealed weapon of manipulative narcissism, is not.

Peter is at my heels. I hear his feet scraping on sand and gravel. I am almost running now.

"We're about to hit the Cliff Walk," he says. I don't look back. "That, my dear, will make you glad you moved to Lucerne. This is a life the drones back in our hometowns will never see because they're too scared to leave the familiar. They're hunkered down in their cotton-wool lives, cemented to their phones, never looking up or taking a risk. You're one of us now, Rose. You're already better than the rest."

I come upon the Cliff Walk. There is no more buffer. The trail narrows to maybe two feet, if that, and it's flanked by a wall of solid rock on one side and a sheer drop on the other. I can see sharp tips of spruce trees and jagged boulders below; it is more than 6,000 feet down if you believe the signage at the cable-car station.

Hikers are protected from a fall by two wires strung between short fence posts. A grown human adult can easily slip through it. The lake is still and plastic from here, like a photograph. There is a peace to this distance, and part of me never wants to return to the bottom. I snap out of it and jump back, realizing I've lost the sound of Peter's feet on gravel.

Suddenly, he's back. He's like a ghost, the way he sneaks up. I'm too close to the edge. I miscalculated. He is next to me. I try to step back, but my foot slips, and I catch myself before I fall hard, possibly all the way down. I feel death taunting me, reaching up to grab me.

The end is physically and figuratively close to me, whispering in my ear. *One more inch, one more half step, one slip. That's all it will take.*

Peter spoons me from behind. I can feel his hip bones grinding into me. I have nowhere to go but over.

"Amazing, isn't it?"

"My husband will be wondering where I am," I croak.

"Trust me. I have you."

He pushes me closer to the edge until I'm forced to step on the cement anchoring the fenceposts, which places me high enough to fold over the wire and tumble down. I open my mouth to scream.

I can hear the group singing and laughing, so near to us, just around the bend. I can't see them for the overhanging rock leaving a four-foot space to walk through.

Peter whispers in my ear, "Scared?"

"*No,*" I hiss, and elbow him as hard as I can in the ribs.

"*Ow!*" He growls, and he has the positioning, the height and the weight, and he pushes again, and I'm about to go down. I feel his knee jerk into mine. I buckle, but he's suddenly backed away, and I scream as I start slipping. I'm grabbing at the air, at the wires, feeling them in my palms, the metal cutting into them as I fight to stop myself from falling. My legs are over the edge and my butt is touching the last bit of ledge before air.

"Whoa!" Someone shouts in alarm. I think it's Kristoff's voice behind me.

Then: "*Shit, Rose!*" That's Wesley.

An octopus's worth of arms are linking under mine, grabbing my legs, taking me by the waist. Four people haul me in, stand me up, and offer comforting words.

"Hey, Rosie, you're fine. You're OK," says Kristoff, his face red with the cold under his beard. He rubs my upper arms reassuringly.

Raj has me by the waist, still, and I suspect he knows if he lets go I might collapse. Teresa is there, holding me under one armpit. Club members surround me until Wesley gets to me, and then the others fall back.

"*Sweetie*," he cries. "You scared me to death! What *happened?*"

My question exactly. I fall into him. He holds me up, hugs me.

"You gotta be careful up here," Peter warns, shaking his head. "There's not a lot Alpine rescue can do if you go over the side."

"What happened?" Wesley asks again. "How did you fall behind? You could've been killed!"

Peter shakes his head in a show of regret and concern. "We were chatting about how nice it was of Rose to bring a hamper to the house the other day, and we simply weren't paying attention," Peter offers a wafer-thin explanation. "Oh, sorry—you call them *gift baskets*, don't you? The kids and I ate all the chocolate in one sitting. Anyway, your wife stepped too close to the edge and slipped, and I was too far away to get to her in time."

I watch Wesley's face. He doesn't flinch, doesn't need a beat to pretend he knew I'd gone to Peter's house bearing gifts. "It was the least we could do," he tilts his head in sympathy. "You need anything at all, we're here."

"I know that, mate," Peter says with a well-placed crack in his voice at *mate*.

He's done a brilliant job of taking the attention off my near-

133

death experience and making it about him, and in the process he's deflected all questions of his involvement in it.

The children are hanging on the wire "fence." Peter's little girl, the one I saw him send off to school a few days ago, says, "Look, Daddy! You can see the hill by our house down there. The one mama said never, ever go up alone because the monsters will get us."

"There are no monsters," Brett says to the girl.

"You might see a runaway yak," Peter jokes, scruffling her head.

"You might as well teach her early," Teresa chimes in from her spot ahead of them. "There are monsters everywhere, kiddo. They hide in crevices and in trees, in caves and in the dark, and unless you know what to look for, you're always one step away from danger. Swiss folklore has child snatchers, baby eaters, zombie children, dragons, snakes with cat's heads…"

"*Teresa*!" Heidi snaps. "That's not appropriate for little ears. Stop that."

Teresa winks and starts walking. "You know it's true. The witches of Belalp, kobolds, Devil's Bridge, the Herwisch…better not make them mad, or they'll turn on their lanterns and lead you to your doom."

The sound of her voice fades as she moves ahead of us.

"Thank god Peter was there to catch you," Wesley breathes, squeezing me, staying with me as everyone else moves on past the Cliff Walk. "I don't want to think about what might've happened if he wasn't."

He kisses my head and whispers, "Are you OK to keep going?"

I nod back. "I'm good."

I'm not. Not even a little bit.

CHAPTER

TWENTY

The trip to London is easier than some commutes I've done between boroughs in New York City. Seychelle picks me up at home and we meet the others at the Bahnhof. The train takes us directly from Lucerne into the bowels of Zurich airport, which is the most convenient, clean, well-organized one I've ever been to.

A Range Rover is waiting for us at London City Airport, which is like a glorified bus station, easy to get in and out of, and off we roll to the salon on Bond Street. A chatty east ender called Zeb paints on my highlights. Nova gets a trim and a blowout, and Heidi's roots are obliterated.

"What's next?" I say as I pay with the credit card Wesley gave me.

"Lunch at Mermaid Depot," Heidi says.

"And then shopping," Nova adds. "Kensington High Street, I think."

Mermaid Depot sounds like a children's toy store, but it's actually an exclusive and suitably dark members-only club.

A man wearing what I hope is an ironic sailor's outfit leads us

135

to our table. Seychelle slips away as the rest of us are seated in a corner with four votives flickering and four rickety farmhouse style chairs. As we situate ourselves, I nod over to where Seychelle has stopped to visit with a man who looks very much like a prince I've seen in magazines.

"Is that guy she's talking to who I think he is, that royal—"

"*Yes*," Heidi whispers, making a point of not looking over at the pack of beautiful people.

She pulls her chair in and accepts a menu from the sailor.

"Her name. It's—"

"Seychelle, yes," Nova replies to me. "Because she was conceived in the Seychelles. Allegedly."

Nova is languid, smiling at me, fucking with me. I decide in this moment to make her like me. However long it takes, I'm going to lure her in with whatever charm I can muster. If I want to thrive here, we need to be friends.

"I meant her last name." She knew what I meant.

Heidi sighs. "And yes, her maiden name is Windsor because…just forget it."

"Not because she's one of the British—?"

"Yes, she's blue-blooded, but *never* bring it up." Heidi is whispering now. "It's all very hazy. She wasn't supposed to take that name. Story goes her father's a love child of Prince whatshisname. But it's not talked about. Strictly off limits."

So, old Seychelle is full-on royalty with a side of shame. She appears at our table.

"Hey, girls." She drawls out the *gulls*, laying a hand on my shoulder and another on Nova's next to me. "Right. It's champagne o'clock."

She wiggles two willowy fingers at the sailor.

"Bobby, *dahling*, a bottle of Perrier-Jouët rose for the table, please."

Bobby dashes off and we peruse our menus. "My favorite is still on here," Heidi says. She turns to me and points to Nova and Seychelle. "These two can't handle spice, so I always split the fiery calamari with—"

She claps a hand over her mouth.

"I can't believe I did that. I guess I'm not used to her being gone…"

Seychelle looks down at the table and we're quiet for a moment.

The champagne arrives, and everyone brightens up, and suddenly the ugliness of reality is wiped away like a sponge over a dirty countertop.

After lunch I try on clothes for hours, and the others buy a few items each, but it's not until the third store I find my fit. I select jeans, three tops, and a dress for New Year's Eve.

I present the credit card Wesley gave me at the register. The cashier runs it, then shakes his head and holds my card out like it's covered in cooties.

"I'm sorry."

"Can you try again?" I ask, gritting my teeth.

He does, then hands it back without looking me in the eye.

"Just use another one," Heidi says.

I didn't bring another one. It didn't occur to me I'd need it.

"It must be because it's from another country," I say.

My friends synch their cringe faces. I am no doubt flushing a deep shade of maroon, as my cheeks have grown hot. Before full-on panic can ensue, I have an idea.

I pick out the two things I really wanted, the dress and the jeans, which add up to 99 British pounds. "Can you only ring these two up, please," I say.

The cashier does as I ask, runs the card once more, then breaks into a relieved grin. "Brilliant," he says. "You're sorted."

It wasn't declined because of a bank mix-up. I was going over the card's spending cap. Wesley put a limit on it.

On *me*.

We walk from the store to the restaurant. London in December is gloomy, wet and warm, but the Brits know how to do the holidays. Everything is lit up with fairy lights and wreaths, and holiday music is everywhere.

When we arrive at a restaurant in a converted firehouse, I order a cosmo and it goes down like candy. I am relaxing now; perhaps I was overreacting about credit-cardgate.

Maybe the bank put the cap on, not my husband. Maybe it *is* something to do with using the card in another country.

"When is the Christmas shopping happening?" I ask my friends. They're all drinking dirty martinis with bleu-cheese stuffed olives.

"Tomorrow morning," Seychelle replies. "We do a power-shop at Harrods before the flight home."

I consider sleeping in. I don't know if I can afford Harrods, and I don't have anyone to buy for. I'm ordering Vi's present online, and I haven't the faintest clue what to get Wesley, the man who can afford everything.

My parents are out of the picture. I grew up in a coastal Massachusetts town with a raging heroin problem, and my mother was an addict who would never get help. We're an old, familiar story. For my mom, she of the comic book-worthy name Sloane Stone, it started with prescription pills. When those became too hard to acquire, she moved on to heroin.

She had a few sober months over the years, mostly when my father would threaten to leave. When he went missing there was no one left to demand that of her, and she spiraled.

Vi and I were freshmen at UMass when the call came in about our fathers getting lost in the storm. Nick Stone and Charles Broussard had sped out in my father's boat in iffy weather at dawn in search of fresh banks to dig for clams, oysters and scallops, but Charles returned to shore alone.

Seagrass Cove and all the fishing towns on the North Shore came together to search. When that was called off, they came to mourn my father's loss and to support Charles, who almost died diving in after my father when the riptide came, flooded Nick's waders, and dragged him away.

Nick Stone, my dad, Clammer of the Year three times since he'd begun digging the flats at fifteen alongside his father, the man who showed me snow angels and told me I was the first person in history to know what the sky tastes like when I'd catch falling flakes on my tongue, was crab food at the bottom of the Atlantic ocean and that was the end of it.

My mother sunk into oblivion after that, and I lost track of her pretty quick. I don't look too hard these days; I'm afraid to find her until I figure out a way to deal with her without letting my rage take over. I have empathy, but it's difficult to hold onto that when she doesn't want help or even forgiveness. Last I checked, anyway.

I look around now at my three new friends and decide there's no way I'm expected to buy presents for these women after knowing them for less than two months. I don't even know if they all celebrate Christmas, but so far I've heard no talk of other religious holidays within the Club.

Nova orders a second round, and this time I join them in their dirty martinis.

I'm a bit drunk. I'm tired of pretending.

I decide to toss a gas-soaked rag onto a gently dancing fire.

"It must be strange to have me here instead of Jacqueline," I say. You can take the girl out of the Dead Newspapers Club, but you can't take the Dead Newspapers Club out of the girl.

As expected, they tense up.

"It is," Nova responds. "She was our friend."

"One thing has nothing to do with the other," Seychelle snaps.

"I just meant that it was nice of you to invite me along when you must really be missing her," I say. "I know it must sound weird, but I miss her, too."

"You have to understand," Nova says, "how hard it is on us *every time* a friend leaves. Midas toddles around with their daughter. Heidi's son is best friends with Peter's boy. The children become intertwined with our lives as much as the parents do."

She gestures with her martini, and vodka sloshes out of her glass.

"Like when Lara left so abruptly last year…same thing. Our girls' nights were quieter."

"They were pathetic," Heidi half-smiles.

"For awhile. We got past it," Seychelle reminds them. "As we will with Jacqueline. She made her choice, and we must respect that. I for one wish her well and hope she's happy."

I'm still not buying it. Yet, if this is a performance, it's Oscar-worthy—and all of them would have to be in on it together.

"You still don't believe us, do you?" Nova leans forward, staring me down.

BINGO. "I want to. I really do."

Seychelle sighs. "Heidi?"

Heidi pulls out her phone and turns to me.

"There's something you need to see," she says, and hands me the device.

CHAPTER

TWENTY ONE

"**H**ave a look at this Instagram account," Heidi says, "and tell us our friend hasn't gone home."

I examine the first photo from *@Jacschihk*. It's an image of Jacqueline in a soft knit sweater, posing alone in front of the Hong Kong skyline, a well-placed junk boat floating by with red sails blowing. Location tag: Victoria Harbour.

I keep scrolling through pictures of her, all of them location-tagged in areas of Hong Kong, all of them dated in the days after she disappeared.

Jacqueline smiling in a baseball cap at an airport: *#expatlife #youcangohomeagain*.

Jacqueline in jeans and a T-shirt with her arm around a young woman in front of a restaurant on a funky city street: *#hongkonglife #hongkongfoodie*.

Jacqueline curled up on a chair with a book whose title I can't make out:

#homeagain #lifeisgood.

I count five new images on this account, which has been active for about eight years. The latest pictures are all dated in the days after she disappeared. Before that, there was a four-year gap between posts.

"Seriously?" I try to read my new friends' faces. "Why didn't you show me this before?"

I hand the phone back to Heidi, then pick my salty drink up and take a gulp.

"We shouldn't have to," Nova chastises me. "You barely knew her. You had no reason not to trust us. We're not horrible people, Rose. We're *hurting*."

Heidi's eyes well up. In this moment I'm reminded of what Wesley has been trying to tell me for days: *You don't know what you don't know.*

"You need to get used to the leaving," Heidi says. "It happens. Fitz took off at Fasnacht, oh, about two years ago now. We adored her—so fun, so cool. Last I heard she's in Big Sur. Or wine country. One of those west-coast type beauty spots."

Left at Faschnact or *disappeared* into the crowd? I remember what Jacqueline said at the gala: *Find someone to hold your hand at Fashnacht.*

"Wait. Another expat went missing? I mean, left?"

I pick up my drink and sip again. An olive, previously sunken into the V at the bottom of my martini glass, bumps me in the nose.

"Fitz was single," Nova says. "But she could've been one of us. She was dating that ER doctor from the French side. If she'd pursued it and gotten married, she could've been promoted at TIG easily. They prefer their top executives to be married, and Fitz could've fit in if she'd only tried."

"The ER doctor was super hot," Seychelle throws in.

"Nonetheless, she ultimately wasn't meant for the expat life," Nova continues. "She got itchy feet."

"Oh, stop it," Seychelle's buzzed now, evidenced by a slight slurring in her speech. "She was bored. She wanted to go clubbing. She worked under that shrew Teresa and that sealed the deal for her, so she bolted."

"When was the last time you all saw her?" I ask.

Nova's eyes go wide. "How in the world would we know that? I don't remember who I saw last Tuesday, let alone two years ago on a certain day."

"We did our annual Fasnacht kickoff drinks," Heidi recalls. "Fitz was fine. She was partying with the rest of us. The next day, Raj told me that Fitz gave her notice that week, but didn't want anyone to know until after she was gone. She didn't want to face us. Didn't want to worry about goodbyes."

"I have a theory." Nova lowers her voice.

I lean in. Heidi and Seychelle remain upright as if they've heard it all before.

"I think Fitz expected expat life to be all glamour and exotic locales, and she couldn't deal with the reality. We're about families and wholesome living. She wanted gritty and wild."

Heidi is nodding like a bobblehead doll. "She thought Lucerne would match the excess and debauchery of Dubai," she says. "but ours is a much calmer existence."

"Or she wanted Hong Kong-level wealth," Seychelle adds. "Lucerne isn't enough for some expats."

"Not to mention the expat packages you get in Singapore," Nova says. "Singapore is what Geneva *thinks* they are."

Suddenly we're all fine, all friends again. I rest my brain for a moment, attempt to reason away my jangled nerves. I haven't had a single good night's sleep since I arrived. I don't count mum's night. I don't count blacking out as a good sleep.

I've seen Jacqueline now. She's OK. Smiling. Comfortable. Safe. I'll study the account later, back at home, to dot the proverbial I's, but I'm thinking maybe she really is OK. Maybe I can let this go.

"They can have all that. Let them brag about their gauche cities and conspicuous consumption," Nova, she of the double dishwashers and two elevators, slurs. "We thrive because we keep our secret. We don't want just *anyone* coming here."

I don't know what to think, but I do know I'm tired enough to pretend I believe them.

"I'm glad I didn't go to the police about Jacqueline," I say.

Heidi reaches out and touches my hand. "Rose, I know Wesley has told you this too, but you must never, *ever* go to the police. They are not here for expats. They're nothing but trouble for non-citizens. When something happens with a TIG employee or their family, the company decides whether to report it to Swiss authorities. It's never a good idea to usurp TIG's authority on that issue. Keep your nose clean."

"Got it," I say as if everything's normal. "Thanks for the warning."

Talk turns to shopping, and I try to absorb what the women are saying about their plans tomorrow, but I can't grip on. There are bothersome issues taking up space in my mind.

What kind of company is my husband working for? In what world does an employer decide whether employees call the authorities about their own families? Not to mention, this Fitz they talked about is the fourth person—along with Jacqueline and this Lars and Lara I heard about at the gala—who seems to have disappeared without so much as a goodbye or a forwarding email address.

Perhaps the darkest question I can't shake is about mum's night. Is Seychelle ever going to tell me what happened to me in Zurich? With Jacqueline going missing the next morning, I've never found the right time to press her.

I'd hoped she'd tell me without my having to ask.

The four of us crowd into one hotel room. Nova drinks straight vodka from the mini bar as a British soap opera plays on TV.

I share a double bed with Seychelle, who sits on the edge rattling the bottles in her purse, aka her traveling medicine cabinet.

"Fresh supply from my London doctor," she says, pouring out some orange tablets. "Benzos help me sleep like a baby. Here—I've got some to spare."

She drops three into my hand like they're Skittles. I take them to the bathroom and bury them in my toiletries bag.

That night, I'm wide awake from two to five. Someone in Heidi and Nova's bed snores like a chainsaw, and Seychelle tosses and turns. I stare at the ceiling. When I start to count sheep, I think about them being sent to slaughter, and I grow more anxious.

I'm wired. I still can't beat the jetlag, no matter how long I stay awake or how determinedly I avoid napping during the day.

When I wake up the next morning, I'm exhausted, and all I want to do is get home and try to sleep again.

CHAPTER

TWENTY TWO

We land back in Zurich the next afternoon. When Seychelle drops me at home, I race upstairs, grab my notebook out of a box of tampons buried in the back of my closet, and head to my office.

Ever since I bought a soft cream rug to warm the room up, the space has become my haven; sometimes I can't believe the view of the valley and Pilatus behind it is real, and its magnificence calms me.

I figure I have about two hours until Wesley gets back. I don't need him around while I dig into his new company. I open my notebook and scribble down the new the information I have.

Paper still matters. Paper can't be hacked or "accidentally" logged into.

I don't know what to believe now. After that carefully timed Instagram reveal by my new friends, I know the only way I'll be satisfied is if I speak to Jacqueline myself—or solve her disappearance.

The timeline has holes. If the men's poker game ended by 1 a.m. on mum's night as Wesley says, and Peter expected Jacqueline to be up for the kids by 7 a.m., that leaves six unaccounted-for hours. If Jacqueline was drinking pints at Pickwick's by herself, that must mean Nova was lying about watching her drive away—but *why?*

Add to this the passport in Jacqueline's drawer, the mess in her closet that I suspect was staged, my blacking out on the same night she went missing, Peter pretending or attempting to push me off a cliff, and the very convenient Instagram account, and I've got as many unconnected strands as a bowl of angel hair pasta flung at the wall.

It's time to dig deeper into TIG. I researched The Group half-heartedly before we left New York, because my focus was on the contract they were asking Wesley to sign rather than on the company itself. More to the point, I was distracted by more than one major life change.

After I told Wesley I would move to Switzerland with him, he stayed on his knees on the kitchen floor for a beat too long—and then he whipped a box out of his sauce-splattered apron pocket, flipped it open, and presented me with a vintage diamond ring.

"Rose Stone," he said, clearing his throat. "Will you marry me?"

I was already so shocked by the Switzerland news I couldn't follow the proposal as quickly as it was happening. I couldn't react like a regular person.

"Oh. We have to get married so I can get a visa…"

It wasn't meant as a challenge. It was brain vomit. I processed the legalities at the same rate as the romantic gesture.

"The opposite," he smiled, forgiving me, used to my awkwardness, his eyes smoldering in that way they do when he's in a particular mood. "I'm taking this job so you'll have to marry me."

"But we've only been dating for three months!"

"I knew after three hours," he said.

I was never going to say no.

The day after he asked me to marry him, I conducted some online searches about The Group, but every result that came back was unrelated to this Swiss firm.

I learned nothing about TIG. I let slide vital questions about its reputation, who runs it, and what its goals are because I trusted Wesley and I had no bandwidth to worry about it.

As Wesley pointed out that night over his homemade marinara—which, to this day, represents the first and last time he ever cooked for me—The Group is un-Googleable by design.

When I pushed for him to tell me what the company does, he answered in vague business-speak. "The Group flies under the radar. It's one of those boutique firms that operates discreetly and makes a shitload of money."

"But what do they *produce*? What's your product? What will you be selling or creating, exactly?"

"We're selling ourselves," he'd sighed. "I don't know how to explain it. Back at Yale—"

"Oh, *stop* it with Yale. You know it doesn't impress me."

"You can't accuse me of being elitist if you're incapable of understanding what I'm trying to say." He aimed his words at me with icepick precision, and I recoiled. "There are a ton of these under-the-radar funds and groups and even non-profits who pay big bucks for the right people. It's all about connections and discretion."

I don't have the luxury of accepting hazy answers anymore. Now, home alone for a couple of hours, I launch into my TIG research again and am immediately reminded that basic internet searches are futile.

"TIG" brings up the face of comic Tig Notaro.

"The Group" + Luzern or + Lucerne brings up a raft of articles about an old apartment building in Manhattan. I find an OB/GYN practice in Florida, a movie, books, a few non-profits, and infinite pages of junk.

I need perspective. I need the ear of someone I can trust. It's time to contact Violet once more and make her answer me, even if I have to employ dirty tactics to catch her attention, because after at least five calls and texts in the past two weeks she's ghosted me.

I text her, *Where are you? Don't make me use 911.*

Finally, after weeks of silence, three dots appear.

Vi: *Don't u dare.*

Me: *I need to talk to you.*

Vi: *Try me after 6 my time.*

Wesley arrives two hours later bearing a large pizza from Al Forno, a cave-like Italian place down the hill from our house. We eat wood-fired veggie slices straight out of the box and pair them with a bottle of prosecco.

"How was London? I heard it was utter debauchery," he says as he waits for me to select a prime piece.

"I wouldn't go that far," I laugh, pulling out a weighty slice that flops dangerously as I transfer it to my plate. "They treat a flight to London like it's a day trip to Hoboken. I want you to come with me for a romantic trip in spring."

"Definitely," he says, choosing a piece loaded with mushrooms and onions.

"How was your boy's night out?" I bite in. It's not New York pizza, because it's something else. It's real; it's the origin story of pizza. We're a couple hours' drive to Italy, so I figure when it comes to pizza, the local Swiss Germans make way for Italians to do what they do best.

"Being mid-week, it didn't pan out," Wesley shrugs. "Worked late, then had drinks with Peter at Seebar."

My stomach knots up at the mention of that name. *Peter.* He's a bad guy, but I know no one will believe me no matter what I say. I know how Wesley would react if I tried to paint a picture of the evil that lurks inside his charming friend: *You're such a cynic, Rose. You're imagining things. He didn't mean it.* Has a woman ever been believed over a man in her life? Maybe. But not me.

"Speaking of which, I heard Jacqueline's been spotted in Hong Kong," he says, tossing me a meaningful look.

"Apparently." I take a massive bite of my second slice.

"Peter showed the posts to me," Wesley says somberly. "She's gone, Rose. I don't know how much clearer it can be. She left him. The guy's humiliated. Are we ready to let this go now? Can we move on and make friends with all the cool people who are still here?"

I nod as I process my deliberately oversized mouthful. My right hand holds my prosecco glass at the ready.

Even after I manage to swallow it all, I don't bring up the credit card problem in London. We're just getting back on track after a chaotic few weeks. *Another time.*

"Don't take it personally," I say as he nods to the last two slices, and I nod back my consent for him to finish the pie. "But I'm going sleep on the futon in the office tonight. I'm gonna pop an antihistamine and see if I can break this jetlag once and for all."

He shrugs, clearly unmoved that his wife will be leaving his side for the night.

"Only if I get conjugal visits."

"That would defeat the purpose," I wag my finger at him. "Curfew's at nine. If you can slip in by then, be my guest."

I'm cautiously optimistic this plan will work, especially because I'll be so tired after my midnight call with Vi that I'll surely sleep all the way through, even through the bustling sounds of Wesley getting ready for work in the morning.

CHAPTER

TWENTY THREE

Wesley visits me in the office at nine. I put down my book and he makes me forget about credit cards and finances. I fall into a deep sleep when he leaves, woozy on allergy medication.

My alarm goes off at midnight, and I bolt up in a panic. I take a moment to remember where I am, then call Vi in the dark.

"Rose Stone," she answers briskly. "I'm in the middle of finals. This better be good."

"You can't possibly still be mad at me for leaving." I yawn big and long.

"I'm not mad. I'm busy."

"Too busy for me? I've been trying to reach you for weeks."

"Married people bore me." She's not kidding.

"Maybe we *are* dull, but I'm not sure there's anyone more insufferable than a first-year law student."

"Touché." I can hear her smiling.

Violet was Seagrass Cove High's first-ever Black valedictorian. Upon graduating we both studied journalism at UMass, but after a few years working in a business with terrible pay and editors who wouldn't let her be an activist *and* a journalist, Vi enrolled at Columbia Law School.

"I miss you," I say.

"Don't push your luck. Hit me, already. What's the big emergency?"

"You're not going to believe it," I tell her. "I'm not as boring as you think. I'm living a podcast-worthy life up in these hills."

Sharp intake of breath. She's talked about us doing a true-crime podcast together since she first heard the word "podcast."

"I'm listening."

I spill it all, recount everything that's happened, tell her about my new friends, my life as a housewife, how having a husband is messy, the strange goings-on with Happy Helpers. About Peter, and about mum's night.

I feel the doubt, fear and largeness of my assumptions seeping away as I share with someone who knows me to my core.

The doomsday-level dread I've felt about Jacqueline leaving suddenly seems melodramatic when I set the story free. Maybe Wesley was right, and I'm bored, and I'm suspicious, and I need to step back.

"Lord, Ro," Vi breathes. "You weren't kidding. This has serious podcast potential."

"Does it? I don't know what to think anymore."

"What does your gut tell you?"

With that question, my doubts crest and crash on me like a Seagrass Cove tide. I'm not inventing problems because of boredom. I'm not imagining any of it.

"The story going around the Club doesn't make sense to me," I reply. "Jacqueline was the queen bee. The woman had it all, and presided over some of the most influential expats in the country. These women have the lives they always wanted. Why throw it away?"

"Maybe that's *why* she took a powder," Violet suggests. "Maybe what you saw as success and happiness felt like crushing pressure or impostor syndrome to her."

"I know you're right," I reply. "And yet…what does *your* gut say? These women seem upset that she's gone, but not worried in the least. They're acting more hurt than anything."

"Sounds like you know what to do. Keep pushing until you're satisfied. You and that unconscious of yours have always been eerily on-point. Don't forget that. Screw Wesley. He's not the boss of you. And by the way, if you don't feel safe enough to tell your own husband that Peter tried to push you down a mountain, that tells you something…"

"I don't think he planned to push me over," I tell her, ignoring the husband comments. I refuse to be the smug married person who tells a single woman *You wouldn't understand.* "I got the distinct impression he might have been sending a message, you know, like, 'stay out of his business or else' kind of thing. Even if he had nothing to do with Jacqueline's disappearance, he might know I suspect him of an affair with the nanny."

"Let's hope that's all it was," Vi says.

"But what if my gut is wrong about all of it?" I add. I'm all over the place. "What if it's not my unconscious talking to me, but a boredom reflex from quitting my job? Too much has changed in my life at once, Vi. My radar is off. I don't know what to think."

"Agreed. What can I do?"

"I need help digging into this company."

"Right. 'The Group.' How original. I can ask D'Shawn to check these TIG fools out. He's started freelancing for the *Wall Street Journal*, if you can believe it. Sellout."

"Good for him," I disagree. "There's no honor in getting paid pennies for clicks at that snarky blog he works for. And on the Happy Helpers thing," I switch gears. "Could you ask Talia to check in with her sources? The time difference screws everything up and I don't want to ask over text."

Violet's drinking something.

"Or am I being ridiculous?" I babble on. "Sometimes I think I am. Being ridiculous."

My friend swallows.

"You remember what Talia said when she was working on that investigation last year," Violet says. "Human trafficking organizations are often operating in plain sight. I think you're right to probe. From what you tell me, something seems hinky."

Her encouragement makes me believe, even for tonight with my exhausted brain and cloudy thinking, that I'm not overreacting or reading something into nothing. There is not a person on earth I trust more than Violet Broussard.

I met her on the playground. The boys were picking on me again, and I saw the new girl in our fifth-grade class alone on a tree stump reading a pick from the eighth-graders' book list, *Things Fall Apart*, watching us out of the corner of her eye.

I had learned to be still and throw in the occasional *Shut up. Go away! Shut up!*

That never stopped the harassment—which, as far as I could tell, was aimed at me because I was poor, awkward, and not particularly pretty—but I was convinced it shortened my time in the fire. On that particular day, the boys moved on to Vi, the girl on the stump, pretty quick. Laughter from the boys ensued, and then Vi turned two deep pools of cool brown on them. This unflinching eye contact confused them, and before long they grew bored and took off.

"The power of ignoring," the girl called to me from the stump when they were gone, "is one of the most effective tools a woman has."

"I'd rather get revenge," I argued back. "Those guys are such jerks."

"So be it," the eleven-year-old girl said. "Just remember one thing: revenge is a dish best served cold."

That was the first time I ever heard that, and it spoke to me like an angel whispering truth in my ear.

For the next week, I watched the new girl ignore the boys every day at recess. And then, one day, our math teacher called the bully up to the chalkboard to solve a problem in front of the class. The bully turned, put his chalk to the board, and before he could draw a single line, the class erupted. Everyone, including his "friends," screamed with laughter.

Violet had smeared baby oil on his seat on a day he came to school wearing light khakis. He didn't feel moisture seeping through as he sat in it, but it made him look like he'd wet his pants.

Vi wasn't a suspect because she'd never engaged with him. It was genius.

The next day, I told her so, and she said, "You need to know your enemy. 'Men are afraid women will laugh at them. Women are afraid men will kill them.' You know who said that?"

I thought for a moment.

"Buffy?"

"What? *No.* Margaret Atwood. She's a writer. You've got some learning to do. Stick with me, kid."

We were inseparable after that. If you have a best friend, you have everything. The divorce rate for best friends is zero percent.

"Get your Instagram up," I advise Violet now as I pull up the account with the new Jacqueline photos. "Oh, wow…"

"What?"

"That account I told you about? It's been set to private." I flip to my camera app and send Vi a bunch of photos I'd like her to examine. "Joke's on them, though. I screenshotted everything when we got back to the hotel in London."

"They're coming through now," Vi confirms.

"I need a fresh eye," I say. "I feel like I'm missing something. I studied them on the plane, but I can't find anything off about the photos that were posted *after* she disappeared. No obvious photoshopping, no alarm bells. You're good with this stuff. Can you take a close look?"

"I'll see what I can do," she replies. "What are these other pics?"

"Jacqueline's not in some of those," I explain. "They're from the night she vanished. When I was at that Zurich club I told you about."

"What are we looking for?"

"Everything," I tell her. "Is there anything weird about the location data, are any images photoshopped or edited? Things like that. Nothing is adding up, Vi. Help me."

I can't bring myself to tell her about Jacqueline asking for my help. I can't articulate how ashamed I am to have waited too long to try, to tell someone, to protect her any way I could.

"Oh, one more thing—I can't find much on Peter online," I add. "I know TIG will have vetted him within an inch of his life, but in case I missed something, can you poke around?"

"I'm on it," she says. "Get some rest."

It's one-thirty in the morning.

I stand, stretch, and feel a welcome exhaustion drape over me like a plush robe. I need a glass of water, and then I'll beckon blessed sleep under my blankets.

I am in the hallway when I hear the noise again. The scratching and tapping from before the London trip that turned out to be nothing. This time I'm up, and awake, and I can react immediately.

I slip along the tiles in my socks and pause at the top of the stairs.

There it is again. *Scratch. Drag.*
THUMP!

CHAPTER

TWENTY FOUR

The *thump* scares me. That's not wind or a mouse or a house settling. I freeze, hear nothing more, then tiptoe to the kitchen and grab the biggest knife I can find. I head downstairs to check the front door. It's locked as always, with no sign of tampering.

I move into the laundry room.

The high, narrow pullout window is still cracked open to discourage mildew from blooming, but it's locked in place with the same slim opening as always.

I pad out to the foyer and plant my ear on the front door. I can't get used to the lack of a peephole, and I'm too foggy with jetlag to be fearful. Curiosity and fuzzy thinking win.

I open the door. There's no one on the stonework outside, not a sound but the gentle whistle of the wind. I step out and accidentally kick a small item across the landing. I look down and see two Oreo-sized wooden discs at my feet. I pick them up, then dash out to grab the one I kicked.

I scan the steep hill and see nothing and no one. I hear nothing. Perhaps ill-advisedly, I venture to the top of the cement stairs. Still no sign of any intruders or animals or burglars.

There is nowhere to hide.

I examine the pieces of wood, and in the dark I can just make out symbols etched into them. I'm no mystic and I'm not superstitious, but I recognize them as runes. From what I remember, these symbols make up an ancient Germanic alphabet sometimes used for divination. To find answers to the unknowable.

A wave of fear ripples through me; there's someone around, somewhere, a stranger invading our property. That I can't see them makes it scarier still. I hurry back inside and lock the door, checking once, twice, a third time that it's truly secure.

Now I have to worry about these sinister gifts left at our door. I don't even know who they're for—me, Wesley or both of us?

It has to be the neighbor. She was up late, couldn't sleep, left me her version of a note. My thoughts are ants trying to move through honey.

I wander to my office in a haze. I need sleep; everything is fuzzy. First, I take the runes to bed, do a quick internet search, and find their basic meanings.

I for Isa = ice

H for Hail = cataclysmic change

Blank is Odin's rune = unanswerable

They beg to be translated into one cohesive message, but all I can manage is a literal take: There is a big mysterious change coming for me that may or may not involve ice, whether metaphorically—as if I'm frozen in place—or literally, which would mean I'll be extremely cold when the change comes.

I'm relieved from my worry when sleep finally takes me.

I wake to the *click clack* of Wesley's shoes passing by my door. The sound machine wasn't enough to protect my slumber, and I'm immediately nauseous and irritable, but I force myself to rush out of bed so I can drive him to work and keep the car for the day.

I leave the house a minute before Wesley so I can knock on the neighbor's door, but I get no answer. The home feels cold and dead.

She has to be the one who left the runes. I'll visit again later.

I turn to see Wesley watching me with narrowed eyes, his mouth in a hard line.

"Let's go," he commands.

He drives, and as he navigates down the steep hill toward town he grumbles, "What was that about? I told you I don't like those people."

I pull the wooden discs out of my handbag. "Couldn't sleep, and I heard a noise again," I say. "I went down to investigate, and I didn't find anything inside the house. But when I checked outside, these were at our doorstep."

He glances at my outstretched palm, then flits his focus back to the road. "What are they?"

"Runes. They have markings that coincide with Germanic or Norse alphabets. Or something," I reply. "I haven't researched what these mean yet, but I think our neighbor might've left them for us."

"That old witch? Surely you don't want to get involved with her. Just ignore it. And her."

"Wait—you think she's a witch?"

He shakes his head. "It's a figure of speech, Rose. The Swiss are weird. I mean, *Jesus*. We're great neighbors, and now she's trying to scare us. Why? Does she hate Americans or something? Thank god for our expat friends."

"That's a bit of a generalization, don't you think? We should try to assimilate, not dismiss and insult them."

"They're rich and white, Rose." Wesley gestures in my general direction. "We can make fun of them. It's practically a sport these days. Wealthy white people didn't do anything for themselves, their talent didn't get them where they are, and if they don't give all their money away they're horrible human beings. Don't you read the news?"

I have never heard him speak like this. I feel a stab of nausea and take a moment to try to squelch it. He's hangry, or in a mood, or playing devil's advocate. I don't have the bandwidth to wonder if he actually possesses deep-rooted resentment of this magnitude.

I don't know if our neighbor is a witch, or a pagan, or a practitioner of Wicca, and in fact I am woefully uneducated in the difference between any of them. But I will be visiting her again, because I have a feeling these runes are related to her earlier warning to me: *Watch out.*

I stop at Bachmann confiserie after I drop Wesley, and when I'm back in the car, I text Heidi: *I'm in the neighborhood. I have Schoggigipfel.*

She writes back quickly:

I've got macchiatos. Come on over!

Heidi and I sit in the sunlight streaming into her kitchen. She pulls apart a croissant dusted with powdered sugar.

The warm hazelnut oozes out of mine and I lick it off my finger. "How do they make these so good?"

"It has to do with real butter, I think," she replies through a mouthful of pastry. "You brought more, right?"

"Of course." I bought six.

Her housekeeper appears at the table. "More coffee?"

This Swiss stuff is potent. I'm sensitive to caffeine at the best of times, but their espresso is ultra high-octane and I've learned I can't have more than one or two a day or I become a jittery mess. It's not helping my jetlag.

"I think we're still going, thank you, Gasira," Heidi replies.

Today I learned that my friend chose "experience" from the Happy Helpers menu. Gasira is sixty if she's a day.

Heidi asks, "How's it going with your help? These girls don't mess around, right? My house has never been cleaner…neither have my kids, now that I think about it."

"Mine unpacked our entire house in half a day," I agree. "I haven't set up regular cleaning yet. I've been fine on my own so far."

She's eyeing the *Schoggigipfel*. I nudge the box in her direction.

"I shouldn't." She reaches in. "Maybe just half."

As she pulls one apart, leaving only the flaky butt of it behind, I say, "They work so hard…but why do they all have that same look? It's a bit dehumanizing, isn't it?"

Heidi makes a face and holds her croissant in mid-air. "Not really...I think it's more about professionalism."

I tell her as casually as I can about my encounter with robo-maid in the closet at Nova's place. "That's weird, right? I'm not being overdramatic?"

If you can drink coffee angrily, Heidi does it, gripping the cup hard, pursed lips suctioning the ceramic edge.

"There's nothing weird about the staff doing their jobs," she replies after she swallows. "You're not in New York City anymore. It's important to have boundaries with live-in help. Happy Helpers trains them to be *staff*. Not members of the family, not best friends. Hired employees."

I tread carefully. "I understand that, I do. But you didn't see her. It wasn't normal."

Her turn to sigh. "I don't have quite as much house as Nova and Brett do, but I bet I can recreate the scene right now."

I'm dying to see what could possibly match what I saw.

"Lead the way."

CHAPTER

TWENTY FIVE

"Gasira!" Heidi summons her help.

When she appears, Heidi spits out three quick German sentences, and Gasira leaves.

I follow Heidi down some stairs to the bottom floor, where she touches a wall. A door slides open with a *ssshhhh.*

Gasira is standing like Irina was: Erect, blank-eyed, arms at her sides.

"Grüezi," Gasira nods to us. She hits a button and the door slides closed.

Heidi smiles in a way I take to mean I was very, very wrong, but we're still friends.

"That's spooky," I admit. "But at Nova's it wasn't an elevator. The elevator was on the opposite end of the hall from where I saw Irina."

Heidi has turned away from me and is walking briskly toward the stairs we descended earlier.

"Nova has two of everything, Rose. Didn't you notice?"

Oh, no. I'm beginning to think I fucked up.

"Irina was using the *service* elevator. The one for the staff.

Clearly, the door opened at the exact moment you were standing there. I'm sure you caught her by surprise."

"I guess…it was just so *odd*." This little show should convince me, but it doesn't.

Heidi stops at the top of the stairs and waits for me.

"Did Irina seem in distress?"

"Well, not exactly…" She seemed like a prisoner.

"There's no *there* there, Rose. We're all sad about Jacqueline, but it was her choice to leave. Sometimes people move on. It happens. But she's OK. We're all OK. Look at her Instagram. She's living the life of Riley."

Ah, their beloved Instagram. Where everything is sharper in color, everyone is faster to smile, and life is frozen in a state of perfection. Where not everything is as it seems. Kind of like this town.

Heidi's walking back to the sunny kitchen where our coffees are growing cold.

Time to start digging myself out. "I'm relieved." I provide a small smile with a hint of regret. "I had all this guilt about hiring help when I don't have a job or kids. I only wanted to be sure these women are happy and treated well."

"I get it," Heidi cocks her head. "That's sweet of you. But I assure you they're happy. How can they not be? TIG gives them health insurance, tuition contributions, a visa for this safe, wonderful country, and a real, livable salary."

"That's…wow." I'm genuinely surprised by this. "My helper, Maira, seemed afraid when I tried to tip her. It got me wondering."

Heidi purses her lips again. "I'm sure she *was* afraid. Afraid she'd lose her sweet gig. Afraid a nosy client was going to tip her and get her in trouble. You must understand this is their springboard to university, or to meeting the partner of their dreams, or setting up a life in a safe, wealthy country. For a poor young immigrant wanting to make something of herself, these jobs are a gift."

I tip my coffee cup back, but nothing comes out. I want more to stay awake, but I plan to push through without more caffeine or napping.

"I'm telling you that TIG and its subsidiaries, including Happy Helpers, is beyond reproach, Rose," Heidi goes on. "They can't afford scandals. That's their brand: We clean your image and give you respectability."

Out comes her phone. "They even get paid time off. Look at this from the other night. I drove my nanny to the nightclub myself so she didn't have to worry about drinking and driving. They're there every Thursday letting loose and comparing notes about us, no doubt."

She taps her Instagram icon and shows me an image of a half a dozen Happy Helpers including Irina, Helena, and several others I think I recognize, though it's hard to tell with their hair down and makeup on.

They're smiling, free, relaxed, and lounging in a place I've seen before. It's a moody bar that turns into a nightclub after eleven p.m. on the edges of Old Town. Wesley and I stumbled onto it during our unofficial honeymoon.

Heidi reaches out and covers my hand with her warm one. "I know it's hard adjusting. Raj and I had quite a time of it ourselves in the first few months. Be happy, Rose. Lean into this life. Embrace all the weirdness and newness.

"I shouldn't tell you this," she smiles and releases my hand. "You and Wesley have made a real impression on everyone.

There's a little surprise for you coming. It's going to be really good for you as a couple. Hang on a little longer and you'll see this place was made for you."

Heidi pushes a button under the table, and Gasira appears.

"We'll switch to prosecco now. Thank you."

Eleven a.m. is generally too early for me to start drinking, but I still have questions. "I can certainly see us staying for a while," I hedge. "It must be hard when friends leave, though…this Fitz you mentioned in London, and Jacqueline, and Lara and Lars I keep hearing about…"

Heidi swats their names away like a swarm of flies.

"They didn't appreciate it here. They're gone. Expats cycle through all the time, but it's the people who choose to stay who are rewarded with endless opportunity and lifelong friendships.

"We found our Eden," she adds, nodding to Gasira, who's back with two glasses of bubbly. "It's people like Lara Rawlings who don't get it. And if you don't get it, we're happy to wave goodbye to you."

Jackpot. Thank you, Heidi. My intent was to learn their last name without having to ask, and she took the bait. And bonus, I now have a way to get to these Happy Helpers outside of their rigid jobs and duties.

Whether or not there's something sinister about the agency, those women know something, and it's time I found out what.

Das Gehminis, indeed.

I'm questioning my judgment, my gut, my unconscious. The dormant part of my mind is always alert, even when I don't know it.

It started when I was young, when I sensed things that adults said I shouldn't and predicted outcomes others couldn't.

"Most people think the subconscious is the hidden room of the mind," Grandma Mixie told me when I was eight. "They're wrong. The *un*conscious is the one plotting and having a grand old time without you knowing much about it. The subconscious is different because you can visit it. It can spring into your conscious thought like a mad rabbit. But you, Rosie—*you're* in touch with your unconscious. You know things. You started listening young. Never lose that."

"I'm psychic, grandma?"

"No, no. This doesn't come from outside you. It is *in* you. You have the key to a door that most others never get to walk through, and it leads to a room where you'll find the tiny details your conscious mind doesn't want to see, the deepest secrets people try to hide from you. You're not fooled. Your unconscious picks up everything."

"Why can't everyone go to the room?"

"The wall between the conscious and unconscious is made of the thickest iron. You bang and bang, and it's as if no one's there," Mixie explained. "It'll never open to most people. But you…you keep listening. Don't ignore it. It could save your life."

I need to find that iron door now, but it's lost in a maze. I can't find a path through my jetlagged brain.

I spend some time in town after leaving Heidi's. I remember just in time that it's Chicken Man day, and lacking any other ideas for dinner, I stop by his van in the lot where we first met. I'm early, so no one's in line yet.

"Ah!" he greets me from the open window, chef's hat on. "Guten Tag, wie gehts?"

I'm pretty sure he's asking me how I am, so I reply, "Sehr gut, danke."

"Schön, schön." He grins proudly, as if he drew the proper words out of me. In a way, he did. My German lessons at TIG don't start until the new year, and in the meantime I have no one else to practice with.

"Mein Name ist Rose. Bitte, Herr…Wie heißen Sie?"

"Ich heiße Karl. Some call me Güggeliman."

My name is Karl. I am…Googly Man? I think I must have heard wrong, but I don't have the energy to figure out how to ask.

He asks me about what I want to order for dinner, and I shake my head, so he teaches me how to ask for a half or a full bird and if I want him to ax it for me. Then he advises me how I should serve it.

After a bit more chatter, the line begins to form behind me, and I take my chicken in its foil bag.

"Next time, we speak English!" I smile, wave, and head home.

I keep dinner warm in the oven while I wait for Brett to drop Wesley off after work. I use the time to pound away on my laptop looking for Lars and Lara Rawlings of Somewhere, United Kingdom.

I discover a handy database that draws from voter rolls, land registries, trusts, telephone listings, and more, and I search every conceivable spelling and combination of their names, but nothing comes up. Not a good sign.

I crawl through social media, and it's clear I'm going to strike out there, too. The Rawlings family is nowhere. I'm convinced they don't live in Great Britain, at least under their real names.

If they went back to England like the Club members claim, they're hiding like they're in witness protection.

Or they no longer exist.

I hear Wesley turn the key to the front door, and I close every tab, clear my browsing history, and shut down my computer. As I rise to go get dinner ready and pray the chicken hasn't dried out by now, my phone vibrates as a notification pops up: *The Dead Newspapers Club has invited you to a Zoom meeting.*

CHAPTER

TWENTY SIX

The chicken stayed succulent thanks to Güggeliman's protective bag, and Wesley eats most of it while I focus on my baked potato and mixed vegetables. I pretend everything's fine, and Wesley goes with it, telling me how everyone's getting along at work and Peter's slowly recovering from the sudden and *totally normal* loss of his wife.

At midnight, I leave Wesley snoring in bed and log in from the living room, as far away from his sleeping body as I can get. I perch on the ledge that rings around the fireplace and face the hallway so I'll know if he stirs.

My eyes go glassy and I choke up seeing the four of them for the first time in months. These people know me. They treat my forthrightness as a virtue and my curiosity as an asset, not as a threat.

Through quick catchups and greetings, I notice Talia, who's wearing her favorite beanie, is more quiet and frowny than usual.

"How's your depression?" I ask.

"Depressing," Talia intones.

"Sorry."

"Eh."

"How's the Dive?"

"Disgusting," Talia replies. "D'Shawn's foot got stuck in some goo on the floor and he had to throw the shoe away."

"What kind of goo?"

"No one knows what the goo was," Talia tells me with regret.

D'Shawn leans in and waves at us.

"Hi! Anyone want to hear what I found out?" He blasts through the chit-chat. We shut our mouths. "On first glance, The Group is your basic AG, which is not unlike an LLC in the States. It's a standard set-up."

He takes a breath and clicks to another window on his laptop.

"It doesn't look like they're up to anything *technically* illegal. They appear to be obscenely rich and operate globally, though, and based on public records, they almost certainly deal with people connected to dark money," D'Shawn continues.

"But what do they *do*?" *Why can't anyone answer this question?*

"Their core business is building connections, managing reputations, and making a shitload of money doing it," D'Shawn explains. "From what you told me, I'm assuming Wesley works in their risk-management department. They figure out what clients are worth taking on and which ones will cost them too much in reputation points in the long run."

"Yes. That rings a bell," I nod. "He's always talking about calculating this and that and risk versus reward, blah, blah, blah."

"Rose, our resident math genius," Vi breaks in.

I ignore her. "Why would someone pay money for an introduction their Harvard pals or PR people can arrange?"

"Think of it in terms of levels," D'Shawn says. "Let's say

you're a tech bro with an iffy profile—maybe you were accused of groping someone or got involved in a sketchy crypto play—and you want to connect with someone whose reputation is beyond reproach. You bring the assets, whether it's cash or stock or oil or whatever you have to offer, and The Group finds a respectable party with a solid reputation who needs those assets. You're leveled up, and the other one gets richer. No one gets hurt."

"And TIG gets a cut," I point out.

"It all sounds very vague," Talia chimes in.

"Perhaps," D'Shawn says. "My friend at the British Embassy did some discreet digging for me and I can tell you there has never been a registered complaint about The Group in Switzerland. There's no pending legal issue, no fines, no reprimands."

He pauses dramatically. We wait.

"But."

"But what?" I bite.

"*But*, the backstory of The Group is wild."

"I *knew* it!"

"So this guy Werner Fiats—"

"He's the CEO. I saw him at the gala. He runs The Group from Monaco," I tell everyone.

"Right," D'Shawn goes on. "He started TIG with a huge hunk of capital but no one knows *how* huge, and almost overnight the company was booming. He had clients lined up before he even finished setting up the AG. But his background is a mystery. He's a ghost. You can find mentions of him online as a 'wealthy financier' before he started TIG twenty years ago, but not much else. Hang on…there's more."

He clicks through some more pages, then goes on, "Here's the bonkers thing with AGs: You can hide virtually everything relating to company leadership. Only one shareholder is required, and however many you have, you can use proxies for them, which means you don't ever know who's really invested. Same for the board. You can have one board member or a hundred. Only one shareholder needs to live in Switzerland, and none of them have to be Swiss. You can issue bearer shares which, come on, is like playing with monopoly money."

He's talking a mile a minute, and when he takes a breath, I shoehorn a question in.

"Surely they're regulated to some degree?"

"Of course," he nods. "Switzerland doesn't mess around with rules. But the regulations only go so far. With all the secrecy allowed, companies can get away with a *lot* under the radar. One financial blogger tried to estimate The Group's assets and balance sheet a few years ago, and he swore they were churning through a billion dollars a year. One of their subsidiaries is into crypto, too, which makes sense because managing reputations isn't a billion-dollar business, I don't care who your clients are."

It's all very enlightening, but I can't figure out how to connect any of this to Jacqueline's disappearance.

"I presume that's how they get away with 'discouraging' employees from going to cantonal police for any reason without TIG's express permission and support," I say.

"That's a perfect example," D'Shawn says, gesturing forcefully at his screen. "Is it illegal to prohibit employees from contacting the cops for any reason? Maybe. Probably. Is it illegal to strongly encourage it? Who knows. But if no one ever protests this unwritten policy or reports it to Swiss authorities, then there's no problem. You see?"

"I think so," I reply. "Do we think TIG's iffy way of conducting business could go all the way to aiding, abetting or at least helping cover up a TIG wife's murder?"

D'Shawn appears intrigued by the question. "I mean…when there's this much dough involved, I don't think we can rule anything out. The question is how far will they go? It's pretty clear TIG isn't directly involved with money laundering and oligarchs and dark money, but some of the people they deal with *are*. The company has a lot to protect, ergo they're picky about who they hire and how they expect their executives and their families to behave. Vi told me about the strange rules you're asked to follow. It tracks that they'd get away with it. Their employees know how connected The Group is, and chances are they won't dare speak out."

"It sounds like some shit out of a Grisham novel," Marty frowns. "Vi was saying they only want married, straight people with kids?"

I exhale. "It *is* strange," I admit, thinking about some of the TIG employees I've met, including Teresa. "Everyone acts as if it's normal. Still, it's not like *everyone's* the same. Wesley's assistant is a single gay man, and I know at least one TIG expat, an American who deals with the board and the higher-ups, who seems happily unmarried."

"Doesn't mean they're not passive-aggressively punished for not fitting in," Talia points out. "Everyone on the Board and the top execs are married and CisHet, yes?"

"By all appearances," I confirm.

D'Shawn ducks his nose back into his files.

"Now. Happy Helpers is a subsidiary of The Group," he says, paging through a sheaf of papers. "They're squeaky clean and run entirely separate from TIG. They pay benefits, secure their workers all the proper visas, the whole nine yards."

Talia breaks in with her piece of the puzzle. "You can rest easy, Rose," she says. "Unless there's something buried *really* deep we don't have access to, I think the company is legit. My research indicates there's nothing nefarious happening at Happy Helpers."

I try to hide my semi-disappointment. I know it's wrong, but I was hoping I was onto a good lead.

"My source at Amnesty checked with their Swiss office and confirmed what D'Shawn found—Happy Helpers is a legitimate platform for educating at-risk women," Talia continues. "These women come from lower-income backgrounds, and Happy Helpers pays them a fair wage with full benefits including tuition. They go out of their way to lift these staffers in society through introductions and education. It's actually kind of awesome."

Heidi was telling the truth. I feel guilty for being surprised by that.

"Well…" I pause. "I don't know where to go from here. I'm worried sick about Jacqueline, but everyone's still acting like everything's fine."

"Sorry," D'Shawn says.

"I wish I could do more," Talia says.

"Vi? Anything from the new photos of Jacqueline or the ones from mums' night?" I ask.

"Nada. You can't get geo data from Insta, and I'm not seeing any signs of photoshopping," she replies. "After finals I can do a deeper dive into the images. But honestly, based on everything you sent and what we're learning, I wonder… is it *possible* she did simply leave town? I'm serious, Ro."

I sigh, annoyed at her question. I'm getting sleepy. And confused.

"Anything more on Peter?" I ask.

Vi says, "Nothing scandalous. He went to Eton and then Cambridge by all accounts. He's on all the alum pages and he lists his degree on LinkedIn. He worked as a portfolio manager at a big firm in London, and he's still connected on social media to a lot of current staff there. TIG doesn't hire without vetting, I'm sure, so we can be confident this isn't some sort of fake profile. He doesn't show up on any revenge-porn type sites or bad boyfriend lists. I don't see any red flags. He's your standard privileged English public-school boy."

That tells me precisely nothing. "Thanks, Vi." I close my eyes, squeeze them shut to flex and erase some tension.

My New York friends go quiet for a moment, and then Marty speaks up. "I can't imagine what it's like trying to make a life in a new country and a new marriage," he says. "All those changes. But I know you, Rose—you'll figure it out. We're here if you need us."

"I know. Thank you," I say, and my eyes well up again, but I blink back tears before they can see. My mind is racing, formulating next steps.

"I really do appreciate you all more than you know," I smile. "Visit me soon, OK? It's friggin' *stunning* here."

We blow air kisses and say our goodbyes. Everyone logs off except D'Shawn.

"Rose?" He leans in. "Wherever this leads you, my advice is to keep your eyes open and your nose out of TIG's business. They're gonna do what they're gonna do, and even if you found evidence of wrongdoing, you'd need proof. And we know what happens to whistleblowers and truth tellers. You can have all the receipts and evidence in the world and still…"

"And still, what?"

He lowers his voice. "Google Deutsche Bank, deaths, and Bill Broeksmit and David Rossi. There were a slew of deaths in a few short years among their executives, including at least one presumed suicide that many people questioned because his demise looked undeniably suspicious. These companies get away with literal murder and rarely get caught. For every rat you see, there's a million you don't."

"I know," I say wearily. "I'm a New Yorker."

I thank him and log off, suitably unnerved.

None of them know why I can't back off. Why I never will. I'm adulterated in shame and hobbled by guilt. No matter what anyone says, no matter how hard they try to convince me otherwise, I know Jacqueline didn't leave on her own.

She rapped on my door one day and told me someone was following her, that she was frightened, and I put off helping her like it was an everyday chore, like paying the electric bill or tossing laundry into the machine.

My investigating is a penance, a driving need, a requirement.

I carry my laptop back to my office, set it on the desk, and finger the runes someone left for me, these pieces of wood that are supposed to hold answers but are dead cold in my hand.

It's all growing odder and odder, especially with Vi not

mentioning my husband or asking about him on that call. She didn't trust Wesley from the day I met him.

I resisted sleeping with Wesley Blackwood for weeks while I waited for him to lose interest—and while I studied up on him. He had virtually no social media presence save for a half-hearted LinkedIn profile with a blurry photo.

I struck gold with a *My New York* magazine story on Manhattan's most eligible bachelors he was featured in the previous year. It told me Wesley is 34 and grew up in Westport, Connecticut, the son of a hedge fund manager named Harold and stay-at-home-mom and wife Bertie. I should have been turned off by the mess of pandering clichés Wesley poured out to the magazine, but they were so much better than the other bachelors' commentary that I forgave him.

Case in point: When he was asked his philosophy on love, he said, "A pretty face can fade by dawn. An amazing personality can see you into your twilight years with love and laughter."

I never read or heard a bad word about him, so I let myself go on our fifth date, on a night we went to a rooftop party and Wesley passed a test I didn't even know I was administering.

When a man bumped me, spilled a beer down my front and laughed about it, Wesley's jaw flexed, he looked me dead in the eye, as if waiting for a signal to jump into action. I gave none. I chased the laughing jerk and unleashed hell until he shrank back and apologized. As I weaved my way back through the fray, I saw Wesley rooted in the same spot, flexing his bicep and mouthing, *Badass.*

We stayed up all night, naked in his sheets, talking in

between, and I knew it was too late for me. I was smitten. I learned things beyond internet searches and magazines: Wesley Blackwood likes to run, lift weights, do CrossFit, can't settle on a favorite workout, but doesn't obsess about it. He's neat, but not as clean as I am. If he can't see the grime it doesn't bother him, whereas if I know there's gunk in the oven I'll get on my knees and scrape it away even if no one knows it was ever there.

He's a carnivore who said he didn't miss meat when he was with me. He started to learn about animal rights, but along with that came the first alarm bell I chose to ignore: He doesn't love dogs. I told him what I thought about that, and then forced myself to forget about it.

I prepared for him to dump me after that first night I stayed over. The chase was over, the prey caught, the rush achieved. Nothing changed, as it happened, but I kept my guard up.

A few weeks later he called me at work and said we needed to talk. He suggested a walk, and I knew "we should take a break" or "it's not you, it's me" was coming, but I went anyway. At least it wasn't a break-up text like the broke poet sent the year before.

We strolled halfway across the Brooklyn Bridge, at which point Wesley stopped and held out a key. "Move in with me," he said. "I'm sick of being away from you."

I couldn't bring myself to say the word *yes*. I didn't believe he meant it. When a parent tells you enough times that you are unlovable, you believe it in your marrow.

I knew it would be a dead giveaway if I asked him the questions dancing in my mind: *Why do you like me? What's wrong with you?*

Instead, I glared at him.

"What's wrong?" He cocked his head in confusion. "I know it's soon, but so what? Life is short."

"Why me?" I couldn't help myself. "And don't say you've never met a woman like me, or I'm not like the other girls, or I'm cooler, more fun and more real. If you do, I'll jump off this bridge right now."

"You're *not* like the others, though." He brazenly defied my orders, grinning all the while. "I've been bored for ten years and didn't know it."

I hung on the gate and gazed down at the dark water of the East River, and then I said yes.

He got me, and even better, he *saw* me. I decided we were oil and water emulsified, two elements meant to remain separate but when conditions were right would create the perfect blend, a delicious new concoction that couldn't physically separate again because of the laws of nature.

When I called Violet to give her the news, she said, "So now you're salad dressing? *Hell*, no. Not until we check him out. You can hate me, I don't care. I've already started digging. Girl, we got some work to do before Imma let you move in with some rando."

I wasn't amused. I was flying high, and she'd poked a hole in my glider.

"You *do* realize how insulting that is? It's medieval, Violet. You're saying a handsome, rich man couldn't possibly love me."

"Come *on*, Rose." She adopted her most exasperated tone. "The guy came out of nowhere and now, after six weeks, he wants you to move in with him? I'm not insulting you. I'm insulting him, if anything."

"He's tired of commuting between Brooklyn and Manhattan. So am I."

"But what do we *know* about him?" She'd pushed. "I'm going to do you the biggest favor of your life and do a background check on this clown. I don't want you ending up on *Dateline*." There was no budging her.

"Funny you never felt the need to forensically examine Rory McDougal when he invited you to move in with him last year," I pointed out.

"Rory McDougal didn't fly me to his friend's yacht by helicopter. Rory McFuckingDougal didn't laser in on me and push aside all the Mitzys and Titzys from the Prissy School for Snotty Rich Girls in favor of a clammer's daughter who makes mid-five figures."

Vi is the only human being the world who can say that to me, because she is the only one who is the same.

"You could be in for a world of pain. Why do you want to move in with a man you barely know?" Vi inquired as if all was lost. "You know they smell. And they leave the toilet seat up. And they—"

"I want to embrace this chance to take the next step in my life. I don't want to regret letting it pass me by because I was scared," I said.

"He's going to hurt you."

"Rory hurt you."

She went deadly silent; I went too far.

"I didn't mean it! I swear, Vi. I wasn't trying to go low. Please know I'm going into this eyes wide open. People get hurt. I accept that risk."

She'd paused, and I worried she was going to hang up at best, or dump me as a friend at worst.

She said three words: "Well I don't."

CHAPTER

TWENTY SEVEN

Wesley scared us up a cord of wood from a local farm, and the fire roars and cracks as I nest in the corner of the sectional and trawl through an internet's worth of gift ideas on my laptop.

I watch him poke at the logs until embers swarm like fireflies. My beautiful pyromaniac plays with kindling and paper and logs every night now like he's responsible for keeping the earth's core aflame.

"If you refuse to tell me what you want, you risk ending up with socks or coal," I warn him. "Or worse, socks filled with coal."

"I trust you," he says, leaning back on his haunches as his latest log alights.

"What about your parents? I don't want Bertie Blackwood to say her new daughter-in-law cheaped out or gives bad gifts. I was thinking—"

"Don't worry about them." He turns to me. "We never made a huge deal about Christmas growing up. I'll order something online."

"You better do it soon if you want it to arrive in time."

He hasn't asked me what I want, so I assume he has a surprise planned for our first Christmas together.

"We're going to have to raise our Christmas game, anyway," I remind him. "Have you seen the social club's holiday lineup? Our application is still pending, so I think we're expected to go to everything."

"We are."

He is gazing into the fire like it's calling to him, like he wants to walk in and become part of the inferno.

I head out on my own after dinner under the guise of secret holiday shopping for Wesley.

My first stop is Pickwick's. The place is packed with sweaty twenty-something backpackers and bleary-eyed tourists, and the line is three-deep at the bar. I hang back until my young Englishman friend is free.

Nova said she saw Jacqueline get into her car in the small parking lot off the riverwalk, about five restaurants down from here. So when did Jacqueline stop at Pickwick's, and where was Nova when Jacqueline was ordering this alleged cider? Or is the British bartender getting his night wrong?

"Cider and black, please," I smile.

He starts pulling my pint, then glances up at me. "American girl," he grins. "Where's the rest of your crew?" He jerks his head toward our usual back booth.

"I'm on my own tonight," I tell him. "I wanted to ask you something. I know you're busy, but—"

"Twelve francs." For what amounts to a two-dollar can of cider. Highway robbery.

I hand him a twenty. "Keep the change."

He sways with shock, and I worry he's going to fall over. In Switzerland the rule of tipping is round up with spare change at restaurants, and nothing at bars. "Wow, thanks!"

"Of course. Hey…remember last time I was here you said you served Jacqueline the previous night?"

"Of course," he smiles. "I haven't seen her since then…I don't think." He studies the ceiling to find the answer.

"The last time you saw her you said she was alone. Do you remember what time it was? I mean a general guess—"

"It was ten-fifteen," he tells me.

"How can you be so sure of the time? And the day for that matter?"

"I never forget a football game. Arsenal was playing Southampton." He makes a sad face. "It was a routing. It still smarts, but at least Jac gave me a kiss on the cheek for the pain."

People are yelling for service.

"Must go," he says, leaving me to serve a thirsty patron.

I sip and ponder what to do. I cannot imagine a more futile exercise than confronting Nova and the gang with this conflicting report of what happened the night Jacqueline disappeared.

I know what they'll say: *You don't understand. Leave it alone.*

I drink, check my phone, drink some more, snap at another pushy drunk, and sip some more. I go back on my phone and, finally, there it is. The post I've been waiting for.

I finish my drink and head out. I pass Kappelbrucke, then wind away from the crowds until I'm in a darkened section on the edge of Old Town.

I move fast, feeling vulnerable on these quiet streets. I am hemmed in by the Musegg wall, built in the 13th century to keep enemies out, its nine ramparts dark, imposing, never resting.

I am not emboldened under their protection; I feel trapped.

I turn down a narrow alleyway and realize too late I've made a wrong turn. The cobblestones are uneven, slick, easy to slip and trip on. I hear footsteps behind me, but it's a busy night, so that's to be expected.

I hold my breath so I can hear what's coming. The footfall is faster, harder than mine. More urgent. I take a quick look back and see a hooded figure, head down, striding toward me with purpose.

I have to cover a good fifty feet to make it to the other end. The figure is stalking toward me, and their shape and power reminds me of the monster who slammed me in the square that night. My throat constricts and my lungs burn as if I've just hiked up our forty-six stairs.

I break into a run, praying my heel doesn't catch on the stonework, and finally, almost feeling their breath on me, I round the corner and see the scratched metal door leading to an oasis, my lifeline, the bar-slash-nightclub where a flock of Happy Helpers are drinking at this very moment, according to their Instagram accounts.

I burst into the nightclub and I'm hit by a blast of colored lights. A disco ball turns the cave-like room into a kaleidoscope. There's no one behind me now, but I know with a cold certainty that hooded figure was following me, and I am still leagues away from figuring out *who* and *why*.

I need the restroom, so I squint through the colored lights and feel my way to the back of the bar. I push open a graffiti-covered door, my heart still working too hard, my head and chest throbbing.

Two women are at the sink.

They're not washing their hands. They're hunched over, heads lowered, and I hear the distinct sound of huffing nostrils.

One of the women turns, sees me, and stands up in a flash. It takes me a moment to realize who it is: It's the quiet, no-nonsense Maira, the woman who helped me unpack my new house, who has just snorted a line of coke off a sink.

I eye the white powder, then meet their eyes. Nothing need be said.

I follow them out of the bathroom and through the club to a back corner where five other young women are drinking and laughing. My breathing is regulating, and I find this encounter a welcome distraction to my recent chase in the darkness outside.

"Hi, everyone," I wave to them cheerily. "Remember me?"

"What do you want?" Maira sighs. "You are determined to get me in trouble."

I'm not used to the Happy Helpers talking back, and I am convinced now that they are not being exploited by the agency. They're fine.

I meet bluntness with bluntness. "I'm not. But my friend has disappeared off the face of the earth, and one of you is having some after-hours fun with her husband," I say. "I need to know if the two are connected."

"Helena and Mr. Pewter-Browne?" Maira rolls her eyes. "I wouldn't worry about it. She thinks he's attractive for an old man, but she's not planning to settle in this little place and become his next bored housewife."

"Don't insult me," I say, perching, uninvited, on the edge of the couch with them. "I know more than you think."

"Helena had nothing to do with Mrs. Pewter-Browne leaving," Maira shakes her head. "Their marriage was messy before she started working there. They didn't even sleep in the same room."

I *knew* it.

"I work in the house too," a quiet, slight woman says from the other side of the U-shaped sofa.

My stomach churns. *Shit.* If this one tells Peter I was here, things will get bad for me. I can only hope our mutually assured destruction over the drugs will keep all our secrets safe.

"They can't stand each other," the woman, a petite redhead, goes on. "He told Helena his wife is frigid."

"Said every man who can't please a woman in bed," I can't help but add.

A few of them crack up, then cover their mouths as the quiet one continues. "Helena's not that into Mr. Pewter-Browne, but she says he's attractive enough, so she's seeing where it goes. She gets plenty of what you call…uh…*benefits* for being with him."

"When did it start between Helena and Peter?"

No one answers me.

"Where is she tonight?" I ask, knowing the answer.

"At work," Maira says unconvincingly.

"She doesn't get Thursday nights off like the rest of you?"

Their faces tell me that yes, she does, and she's choosing to stay at "work" with Peter.

"Hallo," the quiet one signals me. "Do not judge Helena. Everyone believes Mrs. Pewter-Browne was also seeing someone. Maybe before her husband was. I am sorry if she is in trouble, but she is not so innocent."

I watch all their faces as she speaks. "That's fair," I nod as if this news is not shocking. "So...do you all think she was, as you say, 'in trouble?' Or do you think she ran off like Peter's saying?"

The seven of them put on their frozen work faces.

Finally, Maira speaks for them all. "That is not for us to say. We are there to do a job."

"If Peter did something to Jacqueline, don't we have a responsibility to get justice for her?" I ask.

Maira stands and faces me. "Do what you need to do, but do not tell us what our responsibility is. We owe nothing to these families. If no one reports Mrs. Pewter-Browne missing, she is not missing. It is not our job to be police."

I stare back at her, then stand.

"I was never here," I tell them, and they are smart as whips, and they get that my statement is for all our sakes.

I don't leave the club until I see a random group of revelers make a move for the door, and I follow at their heels until they hit a well-lit main road, then walk as fast as I can to my car.

Did someone really chase me earlier? If I tell Wesley I was followed tonight, I know how it will go.

He'll say I imagined it or I should be more careful to avoid pickpockets, and I'll say no, you don't understand, I *know* it's something else but I can't explain what yet, and he'll throw his hands up and say, *I don't know how to help you.*

I'm almost home, driving up the winding hill toward our house, when it hits me I never bought anything for Wesley. I'm going to have to do some explaining about why there was nothing in Old Town worth purchasing for my husband.

CHAPTER
TWENTY EIGHT

I never gave much thought to the winter solstice, but apparently it's a big deal to the Expat Social Club. When the longest night of the year arrives, Wesley and I bundle up and hit the road as the sun begins to set at three-thirty in the afternoon.

"Do you have any guesses as to what this is about?" I ask him for the third time.

He side-eyes me. "It's a solstice party. If I was a betting man, I'd say it has something to do with the sun."

"Ha, ha."

"It's one of the club's annual pre-Christmas gatherings," he says, placing a warm hand on my knee. "All I know is we're the guests of honor."

"That's what worries me."

Wesley guides the car off the main road and the GPS loses its mind. Arrows on the screen flit and flip-flop in a panic, directing us in circles.

My teeth are chattering as our two-door sports car, albeit one outfitted with snow tires because cantonal law requires residents to fit them on in winter, rolls up a winding, icy hill.

"Nothing to worry about," he says with gritted teeth and white knuckles. "Peter warned me it could get a bit treacherous."

"How can you possibly know we're going the right way?"

"It's all up here," he says, tapping his temple with his index finger.

We're almost touching the clouds when we reach a snowy clearing high on the hill where dozens of vehicles, a good portion of them Porsche Cayennes in various colors, are already parked.

The dying strains of daylight push through an opening in the woods. The space is bustling with club members and screaming children making snow angels and throwing snowballs.

Wesley takes my gloved hand and steadies me as we trudge toward a white marquee, and as we approach the opening, I see rows of picnic tables laden with platters of food.

"Rose! Good. I need you," Heidi calls out. "Once I lay this tablecloth, can you set out glasses for the glühwein and cider for the kids?"

"On my way," I call back to her.

"Wesley! Mate, can you help me with this?"

Kristoff, his nose a Rudolph the Reindeer shade of red, is trying to move a large table on his own and failing miserably.

Wesley leans down to kiss me, but sucks in a mouthful of scarf instead. "See you when I see you," he winks, and walks away.

A half hour later, Wesley finds me in the tent. "I think they're ready," he says, handing me one of the glasses of hot glühwein he's carrying.

Suddenly the hustle and bustle has ceased. Everyone is gone.

It's too quiet.

Beyond the tree lines surrounding us, there is nothing but more trees and wilderness as far as my eye can see.

I glance around to find Wesley and I are suddenly alone. I stay rooted in place, and he seems to sense my disquiet.

"Think of it as an adventure," he says, squeezing my hand. "'Step bravely with me into the unknown.' Do you know who said that?"

"Who?" I ask, my teeth chattering.

"I did." He tugs on my hand.

I go along with him, and when we break through the tree line, I'm greeted by a sight so haunting I gasp out loud and inhale a mouthful of glühwein before I can swallow it. I cough it out of my lungs as I take in the bizarre sight.

We've stepped into a clearing between two woods, a patch of mountain scalped by nature or by humans, I cannot tell which.

In the center stands a gargantuan white figure that has to be two stories high. It is rotund, towering and hideous, part snowman, part monster, part nightmare.

What's in front of it, nearly half its height, is the terrifying part.

Two smaller figures stand before the monster as if it's watching over them—or is preparing to crush them. The first is a ten-foot-tall rendering of a blond man. Next to him is a shorter, curvier figure with flowing "hair" the color of dirty dishwater.

Despite the garish features, the hooked noses and exaggerated eyebrows, I know instantly they are meant to be Wesley and me.

The three monstrosities rest atop a pyre of sticks and logs that resembles a gigantic bird's nest.

"What *is* this?" I gasp, staring, watching as the club members begin to wordlessly form a circle around it.

Jesus Christ. I grasp Wesley's hand tighter, and he squeezes back.

I'm getting intense Wicker Man, run-the-fuck-away vibes. I instinctively glance behind me for an exit. All roads lead to cold, unforgiving, unknown wilderness.

I catch Wesley's eye, and I am overwhelmed with pure panic.

My husband is not concerned or apprehensive, but high on adrenaline. His breath comes in a rush of white fog as he absorbs the extreme scene. He is eager for the fire to start, for our effigies to burn.

We have been pushed inside the circle. A hundred souls are holding hands around the pyre, around us.

Heidi stands outside it.

Her voice is carried by the natural amplifiers in this clearing, the rocks and open spaces and sheer breadth of this place.

"I wish you all a safe solstice," she begins. There's that word again: *Safe.* "As the elected Vice President of our club, it is my honor to accept the board's decision, which was made in a closed session this week, that I will become your new president."

She pauses for a round of applause, though the effect is weakened by the largeness of the space and the fact it's two-hundred mittens clapping.

"In my first act as your new leader, I have the honor of welcoming Mr. and Mrs. Wesley Blackwood as permanent and full members of the Expatriate Social Club of Lucerne, with all the benefits, privileges and responsibilities that come with this honor. Our fifty-year tradition of taking care of each other, of embracing everything our adopted country has to offer, has made us like family. Now. Let's fold the Blackwood family into ours, and give them a true expat club welcome!"

All at once, staring like they're drugged, they all start chanting. I can't understand a word of it. The terror is in the tone.

Heidi turns to Wesley and me, her head swiveling as if independent of her neck. Her eyes are wild as she joins the chant, a medieval, ancient verse, an otherworldly call to something sinister.

The sun is almost down and the sky is an apocalyptic mess of pink streaks, depressing grey and darkening blues. Heidi is an apparition across the circle, voice booming, hair blowing in the icy breeze. And as quickly as it started, the chant ceases.

"Do you, Wesley Blackwood, vow to uphold the values and traditions of the Expatriate Social Club of Lucerne, to help your fellow travelers when called upon, to keep its secrets until death and beyond, and to support all other members in the way befitting a steward of Club membership?" Heidi booms.

"I do." My husband's deep voice belts out as if this bizarre ceremony is an everyday course of events.

Heidi asks me the same questions, and I am no less horrified. *No, no, no* is my answer.

"I do," I say with a croak. I clear my throat. "Yes."

Wesley leans down for a hard, fast kiss.

I hear an almighty series of crackling and branches breaking, and my husband pulls away from me and approaches the fresh blaze.

Heidi is part of the circle now, holding hands with Raj and one of her children.

I am alone, as my husband is alone, too, much too close to the fire, and I worry his eyebrows will singe with the heat. Everyone in the circle holds fast to each other's hands and sways back in forth in a synchronized dance, and the mantra, this time in English, begins:

Burn, burn, burn, burn, burn, burn.
Burn, burn, burn, burn, burn, burn.

It grows fiercer and louder as the pyre overtakes the night sky like a sun on earth.

BURN. BURN. BURN. BURN.

My husband is pulled toward the fire as if dragged by the devil himself. I stand frozen, trying to remain still so…so, *what?* So they won't know I'm here and they won't burn me, too?

As my nose transforms from cold to numb, the fire begins to die, and that breaks the spell. They drop hands and the circle becomes a crowd of cold club members finishing wine and the last of the snacks, and the abrupt shift in mood renders this scene odder still.

They're behaving as if nothing happened. My knees are in danger of giving out. I feel like I'm in a cold fever dream.

The children launch into another snowball fight. Some are having meltdowns because it's past their bedtime, throwing themselves on the ground and tantruming in the snow. I cannot distinguish my husband from the other coats and boots and blond heads.

"You can see why they don't show this side of Switzerland in the guidebooks," a voice says in my ear.

I scream, then cover my mouth. It's Teresa.

I'm actually glad to see her, because I recall from the Rigi hike that she seems to know all about Swiss monsters.

"What the hell was that?" My voice shakes when I don't want it to. I can see Nova heading our way, with Heidi and Raj steps behind her.

"*Schneegeiss*. It's a holiday snow monster," Teresa says. "It's a Club tradition to celebrate our adopted country. It's our way of engaging with the locals and respecting their culture."

"It's fucking bizarre." I'm furious, and being a good TIG wife is far from my priority right now. I'm not going to pretend it's fine. "What's the point of it?"

"It's supposed to scare the children into being good. From what I hear, it works like a charm."

"When you have kids, you'll understand." Nova is suddenly here. "Midas! Don't throw ice!"

She's off again. Teresa waves to someone in the distance and wanders away.

Raj sidles up to me. "You OK?"

"No." My teeth are chattering. "Have you seen my husband?"

"I saw him helping Peter pack up the tables." He smiles kindly. "Try not to take it too seriously. There's a monster for every season in Switzerland. You'll get used to it."

I side-eye him, and he laughs in solidarity. "I was the same when I first arrived. Their superstitions are tied to the calendar. Historically, customs and traditions are more important to the Swiss than religion, whether they admit it or not. You moved here *just* in time for high season of customs and festivals. This isn't the worst of it."

"Then I'm in real trouble." My lips are growing numb. "The monster is one thing. It's the effigies of my husband and me that are really, really wrong."

"Ah. I guess if you aren't used to it, this custom could seem sinister," Raj nods. "It's meant to be a welcoming ceremony…sort of a symbolic way to sear you into the club forever. Most people find it flattering. The guy up in this village who made yours does the best work around. He's not cheap, either."

What in the actual fuck. I am speechless, and thankfully, Wesley beckons to me from afar and lets me know it's time to go.

"I can't believe you left me while they burned us to a crisp," I say on the way home as he hunches over the wheel, holding it with an iron grip to make sure he doesn't drive off a cliff in the slippery darkness.

"I didn't leave you," he replies. "There were over a hundred people there. You were getting as much love as I was. I got about a million hugs welcoming me to the club."

"Are you seriously telling me that didn't creep you out? After they burned those monsters I thought we were next."

"It was incredible," he gawks at me as if I'm losing my mind. "I would think you, of all people, a woman who claims she wants to travel and get to know other cultures, would embrace such creativity and spectacle."

"That wasn't culture or spectacle," I hit back. "That was a window to hell. I feel like I watched my own death in real time."

I don't know how he can be so calm. There's not enough glühwein in the world to erase the memory of that incineration of my likeness.

"I'm learning you're hyperbolic when you're tired," he smiles, messing with me, but in a flirty way, so I let it go. "Let's get you home to bed."

CHAPTER

TWENTY NINE

B y the time Wesley and I ring Nova and Brett's doorbell on Christmas Eve, arms weighed down with bottles of wine and Grandma Mixie's famous bleu cheese dip, my unease has been edged out by a zealous pursuit of cultural understanding. Wesley hinting I was showing xenophobic tendencies stuck in my craw. Not me. Not ever.

After hours spent normalizing the burning of my image in front of a chanting crowd, I've found some comfort in a familiar childhood refrain: *We're not in Kansas anymore.*

Irina throws open the front door and we step into a cradle of warmth heaving with the colliding scents of cinnamon, glühwein, peppermint candy, hanging mistletoe and poinsettias. It's a vision of red sweaters, khaki pants, velvety dresses, ornament earrings, a towering tree, and tables laden with savory food, a turkey, sandwiches, sides, desserts of every description.

It's another scene from the same Hallmark Christmas movie I watched outside Peter's house that day. I'm waiting for a harried director to jump out and yell *cut*!

Wesley is whisked away to suffer through The Tour as I'm

beckoned into a cozy corner with other TIG wives. I'm sipping glühwein. They're drinking prosecco.

"Congratulations," Heidi glows. "I can't wait to involve you in our volunteering opportunities. Ooh! And you can write something for the Club website this winter. I promise you'll forget all about going back to work. We could use a wordsmith to give our literature some pizazz."

Ugh. I sip my hot drink, and it burns my mouth.

"You OK?" Seychelle asks. "I didn't get to talk to you, but I heard you were a bit wobbly after the bonfire."

"Can you blame me?" I reply. "Seeing myself burned at the stake was…an experience."

"You think *that* was bad?" Seychelle, always the one with the sense of humor, laughs. "Wait 'til you see tonight's parade of freaks."

"It's all starting to make sense," I half joke, "because you won't believe what else has been happening…"

I tell them about our neighbor's plates and her performance in the rain, about the runes, the noises in the house, and the message I see in the symbols.

"What in the *world*?" Nova is gobsmacked.

"Our neighbor is really into these signs and symbols," I shrug. "It's like she's…I know it might sound like a leap, but…it almost seems like witchcraft. I'm also getting some Satan vibes with the pentacles and pentagrams on those plates."

They all freeze in unison with their drinks in mid air.

"You think your neighbor is a *witch*? Why?" Heidi asks.

"The symbols on the hill…the runes…the warning…"

"About the warning," Heidi says. "Tell us *exactly* what she said."

I tell them everything I can't forget: *Watch out. Take care.*

The three of them exchange unsubtle glances.

"Be careful throwing that word around," Heidi lowers her voice. "The Swiss have a hell of a history with witches. There were all those poor, innocent accused 'witches' who were tortured and slaughtered—no one did that like the Swiss, especially on the French side. These people were executing so-called 'witches' until, like, last week. Well, not literally. Anna Göldi was the last 'witch' executed in Switzerland in 1782."

"How did they do it?" I ask, immediately regretting the question.

"Chopped her head off," Nova whispers.

I know from innocent witches. Violet and I have made a point since childhood to avoid all talk of witches and witch hunters. We grew up fifteen miles from the heart of Salem, and the chest-crushing apparatus and burning pyres were part of school trips in elementary school, and the sights and the stories never left us.

I never forgot the smell of the raw wood inside the Colonial-era courthouses and museums, some slanted and musty from the olden days, others newly rebuilt to be as basic and creaky as the originals.

"But then," Heidi says, "there were the *real* witches. The kind that cast spells and hurt people."

"And helped people," Seychelle adds. "There are some seriously badass witches out there. Just check social media. They have huge followings."

"We need to give Rose the book!" Nova chimes in.

Seychelle asks, "Where *is* it? Jacqueline had it last. Madam

President? Have you gotten it back from Peter?"

"I'm sure he has had other things on his mind other than finding that book," Heidi replies. "But we do need to get hold of it. It's part of our history and our archives."

"What's the book about?" I ask.

"It was written by the founders of the Club. It's about those moments in Swiss history the guidebooks don't tell you," Heidi says. "If you can ignore the overwrought prose, you'll find some real gems in there."

"Sounds fascinating. I'd love to check it out," I say, lying with aplomb.

"I'll pass it on as soon as it turns up," Heidi assures me. "It's supposed to be kept at the resident's home, and anyone who wants to borrow it must promise to take good care of it because it's so old. I seem to remember Jacqueline had just gotten it back from the Evans family…"

They don't strike me as overly secretive about this book. Jacqueline made it seem I was uniquely important for getting an early peek, and now I'm more baffled than ever.

"It's time!" Brett bellows from across the room.

"Godspeed," Seychelle winks to me as dozens of us pour outside into the snow.

I find Wesley and he kisses me on the cheek. We stand together by the roadside to get the best view of whatever's about to happen. Peter barges into a gap between us and throws an arm around each of us.

"Another tradition you'll grow to love," he winks. I recoil and duck out from under him. "Here they come…"

I hear them before I see them. And then I smell them.

The street floods with a procession of red cloaks, black cloaks, and slow, smelly donkeys. The air fills with jingling bells and screaming children, some in delight, some in horror.

"What *is* this?" Wesley asks Peter.

"Think of it like a sinister Santa processional," Peter replies. "St. Nicholas is benevolent—see him there?—he's basically Santa. But unlike the real Santa, old Nicky has a sinister sidekick."

I hug myself as I watch the wall of cloaks approach in short, measured strides, like an army of holiday nightmares. "How bad can this second Santa be?"

"You'll see," Peter turns to me, eyes narrowed and sending a message: *Catch me if you can.* Mine are replying, *I'm coming for you.*

Or I'm imagining the silent encounter. I had one long night's sleep after the bonfire, but that wasn't near enough to clear my permanent brain fog.

Kristoff is next to us now, standing behind Seychelle, his body touching hers, and as he reaches out to wrap his arms around her to spoon her, she recoils. He quickly drops his arms. This coolness between them in public is becoming a theme.

"Here they come!" Teresa trills. I turn to see her at the edges of the group.

The parade is about to pass in front of me. Instead of a velveteen bag full of presents, St. Nicholas carries a knotted wooden staff. He is thin, tall, and wears a Bishop's hat. Instead of reindeer, he is flanked by two donkeys with their heads down.

Leading the animals is a shorter figure in a black cloak with a pointed hat. I can see nothing of his face or features except eyes like hot coal.

The children scream again as he stalks close to us and hisses. I'm no one's mother, but the kids seem genuinely terrified. Bad Santa throws out wrapped candies from a dirty cloth sack a more cloaked figures come up behind them.

Wesley whistles and hoots as the procession passes.

"What *exactly* are they?" I ask no one in particular.

"Child-stealing demons from the Middle Ages," Raj, standing behind us, says in the same tone one might say, *Santa's toy-making elves from the North Pole.* "*Schmutzli* are here to punish the kids who've been naughty." He taps a kid on the head. "Got that, Silas?"

"Yes, daddy," the child replies, holding onto Raj's leg for dear life.

One of the black hooded figures breaks away from the pack, a tangled mass of dead branches held out in front of him. He rushes toward us.

Wesley and I watch, mesmerized, as if the beings are on a screen, as if they can't touch us.

One of them lunges at me. I can see his long beard down to his chest, his mean red eyes, but I cannot distinguish any other features in the second it takes him to reach out and run a grubby finger down my cheek.

The being, the man, whatever he is, hisses in a long *shhhhh*, and I feel tiny droplets of spittle on my face.

I stumble back and gasp. These beings are like walking coal smoke, their faces twisted, their movements jerky and threatening. They are *not* getting me in the holiday spirit.

Peter is cackling and pointing at me. "Whoa! You got the full treatment."

He steps back and stares at my cheek, then swipes the air inches from me. "Ah. The mark of the beast."

"The *what*?"

I pull out my phone and use the camera as a mirror. There is a black slash, like wet coal dust, a mark from a stranger's filthy finger.

I turn to my husband. "Do you have a tissue? Can you get me one? *Hurry*."

"Chill out," Wesley chastises me. "You don't see the kids freaking out. It's just a little fun."

"A man touched your wife's face without her consent. That's not 'fun.' And the kids *are* freaking out. None of you seem to care, though."

"Is it really any different than the Halloween parade in the Village? People touch you all the time and you never complain," Wesley hits back.

"Yes," I reply, trying to figure out who this person I married is. "It *is* different."

I run inside, and I can feel eyes on me, none of them sympathetic. I find a bathroom and scrub my face in the mirror, and it all comes off, but a blotchy patch of red skin I rubbed raw remains.

It's past time to do more than skim the book Jacqueline gave me. There's a section on monsters and folklore, and I'm woefully ignorant about my new country's traditions.

I've a feeling we're not in Kansas anymore. For the first time in my life, I truly understand what Dorothy was feeling when she said that.

Despite the creepy display, that night I manage to sleep until dawn, which makes it easier to push down the ongoing alarm bells about our new life. I wake up less irritable and relieved to have one good night behind me.

I'm happy to have a day just for us with no events, no monsters, no worrying about what to wear.

Wesley didn't ask for a Christmas goose or bird of any kind, and he seems happy with a new recipe I found for a Swiss emmental and onion tart. He says he misses mashed potatoes, so I make a pile of those and cobble together a salad.

After a late lunch, we walk up to Sonnenberg, then wind around the hills and ramble for miles. Wesley stops to *moo* at some cows, and as I walk ahead on the path toward home, I come across my old friend again.

"Grüezi," Rose," Güggeliman nods. "Fröhliche Weihnachten."

"Hello, Karl," I reply with a smile. "Merry Christmas."

His face falls as he sees something behind me—Wesley?—and stops in his tracks. I swivel to see my husband has finished communicating with livestock and is walking back down the hill.

Karl nods to my husband once, and if I didn't know better, I'd say it was a purposefully curt nod. "Grüezi."

Wesley offers a close-lipped half-smile and says nothing as he brushes past Karl on the narrow trail.

I can feel Karl's eyes on us as we crunch down the hill, but I don't hear his footsteps. I suspect he is standing, staring, watching us go.

Back at home, Wesley builds a fire, I pop the cork on a bottle of Perrier-Jouët rose, and we sit cross-legged on the shag rug to exchange presents. He gives me a pair of gold earrings, though I almost never wear jewelry, and I give him a display case for the watch collection he keeps in his sock drawer.

I can't shake the feeling neither of us was thrilled with our gifts, nor were we able to fake it very well. Like everything else that's been happening here, I stuff it down.

We watch *It's a Wonderful Life* by the fire, then settle in to read.

I work so hard to avoid the topic of family and why I'm not calling any that I forget to ask if he contacted his.

CHAPTER

THIRTY

The gap between Christmas and New Year's Eve is calm, with no bumps in the night or strange messages at my door.

And yet my jetlag has ratcheted up to new levels. I've done everything to conquer it: avoiding napping when I can barely keep my eyes open; exercising to exhaustion; fifty kinds of calming tea; no coffee; no screens several hours before bed.

Nothing works. My brain is on fire, my limbs tingle under the sheets, and the unbearable fatigue underpinning the restlessness is no match for my body's stubborn refusal to succumb to sleep.

My main takeaway from online tips for handling chronic insomnia is to steer into the skid. Don't stare at the ceiling, punch your pillow or panic while the minutes tick by. I wake up at one or two most mornings, and I give it an hour, and when I remain wide awake, I rise.

I clean, read, cruise social media. I poke around the internet for mentions of the Rawlings family and Jacqueline. Go through the timeline of her disappearance again. Try to fill in those unaccounted-for hours with logic, supposition and imagination.

And every time, it comes back to Peter and those missing six hours.

By New Year's Eve I'm jittery and exhausted all at once, and I'm more than ready for a change of scenery and the sound of voices other than mine and Wesley's.

Heidi advises me to bring *everything* on the trip to Zermatt and so, on the morning we leave for the big TIG ski trip, Wesley and I engage in a chaotic frenzy of packing, rushing, and checking we have eveningwear, bathing suits, ski pants, goggles, and his new skis.

He makes it downstairs first and wrestles the front door open. "What the hell?"

I peek around him in the doorway. He crouches and picks up three wood chips, runs a thumb over the engraved symbols, turns to me.

More runes. I am at a loss. I visited the neighbor a few more times since the first batch showed up, but she never answers the door.

Wesley holds the discs on his flattened palm as if I'm the one who put them there.

"Give them," I say crisply. "I'll talk to the neighbor. It *has* to be her." I hope it's her. Any other explanation is too creepy to consider.

As I tuck the runes in my handbag, Wesley grumbles something I can't make out, then turns his focus to wrangling his skis and our bags down the endless stairs.

The raven screeches at me from the turret of our roof, and

with Wesley well ahead of me, I look up at him.

"I could use a break from you, bird. You know you can't come to Zermatt. It's too far. Now *scram*."

"Who were you talking to?" Wesley asks as he loads our things into the trunk.

"What? Nobody. I didn't say anything."

Nova brings out a flask on the mountain train and everyone takes a polite sip except me. It's too early for whatever hard liquor they're passing around.

I try not to be too obvious watching Kristoff and Seychelle, but he catches me as he prepares to pass the flask. He rewards my curiosity with a warm smile.

"You want some?" He asks, offering me a drink. "It'll warm you right up."

Fuck it. I take it from him and return his smile. I toss it back, taste metal on my tongue, then wince and cough as the booze goes down like jet fuel. Kristoff stands up, leans over, and pats me hard on the back.

"There you go. You're OK," he says.

I can't bring myself to be afraid of him; I can't even be mildly wary at this point, despite Wesley's earlier comment about him being a wolf in sheep's clothing. Brett, on the other hand, is standing up like a school-bus bully, bloviating, loudly using a spine-tingling falsetto voice to imitate a TIG client whose business he recently lost.

Raj and Heidi are watching with polite smiles, and they strike me as the only grownups on the train today.

Peter, the only single male here, is cracking up and joining in like he's on a boys' weekend, not getting away for one of the first major holidays since his wife supposedly left him.

When we arrive at TIG's chalet on a shuttle—no cars are allowed in Zermatt—the staff descends to open our doors and take our luggage.

Inside the modern ski chalet-slash-mansion, more help is waiting in the grand foyer holding trays of steaming mugs. I tilt my head to get a good look at its high ceilings and a spectacular chandelier dripping with crystals, then snap back to attention when a woman offers me a drink.

"Rum toddy or Irish Hot Chocolate," she says, and I realize with a start that it's Helena.

I guess Peter, the only one of us without a spouse in tow, won't be so single this weekend after all.

I grab a hot chocolate. One by one, a staff member leads each couple to their room. Ours is downstairs, with a view of a snowbank, but it's cozy and quiet and I'll take it. I get my husband to myself, far away from everyone else.

We take our time freshening up, then meet everyone upstairs for dinner. The table is laid like a medieval banquet with elaborate centerpieces and slender candles flickering in the dimly lit room.

I take my seat next to Wesley, who reaches out and massages my thigh, which has the exact effect he meant it to and I'm glad no one can see me blush.

Servers swarm the table and deposit steaming entrees in front of us. Everyone has chunks of meat, but I get a rosti, no bacon. I make eye contact with Heidi, who is clearly supporting me as a vegetarian-in-progress, across the table. She smiles and raises her glass to me, then turns to the others.

"I'd like to toast to good food, friendship, and the annual New Year's trip. May this one reach new levels of relaxation," she says.

"And debauchery," Brett talks with his mouth full.

"And debauchery," everyone agrees, and we clink glasses.

Two courses later, as we're sipping digestifs, Brett stands. "Would the menfolk like to join me for Blanton's and Cohibas in the lounge?"

Chairs scrape on tile as the men push away from the table. Wesley kisses me on the cheek before departing. "You'll be OK?" He whispers.

"I'll try to manage without you."

When they're gone, Seychelle makes a face at the door the men just disappeared through. "Bourbon and cigars? How basic of them," she observes. "Who's up for champagne in the hot tub?"

There are whoops and cheers, and then we all head out to change. I wriggle into a one-piece, wrap myself in the fluffy white robe hanging in our bathroom, and meet the rest of them on the freezing outdoor deck. It's suspended over the valley next to the pool, and everything is steaming. I imagine that from a distance it might appear like our chalet is on fire.

I step to the edge of the oversized hot tub and lower myself in. Someone hands me a glass of champagne, and as I take a sip, Seychelle eyes me from across the tub.

"So, New York girl," she says through the steam rising between us. "How are you faring as an expat? *Real* talk. How are you adjusting?"

I smile, stall, think of what I can share that won't circulate around TIG and get back to Wesley.

"Uh oh," Seychelle laughs. "That bad?"

"No! Not at all. It's just…" I'm thinking on my feet. "Obviously, everything's amazing, and Wesley and I are doing marriage pretty well, I think. But…I miss working and making my own money. I miss my career."

"Don't worry about *money*," Heidi, her curls pulled into a messy top knot, furrows her brow. "Wesley makes plenty for both of you and then some. All the top TIG guys do. Just look at this year's Christmas bonuses."

What? I haven't been informed of any Christmas bonus, but I nod and mumble my excitement about the alleged cash infusion.

Nova gestures with her drink. "No, no. I get what Rose means. I met Brett when he was on business in Stockholm, and at the time I was the star of the national surfing team. When he proposed and asked me to move to Lucerne, a part of me was sad to leave, and to give up my spot on the team."

Her platinum locks turn dark as the bubbles soak the edges of her bob.

"You'll get used to it," Nova assures me. "You'll forget about these doubts when you have your first baby. I know it's a cliché, but I didn't understand my purpose on this earth until I gave birth."

Don't roll your eyes, Rose. Don't say a word.

Heidi sets her jaw and sends Nova an evil eye. Seychelle sips champagne.

"We all had careers," Seychelle says. "We all had a choice to make."

"Oh? What did you do?" I ask.

"I ran a PR firm. I did well, too."

Nova scrunches up her face. "You still kind of do, don't you, though?"

"I keep my contacts up," Seychelle replies. "Networking is always a good idea."

She adds, "Heidi over here was a lawyer."

Heidi shrugs. "Eh. I practiced for a couple years. Some civil litigation, stuff like that. I met Raj online and went to London to visit him, and that was all she wrote. He got me out of Ohio. For that, I am forever grateful. Don't get me wrong, I won't tolerate anyone slamming my home state, but I wanted to see the world, and Raj gave me the impetus to do it."

We are all quiet for a moment, and I hear the caw of a raven above me over the roiling bubbles of the tub. I glance up and want to yell at him to *go away*.

"What about Jacqueline?" I ask.

My new friends don't miss a beat. They've become deft at acting like her absence is normal.

"Jacqueline was a portfolio manager for an investment firm in Hong Kong when she met Peter," Seychelle informs me. "Who knows. Maybe she's back at it now."

The delicate conversation is halted by the men bursting out of the glass doors.

"Hey, hot ladies," Brett calls out, arching his back and doing a little dance to show off his gut, much to everyone's amusement.

Peter gets ahead of him and dips a toe in the hot tub, wincing at the heat. Kristoff is in a Speedo, and Wesley and I lock eyes. We made a bet before we moved to Europe about when we'd see our first banana hammock. I had May. He guessed June. I win.

Wesley nudges Heidi and she scoots over. He sinks in next to me, moaning as the hot water inches up his body. "This is the life," he sighs.

Two servers breeze outside with more champagne.

"Look at those stars," Wesley says, throwing his head back to see the sky and snaking a hand between my legs under the water. "You don't see that in New York."

"No light pollution here," Raj observes. Heidi is now tucked in the crook of his shoulder. Nova is on Brett's lap.

It's as if I was imagining a month's worth of drama. How could this many people act so normal and happy if Jacqueline was truly in danger? She left on her own.

Right?

CHAPTER

THIRTY ONE

Wesley hangs back as the gang wrangles their skis out of the shuttle when we arrive at the lift the next morning.

"Are you *sure* you'll be OK? I can stay and set you up with a lesson on the bunny slope…"

"I'm not ready for that yet," I tell him. "I'm excited to hike and explore."

"We'll have a great time," Seychelle says. "I'm not skiing today, either. I fancy a bit of a walk."

The rest of them clamber to the lift line, and Seychelle and I start our ascent.

"Are you prepared for tonight?" She asks as we huff and puff up a mountain trail that snakes around the ski runs.

"I have no idea," I laugh. "Should I be worried?"

"Eh," she hedges.

"It's been fun to hang out with the guys a little more," I say. "I like Kristoff. How did you two meet?"

"At a family wedding." Her tone tells me to drop it, so I change tack.

"How long have you been together?"

"What are you getting at?" She flicks an evil eye at me between steps. "It's been five years. Yes, I've struggled with fertility. That's why I'm on this sad little hike with you. I've been injected, I'm supposed to ovulate soon, and Kristoff thought it would be safest for me to stay in one piece."

"I didn't—I'm sorry, I didn't mean to pry—"

"Hey. It's fine. I know you didn't," she sighs heavily. "I'm sorry, Rose. It's these bloody hormone injections. They make me homicidal. Not everyone is like you and Wesley…it's not all lust and meet-cutes. We get by. We're good for each other."

It's the first time she's ever snapped at me. Either we're true friends now, or we never were.

We trudge up above the tree line, and the movement and sun beating down keeps me from freezing.

I can feel her relaxing some, so I get up the nerve to pose the question I've needed to ask for weeks. "What happened to me that night in Zurich, Seychelle? Mum's night?"

She doesn't miss a beat. Keeps walking, doesn't change her expression.

"Whatever do you mean?"

"I don't remember a thing after one vodka tonic. I woke up at noon the next day with no memory of how I got home."

"I *did* give you that pill, darling."

"I didn't take it."

She raises her eyebrows. "Well, now."

"I'm worried something happened. If my memory is blank, anyone could have done anything to me." The implication is clear.

Seychelle halts in the snow and clutches her chest. "Oh god, Rose! Don't even think like that. I'd *never* let anything happen to you."

I feel tears welling up. Jacqueline disappeared that night, so I suppressed all my questions and concerns about my blackout because I told myself my problems paled in comparison.

"Look," Seychelle faces me. "I remember you swaying and dancing and being a bit flirty with some of my friends, but that was as scandalous as it got. Maybe that drink was stronger than you thought—and I remember you had a shot or two. You had a great time, and my sober mate drove us both home in my car since I was in no condition."

She stops dead in her tracks, and I follow suit.

"There!" She points to a looming, crooked, pointy rock in the distance. "The Matterhorn. We're so close. Take a good look."

I do.

"Majestic, isn't it?" She's moving back down the mountain. "Now. Let's get to the fun part. That's enough scenery and exercise for one day."

It begins to snow as we approach a chalet plopped alone in the middle of the mountain, and I can just about read the sign through the big, fat, meandering flakes crowding the air: *Hennu Stall. Welcome.*

We stagger toward the oasis like we're returning from a months-long expedition.

The place is straight out of Swiss Ski Bar Central Casting with a pitched roof, dark, unfinished wood, an outdoor balcony, and a rustic loft for the overflow to drink on.

"I'll tell you a secret," Seychelle whispers after we order drinks. "I've always fancied après ski more than actual skiing."

She pulls up her coat sleeve and checks her watch. "They should be here in an hour or so."

When she takes a bathroom break two drinks later, I sit in a corner and Google Seychelle and Kristoff. I'm intrigued by their union, one that seems tight yet miserable at the same time.

The European society pages pop up with talk of their glamorous wedding, and apparently *Hello!* magazine had the exclusive:

Liechtenstein playboy Kristoff von Verling, who is twelfth in line for the throne, marries the stunning South-African-born Seychelle Windsor of the British aristo set.

We can exclusively reveal that the new golden couple is sure to reign in the popularity stakes. Liechtenstein might be the least-visited country in Europe, but this little principality— the continent's only absolute monarchy—is also the wealthiest.

Says one royal watcher, "This beautiful couple are the future of the royal family. Young, hot, and already extremely popular. It's a match made in royalty heaven."

I'm surprised Kristoff doesn't use a title, but I guess twelfth in line for the throne doesn't qualify for much fanfare. I see Seychelle weaving her way back to me, and I close the tab and slip my phone back in my pocket.

By the time the others arrive, we're merry from our wine, and they all do shots to catch up.

"I can't hear anything!" I shout over the music directly into Wesley's ear five hours later when we're packed into a nightclub. I'm too old for this.

He winces, then pulls me close. "Let's get you another shot!"

Brett leans forward and says to Heidi, "Have you told Rose the Zermatt Rule?"

"Not yet." Heidi nods and fixes her gaze on me. "What happens in Zermatt, stays in Zermatt."

What happens in Zermatt is not my idea of fun. One by one, my new friends bring out a favorite drug. There are pills, lines in the bathroom—including Wesley, who I didn't know enjoyed the occasional bump—and vaping, all on top of free-flowing booze served by a woman in our own VIP area.

I'm offered a rainbow of choices, and I finally accept a pill from Heidi to shut them all up, and I palm it like I did in Zurich. I sip champagne, and I barely register our private server topping it up every time I get close to finishing a glass.

At one point everyone gets up to dance, and drunk as I am, I join in in my own shy, self-conscious way. Wesley is as zoned out as I've ever seen him, but soon I am too, so he and everyone else become a blur. It's late when I figure out my friends seem to all be dancing with other people. Strangers.

Peter is clinging to a young brunette, Brett is grinding between two women, Nova is sitting on a random man's lap, and Wesley, my Wesley, I think, is making out with a woman, but I'm unable to react. I don't even care; maybe it's not him, after all. Kristoff is perched on the sofa alone watching Seychelle, whose legs are draped over another man's lap.

I stumble in their general direction, but they disappear before my eyes. Someone taps me on my shoulder and there he is, my husband, and now he's kissing me.

We left the chalet with nine people, but more than a dozen

end up back home with us, and I'm determined to grab my husband from the pull of this hazy, weird, clothes-on orgy.

A hand pulls me to the sunken living room where everyone is congregating. "You were kissing someone else. We're married." I can hear myself slurring.

My husband plants his face on mine in front of everyone. I pull away.

"So were you," he says. Wesley's eyes are as vacant as I've ever seen.

"No. I would never do that. We took vows…"

Seychelle is sitting across from me on the lap of a gigantic man who looks no older than twenty-one.

Slick bodies intertwine in the hot tub and the pool. Couples sneak off down hallways and up stairs. Everything is hazy and out of focus, especially with the deliberate low lighting throughout the first floor, but I keep myself unmolested and my space my own.

I know in my heart this is not alcohol making me this way, but I can't construct a narrative with my fuzzy brain. I feel like I'm slipping in and out of consciousness but still awake, still on my feet.

It is, as Brett had hoped, pure debauchery.

CHAPTER

THIRTY TWO

I have to get away. This is not me; this is uncontrolled, unplanned, unsupervised pandemonium. I slip away from the group, and on the way to my room, I can't find the light switch, so I yell at the house: *Turn on.*

Nothing happens. I feel the wall, trying to get by with the nightlights. I don't know where I am.

I see a shadow. The shadow touches me, and I scream.

"Hey! Hey, calm down, it's just me."

Hands reach out and grab my shoulders. The accent, the calming voice, the slick delivery. *Peter.* I can make him out now in the dark, that one floppy curl always in danger of falling in his eye.

"Leaving so soon? I was hoping we could spend more quality time together."

More?

He leans down as if he's going to kiss me. I can feel his hot breath on my face, smell the bourbon. He moves his hand up and starts stroking my hair with a feather-light touch.

He's resting his left shoulder on the wall, his right hand is firmly on my hip, and I can't move. The hallway is dark and empty.

"There's something about you, isn't there, Rosie." His voice is lower, scratchy. "You do something for Wesley. I want to find out what's so special about you."

I think I hear footsteps, gentle, quiet. Maybe.

"Hello?" My voice echoes in the hallway. No one's there.

"You know," Peter says, pulling slightly away to look directly into my eyes, "if you wanted to know about me, you could've asked. You don't have to spy and harass people close to me."

I am frozen, as if he's paralyzed me. My throat feels as if it's closing up.

"Did it turn you on, being in my bedroom?" He brushes his lips on my ear. "Did you smell my pillow, Rose? Did you think about me coming in there and tearing your clothes off? Fucking you?"

He wrenches me into his body so I can feel his erection.

My unconscious takes over from my stalled conscious.

"Where's Jacqueline? *Where is she*, Peter?" I don't know how I got the courage to blurt it, but I know his wife's name will pour an ice bucket on his cockiness, and it's the only thing I can think to do, because I am no match physically.

Footsteps again. Now I see another shadow, standing still, watching. Then it moves toward us. Peter lets go of me and whips around.

"Wesley! Oh my god." I scream, step around Peter, and fall into my husband.

He laughs. "What's going on with you? Everyone's partying upstairs. Come back up!"

He isn't capable of helping me, or protecting me, or putting Peter in his place. Wesley is high, wired, and it's dark, so he can't see what's gone on. I'm on my own.

"Walk me back to my room," I say, and I pull him along, and he stays with me.

I *know* he couldn't have been there all that time watching Peter touch me, threaten me, traumatize me.

The man I thought I married would have stepped in and knocked him out on sight.

I bolt upright at four a.m. It takes me a moment to figure out where I am, and then I remember it all.

Was I drugged? Here *and* in Zurich? I can account for all my time last night. I remember not understanding everything going on around me, but I was awake and in control of my body.

I can't fall back to sleep with my mind racing and my stomach in knots, so I leave a snoring Wesley, slide into my slippers, and head upstairs. Anything to distract myself until I can talk to him about how I *think* I saw him with another woman and tell him what Peter did to me.

I heard mention of a library when we first arrived, and I'm curious to know what a ski chalet owned by a faceless Swiss company will contain.

I find it on the main floor at the back of the house, far from the pool, the kitchen, and the main living room where the party raged not long ago. I can smell the old bindings and the newer paper of modern volumes as soon as I step inside.

I pad over the hardwood floors, immediately drawn to a shelf of vintage and antique books including early editions from Dickens,

Austen, Tolstoy and Poe upright on a wooden shelf, unprotected in a place where any visitor could slip one in her bag and walk out. I move to pull one out when something catches my eye.

I gravitate to the self-help shelf. It's a mantel of platitudes, hollow wisdom, and guidance for pursuing comfort for the self above all else.

What did I see that drew me to this part of the room? What is my unconscious trying to tell me?

I run my fingers across the smooth bindings. One stands out. It is yellow. It is the one I saw in my mind's eye minutes ago, and it could hold the answer to at least one huge question I've had since before Jacqueline disappeared.

I slide it out carefully, then open the front cover. *The Secret* is the mother of vision boards, if I remember correctly. I flip through it, and it takes no time to discover this book indeed holds the secret.

The secret to an affair Jacqueline was having.

Two unnamed paramours have underlined certain passages and left little notes in the margins throughout the book, and I know one of them is Jacqueline because the handwriting is slim and elegant in the way it was on her vision board.

Through their fog of lust, the pair chose a code any fool could crack. Notes include, *I am available for a reading session this evening at the usual place.*

The library will be empty at noon. I'll be napping…

I want to get my hands on YOUR book, K?

"You don't give up, do you," a voice I recognize says coolly from behind me. I whirl around. "I see you've discovered *The Secret.*"

There she is, up early or up late, I can't be sure which, her bun perfect, her posture erect.

"What is going on, Irina?" I cry. "Will somebody *please* tell me?"

I'm too tired to play it cool.

Irina retains an expression in a Happy Helpers shade of neutral, and says through barely moving lips, "They are always watching."

I shake the book at her. "Is this what I think it is? Jacqueline was having an affair? With whom?"

"You can guess," she says through gritted teeth. "They were very careful. The only reason I knew is because I picked this book out last year to show Helena. She is into messages and signs from the universe and all that. She was interested in the money part. She paid no attention to those little notes, but I found them… interesting."

"Are you saying you don't know for sure who the guy is, if it is a guy? They were never caught in the act?"

"This group, *your* group now, they are all very careful. They learned to hide their…activities. They don't like to show weakness or problems."

So the guy is one of ours. It's not Peter, obviously, nor Wesley, because we just got here. That leaves two others, and I know who my money's on. Whoever wrote a sweeping "K" in the book was trying to pretend it meant *OK*.

"Irina," I say, "She was having an affair with Kristoff, wasn't she? I heard you and Jacqueline arguing at the vision board party. What was that about? She went missing not long after that. Whatever you were arguing about might be important."

I've finally rattled her. She goes pale, closes her eyes for a moment, then recovers. "Jacqueline was a good one," she says. "Always nice to everyone's staff, gave out bonuses every year. Yes, she could be intimidating, but only if you are afraid of smart, beautiful women. Those children loved her as their mother. She read stories to them when Peter was working late—which was a lot. She nursed them when they were ill. But toward the end…well, she became paranoid."

"You know that saying, just because you're paranoid doesn't mean they're not out to get you?" I ask.

"Exactly," Irina nods. "She put me in an awkward position. She demanded I tell her if Peter and Helena were getting close, wanted me to spy on my friend and betray her, but Helena didn't do anything wrong. Peter went after *her* and bought her expensive gifts she wasn't supposed to accept. She ended up giving in, but it wasn't her idea. *Peter* is the bad one. It was, what is the word…"

"Icky."

"Yes. It was icky the way Helena's boss went after her."

"You're saying Jacqueline was turning on you all of the sudden, and you tried to defend yourself by letting her know that *you* knew she was sleeping with her best friend's husband?"

Irina nods. I'm shifting gears, discarding Peter as my only focus, tearing away from the smirking face I can't seem to get away from, and giving Kristoff some thought. Mr. Nice Guy. Mr. Unassuming. A wolf in sheep's clothing, indeed.

If Jacqueline was sleeping with Seychelle's husband, that would give a whole new batch of people a reason to want her gone. It makes me sad for Seychelle to think her husband might have betrayed her, but if she knew about any of this, it could give her a motive to force Jacqueline out of the picture.

This feels out of control now, like I'm way out of my depth. Like my assumptions were wrong all along. Like I'm missing too big a piece of the puzzle to make any sort of cogent case for what happened to Jacqueline.

"Am I in danger, Irina? Are *we* in danger?"

"I don't know," she replies. "But I will tell you this: two years ago, another expat woman goes missing from Lucerne. This one at Fasnacht."

"And Fasnacht is coming up in a few weeks."

"Yes. Things are getting weird around here," she whispers. "I've put in for a transfer. Don't tell anyone, but I've got a job lined up in Provence. This is too strange for me."

"But what is this all about? Are we saying there's a serial killer in the club?"

"Like I told you, I don't know," she says, her voice a husky stage whisper now. "But Fasnacht is coming up, and I intend to be long gone by then."

She turns to leave.

"*Irina*," I hiss. She turns back. "What time did Peter get home the night Jacqueline went missing? You and Helena talk, right? She'd *have* to know if something happened that night…if there was a fight or if he did something to his wife."

Her neutral face is obliterated, replaced by wide, blinking eyes and trembling lips.

"Helena didn't mention anything was off that night. That's all I can tell you."

"What about Kristoff?" I ask. "When did he leave?"

She pretends she doesn't hear me as she hurries out, never looking back.

I take a few quick pictures of some of the love notes, then cram *The Secret* back in its slot.

Back in our room, Wesley is snoring like a Mack truck and the white-noise app is whirring. I pull the runes out of my robe pocket and kneel on the faux-bearskin rug by the antique books, then jiggle them in my hand and toss them on the floor like dice.

I crawl to where they landed in a lopsided triangle.

I punch descriptions of the shapes into my phone in order:

1. PERTHRO: Fate. Mystery. Secrets.

2. TIWAZ Battle.

3. ISA again. Ice. Waiting. Watching.

I read through the vast rune-related literature available online, and it hits me there's no point trying to decipher a complex message or prophecy with only three runes. Your own hand is supposed to reveal the answer in the way it throws a *bunch* of them, and you're supposed to follow your instincts to choose three to reveal the answers you seek.

In this case, someone's already chosen for me.

The runes themselves are the message.

Someone is deliberately fucking with me, and I sense the danger, but whoever's behind this is too good. It could be my neighbor. It could also be my new "friends."

It could be Wesley. I know this, even as I pray it isn't, even as I know it's a slim chance. It's still possible.

It's not like Violet didn't warn me.

CHAPTER

THIRTY THREE

Violet pestered me with the truth like a fly buzzing around my head, and I swatted it away at first. She knew I would eventually buckle, which I did, and gave her my blessing to dig deeper into Wesley Blackwood's life.

I wear my cynicism like a skin, let it live in my bones, swirled in with my marrow like a soft-serve twist cone. Hitching my name and my life to this man required due diligence.

I could almost accept this beautiful, smart, popular, wealthy man appeared to be besotted with me, but why he was rushing us through the stages of courtship was another question entirely.

When the facts were in, the Dead Newspaper Club met at the dive bar in a Hell's Kitchen-adjacent neighborhood, where the *Daily News* building used to be, or still is, though it's less of a newspaper now and more like a pamphlet.

"I think it's a love story for the ages," Talia said when we were seated at a scarred wooden table clutching local beers. "There *are* good men in New York. Rose has proved it."

"No, there aren't, and no, she hasn't," Vi shot back.

I felt the proverbial lump in my throat. "Does that mean it's bad news? He's a white supremacist or an ex-con, or…"

"Came back negative." Violet reported with mild disappointment. "No DUIs, no foreclosures or evictions, no sex assault charges at Yale. Oh, and he did go there. Got the records and a photo to boot—it's him. I've got an entire virtual file if you want it. A friend in my torts class knew a friend of his back then."

I picked up my beer.

"So the man I've chosen to spend my life with, the one I've been sleeping with for the past three months, is a good guy? What are the odds?"

"I wouldn't go that far," Marty said. "He spent a semester abroad. There are no records of that period. He could've been sex-trafficking his way around Bulgaria and we'd never know it."

"What's his *motive*?" I asked them. "What would Wesley's endgame be in marrying me for anything other than true love?"

"Money," Vi said.

"Oh, stop it," Talia said. "You know Rose comes from the lower-middle class. There *is* no money."

"It's true," I said. "His family's got plenty."

"But he can't tap into it."

"He doesn't *want* to tap into the trust right now. Big difference."

"So he says," Violet says. "Have you seen the paperwork? There's always life insurance, too. Yes. The life insurance! He can get a huge policy on you and will become filthy rich if you kick the bucket. More to the point, if *he's* the one who kicks your bucket."

That's the one thing that got me—the life insurance.

I wrote an article once about a husband who had a secret

policy on his dead wife. I learned the policy holder *must* alert the person whose life is insured, which made me feel better for a hot second, until I read about the punishment: *For those who forge insurance documents, there is a very stiff fine.*

So my body will be burned to smithereens in a furnace after a clever murder, while my husband the killer is paying a stiff fine with the $5 million policy he had on me that I never knew about.

I decided we needed to learn about his past love life to put it all in perspective. I asked Vi, "What about girlfriends? Ex-fiancés? He only told me about flings in college and in New York. I want to know what his type is."

"You," Violet replied. "*You're* his type, as far as I can tell. I found one alleged girlfriend by the name of Darlene DeWitt of Hamden, Connecticut. She went to community college and they met at a bar in New Haven. After graduation he refused to marry her and she disappeared off the radar."

"Great! Job done. Let's eat," I said, planning to cyberstalk this "Darlene" as soon as I was alone.

"I'm with Rose," Talia said. "There's a fine line between diligence and paranoia. This isn't the first time two people met at a party and fell head-over-heels for each other. Let the woman be happy."

"You know what they also say," Marty held up a finger. "Just because you're paranoid doesn't mean they're not out to get you."

"Rosie, girl, I don't know what to tell you," Vi said. "Something feels wrong."

"Can you forget that, though? Can you just be happy for me? The wedding's going to be a small affair at their Westport estate.

I'm not canceling it on a feeling."

"I am happy for you, Mrs. Thurston Howell III," Vi pretended to put it all aside. "Will I have to start calling you 'Luvvy?'"

"Violet."

"What."

"Will you be my maid of honor?"

"Shit, girl! What took you so long? Oh my god, damn, I'm already behind organizing the bachelorette and...don't you dare make me wear a strapless dress. And I don't wear dark blue— ever. When are we going *shopping*?"

The other three were quiet, letting us hash it out while they sipped their beers. Marty offered to go to the bar and put in our onion rings order, and moved his wheelchair away from the table.

"Where you going?" I said to him. "I need three others up there with me. Talia, D'Shawn, Marty: Will you be my bridespeople? Tux, cheap suit or dress. Your call."

They all said yes.

Vi and I went shopping the next week, but it turned out there would be no fancy wedding after all. We were stuck with City Hall when TIG called and told Wesley we needed a marriage certificate *immediately* so they could secure our visas.

Both our wedding parties wore whatever made them comfortable, and Vi insisted on a stunning gown in deep magenta even though there were no photographs of the affair because Wesley didn't want them.

I told him that was an absurd and unfair request. He begged me to relent.

"This is not the wedding I wanted to give you. It's not the

wedding my mother wants," he pleaded. "I want you to have an amazing celebration at the yacht club or a destination wedding in Italy. Something spectacular that we'll *want* to remember. We'll be in the *Times*, and my mother refuses to allow that when it's a City Hall wedding. Consider this our placeholder. Please?"

I agreed in the end, because it actually made some sense. Instead of a swanky reception, there was lunch at Houston's with his parents, my four friends, and three of Wesley's.

It turned out to be a blessing. A basic ceremony with no fuss spared me from having to think about who would walk me down the aisle.

After my foray to the chalet's library, I jump into bed, pull the blankets off Wesley and wrap them around me.

"Hey," he groans, turning over and sliding the comforter back his way as I hoped he would. "Everything OK?"

"No. It's not." I sit up. "I know everyone was messed up last night, but we need to talk about what happened."

"Whoa." He sits up, rubs his eyes, and turns on the light next to his bed. "What do you mean?"

I tell him everything: That I saw him kissing someone else, that Peter groped and threatened me, that I was followed around town again. He listens, blinking and confused, as I run through it all.

This is his test. This is how I know if he's in my corner.

"Hey, come here." He opens his arms and I fall into them. "I have never and *would* never cheat on you. We were all shee threets to the wind last night. It must have been someone else you saw."

"I think maybe someone is *still* 'shee threets' to the wind," I say.

He closes his eyes. "Ugh. I probably *am* still a little drunk. You got me. Three sheets to the wind. In any case we were together most of the night, and if someone came on to me, I certainly don't remember it."

"I *know* I saw you kissing one of those women from the bar."

"*What*? No," he cries. "Stop it. Seriously. Everyone was totally out of it. God knows all the stuff we took was enough to make us hallucinate."

"I don't do drugs."

"You took something," he insists. "Maybe just a tranquilizer, but come on. How much champagne and how many shots did we have? Don't be so hard on yourself—on us. What happens in Zermatt stays in Zermatt, remember? Leave it behind, OK?"

I can't.

"I don't know what else to say," he goes on, "Except I need you to trust me. And anyway, I'm more concerned about Peter touching you. If I'd realized what was happening in that hallway, I *swear* I would've…"

He flexes his jaw and shakes his head. "I'd say he was out of his mind, high and drunk, but that's no excuse. Leave it with me, OK? I'll talk to him. I'll make sure nothing like this ever happens again."

I almost cry with relief. I was braced for the denials I've gotten in my life before him, the ones women are so used to: *He didn't mean anything by it; he was being friendly; you misread his intentions; he's a good guy, trust me.*

"Thank you," I say, and we are quiet, resting, for a few moments.

"I'm starved," he says after a while. "Should we go down for breakfast?"

When the trip ends, the holidays are over, and the work begins. Through frigid air under the vivid blue skies of January, I venture inside TIG's glassy riverside offices for our first German lesson. The lobby is welcoming and bright, and picture windows draw sunlight in even in a city where it starts to get dark by three p.m. in deepest winter.

Wesley's assistant, a red-headed Swiss man with a mustache, fetches me within a minute of my checking in.

"Hello, Mrs. Blackwood. I am Pieter," he says. "It's a pleasure to meet you. If you'll follow me…"

I do, and we pass by a dozen quiet offices with lake views and well-dressed workers hunched over computers.

Pieter stops at an office I would know was Wesley's even without a guide: It's immaculate and low on clutter.

"Can I get you anything, Mrs. Blackwood? Coffee, tea, water?"

"Please—call me Rose. Could I get a macchiato with two sugars?"

"Right away. Please, make yourself at home. Wesley is in a meeting but I will let him know you are here."

"No need, Pieter," I smile. "I can wait. Our lesson doesn't start for another fifteen minutes."

Enough time to search the office.

I sink into Wesley's ergonomic chair, keep an eye on the frosted glass door, and start opening drawers. They're unlocked and organized with accordion folders. I ignore the labels—when people are hiding something, it will always be filed under the opposite of what it actually is—and rifle through the first folder I pick out.

Most of the pages are rows upon rows of numbers. No wonder Wesley never wants to make dinner conversation about his life at TIG. It would be conversational Valium.

I check his "Employment Documents" file next, and what do you know—jackpot.

I glance up and see a head bobbing along the hallway.

I duck down and scan the documents as quick as I can. My name's on page three: *Rose Stone Blackwood: spouse*. It's a copy of the contract I studied in the kitchen the night Wesley asked me to move to Switzerland.

There is a life insurance policy I never saw. It's tacked on to the signed employment contract, and I get the gist quickly. It's provided through TIG as a standard benefit, it costs us nothing, and if I die, Wesley gets two thousand francs to help defray cost of burial.

I look up, but the head wasn't Pieter's; it has passed by, so I read on. If Wesley dies before me, I get five years' salary in a lump sum. *Holy crap.* For the first time, I see how much Wesley makes. Five years of it would be millions.

I flick through the folder and find a bank statement from a German bank I've never heard of, and I see a substantial Christmas bonus he didn't tell me about. He truly doesn't need life insurance on me. It doesn't mean there's not another policy floating in the ether, but I believe the chances are dimming fast.

I shut the drawer just in time, as Pieter returns with my coffee. He escorts me and my macchiato to the mini-conference room.

Wesley rushes in late, out of breath and stressed.

"Sorry, sorry, sorry. Back-to-back meetings today. I don't know where the time goes," he breathes.

Our teacher, a slight, greying man with a briefcase and a frown, wordlessly hands us each a textbook and a workbook, then launches into the lesson.

It's like being in first grade again. We must learn to communicate with the most basic words. To count. To recite the alphabet, to say hello, please, thank you and sorry.

Wesley and I sit thigh-to-thigh across from the teacher. After a forty-five-minute lesson, he gives us homework and sends us on our way.

My husband leans down and kisses me on the cheek after the teacher shuffles out with his briefcase. "I'll be late tonight," he says. "Don't wait for me for dinner."

After I eat soup and bread alone that evening, I stretch out on the sofa with my laptop and force myself to face the financial music, so to speak.

I poke around online and find a reasonable airfare back to New York, one that is still far over the spending limit I suspect Wesley placed on my credit card.

I begin the process of booking it. If the card he gave me works, great. I'll have a long weekend back home to center myself and clear my head. I'll take a breather from the drama and darkness. I will see my old friends, hug Vi and laugh with the wry, unfashionable and quirky Dead Newspapers Club.

If the payment doesn't go through, Wesley will get a notification from the company that I made the attempt. I won't have to think about gathering the courage to confront him anymore.

I click *Book now.*

The alert flashes up in red: PAYMENT DECLINED.

CHAPTER

THIRTY FOUR

I wait in the living room for my husband's return. I hear him coming up the stairs, watch him make to the landing. His tie is off and his top two shirt buttons are undone, but I don't have the energy to worry about what that might mean.

He blinks at the light from my e-reader across the darkened room.

"Whoa! You scared me." He clutches his chest.

"I tried to book a flight home today for Vi's birthday," I say. "My credit card was declined."

"It's been a helluva day," he shakes his head and flips on the overhead light. "I can't do this right now. I'm going to bed."

"When I agreed to leave my job, you swore that we'd share our money." I stand up to face him. "We're married, but I feel like a child on an allowance. By all means go to bed. This won't take long. I want a debit card, access to our accounts, and a card with the same credit line you have. Conversation over."

He raises a hand to loosen his non-existent tie, then runs them through his blond hair instead, slicking it back.

"Wait a minute." He shakes his head. "You said you never

cared about my money. That you weren't like the rest of them."

"I'm your *wife*," I reply. "You gave me a credit card with a useless limit. Why? We need groceries. We need things for the apartment—we don't even own a vacuum. How do you propose I pay for that?"

He is glaring now, look of contempt crossing his face.

"You know about my last girlfriend," he says. "How she used me. She ran up my Black Amex shopping in Soho, Fifth Avenue, online. She never even bought *me* anything with it."

"Interesting an old girlfriend got a Black Amex but your wife can't afford to buy a new pair of jeans."

I can see his jaw flexing in the moonlight.

"What I feared has happened," I say. "I gave up my power, and our dynamic changed. I left my job and you promised you wouldn't punish me for it."

He's gotten used to manipulating me, making me feel I'm starting a fight when I mention money. The more I stand up to him, the better it feels.

"And look where you are." He gestures to the grand Pilatus outside the picture window. "You wouldn't be here without me."

I exhale long, loud and slow.

"You finally said it. It took you—"

I check my wrist for effect, though I don't wear a watch.

"—five whole months to say it out loud. To say what everyone's been thinking since we met: you're too good for me. Ordinary Rose drags you down. That—"

"Stop it." He barks like a drill sergeant.

"Or what?" It comes out shakier than I wanted it to.

That throws him. His eyes are hard, hands are on his hips now, and as he seethes, he thinks.

"Fine. You want to get some stuff out in the open? Let's do it. What are you going home *for*? Think about that, Rose."

He waits. I say nothing. "Neither of us can stand our mothers for more than a few minutes at a time. I don't know what the story is with yours, but I know you haven't seen her or talked to her in months, maybe years. And your father..."

His eyes are ice, lacking all feeling or empathy.

"...I assume he's dead. You never told me anything about it, so I can only guess, because at night you scream *dad*! Like you're in a horror movie. Get over it, Rose. Life goes on."

"Fuck you," I say, and stalk away to lock myself in my office.

I have no interest in explaining my wretched family to anyone, including my husband. He knows the basics; he knows enough. I pull out the futon and lie flat on my back, close my eyes, think about what to do next with my life.

I'm shocked when Wesley knocks gently on the door fifteen minutes later. He'd been so tense, so angry, I figured I was in for an endless standoff.

"Please, Rose," he says, his voice muffled through the thick wood. "Can we talk?"

I'm not even *close* to deciding whether I want to see his chiseled face ever again. I ignore his knocks, his apologies through the door, his texts for a few minutes.

"Rosie," he says again. "I'm *sorry*. That was a low blow. I'm new at this marriage stuff. Forgive me?"

I hear his palm *splat* against the door and I picture him leaning on it, ear pressed against the smooth finish.

"You know what happened with my father traumatized me,"

I finally respond. "You're the *one* person who's supposed to have my back. If you're going to hit me in the most tender spot at the smallest disagreement—"

"I'm *sorry*."

"Go away!"

I feel trapped in this room. He has never made a move toward me or laid a hand on me in anger, but I have a heightened awareness of our size difference, of his rage, of my vulnerability on this quiet hill.

There is quiet as I wait for his reaction, then I hear him give up and shuffle away in his socked feet. I knew this would happen. There's a reason the divorce rate in my home country is so high. I went in eyes wide open, because I knew no piece of paper, no flowery vow, can stop the inevitable. I always found comfort in knowing they'll leave. *They* meaning *everyone*.

Even Vi. I'll never ditch her as a friend no matter what she does, but I've spent nearly a lifetime bracing for her to get sick of me, for one bad fight to end with her being done.

That made it easy for me to say yes to Wesley after knowing him for three months. Everything is temporary, so why not have some fun in the meantime?

I've managed to squirrel away cash a little at a time, and I've amassed five grand in dollars and francs in my sock drawer with which to start over, to find an apartment, a job, pay for food, make my way home. *If* that's what I want to do.

I tuck a couch pillow behind my head. I've locked myself in the office without bedding, a book, or my laptop. I have nothing do to but think, and I have no desire to step out and see that man.

Then I remember I *do* have a book. I paw through the back of the closet where I'd left it wrapped in pre-marriage undergarments I can't bring myself to throw out, stuffed in the bottom of the box they arrived in.

I lie back and crack the book open again. It reminds me of the old Bible Grandma Mixie used to have in her nightstand with its floppy cloth cover, pages so thin you can see the words on the next page, and crowded text that makes me squint.

I flip to the chapter with wordy tales of discovering and exploring the Swiss Alps, including mention of the folklore up in them hills. There are the monsters Teresa mentioned on the Rigi hike, there are child snatchers, soul stealers, demons, mischief makers, serpents with cat heads, thieves of Alpine livestock (I figure I'm safe from that one). Dragons are hiding everywhere, according to the early explorers.

There were people, too, tucked up in the caves. One passage reads, *Explorers encountered hideous visions in tiny villages cut off from polite society, its population stout, riddled with incest, grunting men with grotesque goiters protruding like levers out of the neck…One such village was suspected to be a haven for witches covered in warts with hooked noses that made children cry and grown men wail.*

I wince at some of the descriptions. This book needs some serious modernizing.

I flip through a few more pages until the Alpine Games, or "Schwingfest," catches my eye. This is apparently an occasion for the Swiss to wrestle each other in sawdust while the country's best yodelers and alphorn players compete in the background. The Games also feature unknowable events called "hornussen" and the tossing of the "Unspunnen stone."

Witches are touched on in Chapter 4 and expanded upon in Chapter 5, intriguingly titled *Understanding the Mess of Witches, Monsters and Folklore in the Swiss Culture*. I pull the blanket up to my chin and read about how the Swiss hunted, burned, hanged and decapitated "witches" well into the eighteenth century. Some say you can still hear screams for vengeance from their ancestors up in the mountains.

I try my best to figure out what Jacqueline was trying to tell me, but I can't find answers in these rambling and occasionally offensive stories. I also can't figure out why only pregnant—or "expecting" women as Jacqueline put it—are allowed to read it.

I fan the pages out again. Nothing.

I gently wiggle the binding with my thumb and forefinger, then work a finger down as far as it will go—and I feel something lodged in the spine.

I don't want to wreck the binding, but I'm presently less worried about the survival of old paper than I am about my and Jacqueline's safety. I'm careful and patient as I slide a tiny piece of folded paper out a millimeter at a time.

I work it out with my pinky, then gingerly unfold the triangle, and when it's laid out, it's the size of a quarter. Two words are written on it.

They assault me like a punch in the face.

CHAPTER

THIRTY FIVE

Find me.

F The words have so much power it's as if I can I hear them leaping off the paper. The ink speaks to me in an unfamiliar voice. The paper is clean, modern, crisp.

The words are in block letters so the wrong person couldn't recognize the handwriting if they found it. It has to be Jacqueline. The generic voice in my head morphs into Jacqueline's: *Find me.*

I want to find her, and then shake her. She went to all this trouble, and this clue is *nothing*. This gives me zero information to go on, except maybe to tell me she believed she'd be taken, not murdered. Or not—maybe she means find her body, which is a sickening thought.

I examine the paper. There are rough edges around some of the letters; I grab my phone and use the camera as a magnifying glass. My heart is racing, because I can see now *there are words within the words.*

What I thought was a blurry, messy letter is made of letters itself. I make out an *f* and a *d*.

I increase the magnification, and there it is: *Find CM.*

And suddenly, I'm trapped in this country again whether I want to be or not. I can't go home to New York yet; I must venture farther down the rabbit hole. I can't leave Jacqueline where she is. It's not in me.

I fall asleep after three a.m. and wake up five hours later with a knot in my stomach. I can hear Wesley in the shower, the water pelting on the walls, rhythmic, then splashing as it falls off him down to the drain.

I am dreading seeing him, talking to him, feeling his anger, knowing I'll have to stand my ground no matter what. I'm not sure if I will, or if I can.

I hit the button to raise the shutter, and light pours in one inch at a time. I think about the bombshell I found in the book binding, and in the bright light of day, it doesn't seem the definitive game changer it first appeared to be.

The missive could be from anyone, to anyone. It could have been a parlor game of hide-and-seek in a dusty Expat Social Club chalet somewhere. I wouldn't put anything past these people. What happened to Jacqueline all comes down to mum's night, and I need to nail down a timeline.

I hear Wesley's shoes slapping on tile, then feel the vibration of the garage door opening twenty feet below. I won't have a car today, so I'll walk to Peter's and call it exercise.

I grab a bottle of Chablis and set off under grey, pregnant skies. We're bracing for another eight inches of snow.

The door to Peter's home opens within a minute of my knocking.

I open my mouth to start charming Helena immediately, but

she's not standing in the doorway. Another Happy Helper—this one clearly from the EXPERIENCE roster—greets me with a dour expression.

"Oh—um, good morning," I smile. "Is…is Helena here?"

"Helena does not work here."

"But—"

"She is gone. Can I help you?"

"No, uh, I understand. Thank you. Auf Wiedersehen."

I take my wine and leave, crossing my fingers that the new woman doesn't mention this to Peter. I'm wrapped up in a hat, scarf, sunglasses and a puffy coat, so she'll have no good description to offer.

So now Helena has disappeared. I have a sick feeling in my stomach again. Another one leaves town so soon after Jacqueline? Whoever's doing this is tipping their hand if they eliminated Helena.

I check the Happy Helpers website as I walk, scanning for Helena's photo, and I'm relieved when I see her face on page two. She's still there. That's a good sign, but it's not definitive proof she's OK. I block the caller ID function on my phone and call the office.

"Grüezi. I am new in Lucerne and I'd like to hire one of your staff to help around the house," I say when a woman answers. "I like the resume of Helena I saw on your website. We'd like to interview her, please."

"Ah, well, unfortunately Helena is working with a family in Lyon now," the woman replies. "But we have a wonderful array of other qualified—"

I end the call and look up at the heavens as if God herself is smiling down on me today, even though I'm not religious, even though my parents took us to church a total of five times, and only on holidays. If Happy Helpers placed Helena in Lyon, *she's OK.*

The bad news is I have no way of nailing down the timeline of that night. Everyone agrees the poker game went until 1 a.m., but what happened after that, what went on inside Peter's four-story home in the subsequent hours, is unknowable from my perspective.

Assuming he ensured his children wouldn't see or hear anything disturbing, the only way to reconstruct the events of that night after both Jacqueline and Peter returned home is with a witness, or with location data from their cars and/or phones. I have none of those things.

I'm going to have to steer around this mystery. Like my father showed me when I was young out on the flats, I'll circle it from different directions. *Dig around the clams,* he'd say. *Don't stab at them. Be crisp but conservative. Don't let them know you're coming, and don't disturb them until you know exactly what's underneath that first layer.*

I'll have to speak to Wesley at some point today, unfortunately, to make sure I have the car tomorrow. If things don't go well, I'll probably take that trip to New York.

When I arrive home, hands numb and quads burning from the three-mile trek, I go in search of my American credit card and my passport, both of which I'll need if I flee my new marriage, even temporarily.

I head to my office and pull out the top drawer. My pink

faux-croc passport wallet, the one Vi gave me as a going-away present, isn't there, where it always is, ready to grab at a moment's notice. I rifle around. It occurs to me I don't recall putting it back in the drawer after Zermatt.

Have I seen it since that trip? I check my tote, my purse, and the now-empty backpack I traveled to the resort with. It *has* to be in there. I check every pocket, feel around, dump everything out. My passport is nowhere to be found.

I race away and look under the bed. I check all the bathroom cabinets and under the sofa cushions.

I throw on my coat, slip into my furry boots and race out the door to search the garage. I shine my phone's flashlight in every nook and cranny. Nothing.

That tiny government-issued book with the navy matte cover is a lifeline. It is a key to a prison cell. I trudge back upstairs. It could be in the car, or maybe it got packed with Wesley's things when we left Zermatt.

I'm overcome with a creeping panic that wheedles its way through my exhaustion. I decide to keep going—I'll tire my body out until it's forced to sleep through the night.

We need milk for the cappuccino machine and I need more wine. I need a purpose. I grab my backpack and set out in the cold, before it snows, for a shopping trip to Coop.

I'm distracted as I peruse the still-unfamiliar aisles and brands, picking up the essentials, and I'm OK until I reach the cheese section.

The cheese section enrages me. I can't find any fucking *cheddar*—you can get every form of cheese in this canton except the most basic one in the history of the world—and I almost have a breakdown in the middle of the aisle. I angrily grab a wheel of brie, full of hate for it.

I wipe stray tears away as I wait in line behind three people with full carts. When it's my turn and three others are waiting behind me, the teller holds up a bag of tomatoes.

She stares at me.

"What?" I snap.

She turns and points to the produce section. "Price," she says. "*You* price. Bitte."

Fuck it. *Goddamn motherfucker shithole ass.* I forgot again. You're supposed to weigh and price your own produce here. Print out the sticker. Slap it on. And do it all in German with kilograms. She blinks at me and points to the tomatoes, hanging in their bag like distended, red testicles.

"Self. *Weigh.*"

"Take it back," I say. "Keep it. I have to go. *Entschuldigung.*"

I run out without my groceries. The convenience store is on the way home, and I run in for milk, bread and wine, then race back up the hill to my empty house, my legs throbbing with exertion. I'm acutely aware there's nothing on this hill for me. It happened in one tick of the second hand: my life went from 11:59:59 to midnight, and with the faintest movement I was cut off from my old way. From my independence. To use another analogy, I was boiled like a frog.

My health insurance is here. My job is long gone. My income and assets are zero, not counting the sock drawer. My passport is missing. Wesley has my B permit, my essential Swiss visa, at work. Wesley owns me, just as I feared when I agreed to come to the land of cheese and chocolate.

I drag myself up one step at a time, my backpack and dread weighing me down, the uneven sounds of ravens and crackling tree branches adding to my anxiety.

With no one around to see or hear me, I begin to sob. With every step, I cry out. Up one. *Wail.* Up two. *Bawl.* Two more. *Howl.* I glance up to see if I'm close. I am six stairs away.

At the top, a dark shadow awaits me.

Standing, staring, waiting.

CHAPTER

THIRTY SIX

I scream when I see her. The sight of another human being shocks and embarrasses me; she must have heard every overdone sob and wheeze, witnessed my splintering apart in blazing color.

I'm three steps from the top, and I can see her eyes and tufts of thick grey hair poking out from under her knit cap. One puffy black glove robust enough for an arctic expedition stretches out.

She wiggles her oversized fingers. "I take. Give. Please."

I hand her my backpack and haul myself up the last few stairs. My nose is running and my face is wet with tears.

"Come," she says, beckoning me to follow with one hand as she hikes the pack on her opposite shoulder. "Please."

I'd go with anyone to avoid being alone right now. The wine bottles clang together in the pack as she carries it with ease. She has to be in her seventies, but with her hill walking and the clean Swiss air, she's as fit as I am.

Sore and sniffling, I follow her up the same kind of wide, tiled stairs we have in our house across the way. The place smells of anise, fresh earth and the smoky residue of blown-out candles. At the top, instead of a sterile expanse of hard floors with the largely spare, cold decor Wesley and I have, there is a hodge-podge of furniture, collectibles, throw rugs, sculptures, decorations.

The woman sets my bag down, holds up an index finger for me to wait, and walks to her kitchen. I move to the balcony. She has the same view of Pilatus that we do, though a couple dozen yards to the left.

She returns with tissues in one hand and a steaming mug in the other. I follow her to the dining-room table, sit with her, and accept the tissue she offers. I dab my eyes and blow my nose as delicately as I can.

"Drink," she says, nodding to the mug. "It is for…beruhigen. It is good for you. *Beruhigen.*"

She makes an *aahh* sound, a soothing one, using her hands to suggest bringing things down.

"Calming?" I ask. I bring the cup to my lips.

"*Yes,*" she says with obvious relief. "*Calming.*"

"I am Rose," I say, pointing to myself.

"I am Astrid."

She watches me sip the tea. It is the exhaustion, the loneliness, the self-doubt, the attention she is paying me, the way she waits for me to tell her why I've been screaming and crying on the hill—*that's* what makes me tell this stranger what I haven't been able to spill to anyone before now.

"Something is wrong," I blurt. "Something is…bad."

I can say it out loud here, once, and it won't trigger or upset anyone in my life, in my home, in the Club.

Astrid nods. She doesn't flinch or look away; she is unsurprised and seems to understand key words, the same way

I've gotten along in Lucerne picking out certain recognizable terms.

"Genau," she says, not seeming to require further explanation. *Genau. OK.* It's as if she's reading my mind. She holds up a finger again and rises.

I am thinking about the runes, and how my inner voice is telling me she did not leave them. Yet she had to be the one; it is the most logical explanation.

Astrid returns carrying a flat piece of wood that has seen better days. She sets it on the table between us. A cold fear ripples through me, and I'm not sure why. It's a talking board, an ancient one by the looks of it, but this is not mass-marketed entertainment.

I've participated in a fair number of séances and Ouija board sessions in my day. It started in sixth grade and always went the same way: One girl whispers that a spirit is moving the planchette. Another pipes up that one of *us* is obviously pushing it. We all remove our hands. The thing doesn't move. We put them back. It moves. We all scream and agree it's a ghost.

Astrid's board is not a toy. It is peeling and weathered and painted with symbols and pictures: an angry owl, a rotting apple, a pentagram, a hand, an urn. A hornet. A lion with wings.

"Yes? OK?" Astrid tilts her head and jabs the board toward me in three quick motions, which I translate as, *Are you sure you want to do this?*

"*Ja,*" I nod. "Genau. I've played games like this before."

She wags her finger at me and shakes her head. "Not a game. *No* game."

Her voice is raspy and her eyes are telling me to take her

seriously. I study the board for a moment. It has letters and numerals, but they're arranged differently than a Ouija.

The word *Abschiedsgruß* is stenciled across the bottom. Under the table, I punch the letters into my translator app: *Farewell* comes up first. At the top is written *Gute Nacht*. Good night.

I wish I could ask her what she's trying to do, how this can help, what it will accomplish. Why she warned me weeks ago. But I don't, because blurted, mispronounced, disjointed words thrown at the locals have gotten me nowhere in this town, and I won't bother now.

Astrid sets out a wooden planchette and lays her fingers on it. I apply my index and middle fingers lightly across from hers.

It's deadsville in Ouija-land. I wait. She stares at the board. I sigh without meaning to in a loud, quick whoosh. And then the wood moves.

It scrapes across the board, pushing past tiny hitches in the worn surface, and I am certain I am not pushing it. I cast an eye to Astrid and her fingers are so lightly on it I can't believe it's her, either.

"They are here," she says. "Geisterwelt."

I pick *ghost* out of that, and then extrapolate to *spirit*.

"Who is here? Are you seeing Jacqueline? My friend? JAC-QUE-LINE? Or…my husband? Me?"

She shakes her head.

It stops short on the letter "C."

Astrid raises her eyes to mine. Off we go again. It lands on "M," and again Astrid gazes up at me. She lays one knotted finger to her lips. "Shhhh. Listen."

C and *M.* I remember where I've seen these letters together:

Find me. Find CM. The plea on Jacqueline's note tucked in the book's binding.

My blood is curdling. The planchette moves again, faster this time.

W

A

R

N

H

E

There is a pause. What does *warnhe* mean? I hope I'm remembering the letters in the correct sequence. The planchette moves again, faster this time.

R

G

O

It doesn't take me long. The letters spell *Warnhergo.*

Warn her.

Go.

I remove my fingers like the wood has caught fire, and I try to inwardly joke myself out of the fear: At least we know we have ourselves an American ghost. Or an English one.

Or a Hong Kong native born under British rule.

My neighbor gestures for me to lay fingers on the wood again. "We *must* finished," she says.

Against every fiber of my being, I do as she requests, but nothing happens. Astrid frowns at the board, as if to force it into action.

She makes eye contact. "You," she says. "You speak. Understand? Ask."

"Ask the spirit a question?"

She nods.

"Is someone in this room in danger?"

The planchette moves to *Ja*.

"*Who* is in danger?" My voice cracks. I really hope the spirit doesn't think I'm afraid of them.

The planchette doesn't move.

"Are we in danger? Both of us?"

It moves slowly to *Ja*.

"From whom?"

The planchette moves agonizingly slowly.

A.

Not Wesley. Not Heidi, not any of the others. *Good*. A for Astrid? I shoot her a furtive look. It's moving again.

L.

L.

E.

S.

Alles.

All. Everyone.

Watch out. Watch out watch out watch out.

Who is saying that? It's *me*. That's my voice. I'm in a trance and I say it unconsciously out loud, and I have to clap my mouth shut. Something outside of me controls my voice. *What is going on?*

Was it something in the tea? Is sleep deprivation driving me mad? Is it my unconscious banging down that iron door Mixie told me about? Astrid's expression has morphed from in-control to freaked out, her lips pursed, her chin trembling.

The planchette is moving again. It feels like a string is pulling it away from me, down, down, down the board. It points to *Guten Nacht*, and it stops dead. I feel the life leave it.

Astrid takes in a deep breath and lets it out. I don't know what to think, and I don't know how to ask. She rises and takes two long strides to a bookshelf at the back of the room.

She returns with something in her palm, then moves closer to me until we are chest to chest. She presses a silver piece of jewelry into my sweater. It hangs on a black satin necklace that spills between her fingers like squid ink pasta.

"*Der Schutz*," she says. "For you. *Der Schtuz*."

She lifts her arms and I instinctively duck my head to let her hang an amulet around my neck. I pull the piece off my chest and examine it upside-down.

"Danke schön," I say, wanting to hug her but resisting, because her body language does not ask for it. "Thank you."

She nods as if to say, *You will be OK*.

But I won't; I'm not. "What is happening?" I cry. "What did you see? What do the runes mean?"

She furrows her brow and shakes her head slowly. "Runes? *Nein*."

"You left me runes outside my door. Little wooden symbols. Ice. Secrets. What are you trying to tell me?"

She continues shaking her head, holds out her hands and gently guides me toward the stairs. I clutch the railing so I won't fall.

I turn back. "Bitte."

She pats her own chest. "Do not lose this."

I leave her house, and as I wrestle open my front door, the

raven perched on the hill *caw, caw, caws* into the air.

I turn and direct a stream of pent-up anxiety at him.

"*Shut. Up! Just shut up!*" His yellow eyes stare back at me.

I step inside and slam the door, checking the handle three times to make sure it's locked.

CHAPTER

THIRTY SEVEN

Wesley comes home late. I'm reading on the couch and absorbing none of the words or sentences or pages.

I hear rustling as he mounts the stairs, and my adrenaline is firing, because I have no idea how to be married in any healthy sense of the word.

"I'm sorry," he says, his voice startling me as it echoes in the room. I raise my eyes from my e-reader and see the world's biggest flower arrangement in his arms. "I'm unreservedly, off-the-charts, no-excuses *sorry*. In this day in age, I should know better than to leave you hanging like that."

It's *day AND age,* I want to shout back. I set my device down. He sits next to me. I take the flowers, a bouquet of one-dozen gross carnations.

"Ah, you remembered my least-favorite flower. That's one way to go," I say, half-smiling at the cockiness of it, and when he leans in for a kiss, I meet him halfway.

When we pull apart, he reaches into his pocket, grabs his wallet, opens it, and slides out two heavy silver cards.

"The first is a Visa. Pretty much no limit, but let me know in advance if you're going over twenty K in one day. The other is a debit for whenever you need cash. Same deal."

I take them both. "All I want is to feel secure and be equal with you," I say.

"I know," he replies. "I just...I didn't *get* it before. They're ready to use, but I can't get you into the accounts this very minute because they require those fob thingys to log on, and I only have one. The process of getting a second one is underway."

I smile and kiss him, and I feel a warm flush, and I think, maybe he's got my back. Maybe this move, this change, is hard on both of us, and this was all a terrible reaction to the disruption of our lives.

"Now for the pièce de résistance, your favorite: Veuve Clicquot rose." He walks back to the stairs and picks up the bottle he'd stashed there.

We talk about our day over crystal flutes of bubbly, and I avoid mentioning today's talking board session with Astrid. I'm not sure what to make of it yet, and he already doesn't like our neighbor.

I feel the weight of the amulet resting on my chest under my sweater. I examined it after I'd absorbed what had happened, tried to make sense of it. It's a pentagram inside a circle, otherwise known as a pentacle. It's a well-known symbol that television shows and social media-influencer witches have absconded with, but the meaning behind it, Astrid's intent, cannot be cancelled with sloppy cultural appropriation.

She meant to offer me protection; I feel that energy; thus, I am protected.

I finish my first glass and notice Wesley is scratching up and down his arms.

"By the way," I say. "Have you seen my passport?"

"Sorry, no. When did you see it last?" He takes a sip of champagne.

"When I packed it in Zermatt."

"Well, that's it, isn't it? Either you *thought* you packed it, or if fell out."

"I'm quite sure I put it in my backpack. It was nice and snug under a sweater."

"Keep looking. It'll turn up."

He tilts his chin at me. "What's that around your neck? What happened to the Tiffany necklace I gave you?"

I pull out the amulet. "The neighbor gave it to me. Isn't it cool?"

He examines it and then rolls up his sleeve to scratch some more.

"Now that you mention it, I swear that old witch put a hex on me," he says.

"You mean a spell. And stop calling her that old witch," I chide him. "It's dehumanizing. She's done nothing to us except clean up all our storm damage by herself."

"I'm calling her an old *witch* to be nice."

I don't like this side of him, not at all. "When have you ever even talked to her?"

"I've seen her around. She almost got you killed in that storm you mentioned. I need a Benadryl," he grumbles, heading back to our bathroom.

I watch him go, and the warm glow I felt earlier is fading.

Since moving abroad and feeling out of control, I've treated my passport like a baby. You never leave your baby behind, and you know where your baby is at all times.

That night, after Wesley falls asleep, I curl up on the sofa, moonlight streaming in, and travel down the rabbit hole of witch-related social media.

Witches are trending right now, and there's too much information to sift through in one night. So far, nothing I'm reading fits authentically with what I experienced with Astrid.

I don't believe for a second there was a spirit speaking to us today. Talking boards are fun because if we're playing honestly, we often *don't* know we're moving the planchette ourselves. I looked it up in seventh grade. It's called the ideomotor effect, in which our unconscious mind directs our muscle movements so our body is moving it, but our conscious mind doesn't know why.

Our unconscious sees things and knows things our conscious doesn't. Mine sees things in Peter Pewter-Browne that I can't articulate. It probably sees things in Wesley, too, those unknowable, hidden parts that make up a person, the things a background check like Violet's could never find.

Whether it is the spirit of this unknown CM warning me, or my own brain, it's time I figured out why.

I call Violet, and in a miraculous turn of events, she answers. I update her on everything from Helena to the book to the runes and the talking board, and I can hear the gears turning from across the Atlantic: *How can I spin this so it makes a great podcast?*

She's chewing something. "I think it's time we got you some help."

I snort at that suggestion. "I don't even know if they have psychologists in Switzerland. I don't have a gynecologist yet. I don't have a *dentist*."

I hear Vi swallow, then clean her teeth with her tongue. "I mean academic assistance," she says through a sucking sound. "You need an expert. I know someone. They're a witch or a Wiccan. Or both, I never know the difference. Is there one?"

"You want me to talk to your witch friend, why?"

"I know you, Rose. Your radar is jammed. You don't know who to trust and you're reading things into these symbols. I think my friend can help. Send me pics of your neighbor's plates and the runes and I'll set something up." She takes a breath. "Just one thing. They are wicked smaht. Have your questions ready."

"They?"

"They're nonbinary. They know their stuff and they don't have time for drama. Do your homework before you meet them. Wait for my call."

Heidi calls the next day and informs me I *will* be going on a hike with the girls.

"I'm not going to pretend the exercise is the selling point," she says. "After we walk, we're going for raclette at the coziest restaurant you've ever been to. It's nestled in the valley and it's *heaven*."

I attend the hike-slash-cheese outing as ordered, and I'm glad I came. The hike is drenched in dramatic scenery, like we landed in a Scandinavian TV mystery, an endless snowy landscape with gorges and dips and gigantic boulders and peaks as far as the eye can see. When we make it to a stunning rock formation, one that *almost* makes for an arch, but doesn't quite meet in the middle, I stop.

"I've got to get a shot of this," I say, staring up at the imposing natural formation. The other women wait as I snap a picture, and as we trudge on, I open Instagram to find a good filter, and I notice something odd. "Huh."

Seychelle is walking next to me and peeks over my shoulder. "What?"

"Jacqueline hasn't posted since we were in London," I say. Her account is unlocked again. "There were like five or six photos right after she left, and then…nothing. I hope she's OK."

Nova rolls her eyes. "Forget about her. I'm sure she doesn't want any of her Swiss pals seeing her glamorous new life and whatever new man she's ensnared. She won't want anything getting back to Peter before they can reach a settlement. That woman is like catnip to men. She *loves* the attention."

Heidi is bouncing on her toes to keep warm. "Shall we head back down? I'm starved."

I stop cold.

"Nova," I ask, "are you saying Jacqueline has been in touch with Peter about a divorce?"

CHAPTER

THIRTY EIGHT

Jacqueline and Peter engaged in a messy divorce would be the *best* news. It would give me permission to exhale, to focus on my own life, to figure out how to navigate my new marriage and focus on the man I vowed to spend my life with.

Jacqueline, who I met in the flesh only a few times, is barely real to me at this point. She is an idea. A concept. Jacqueline is a possible victim, a woman in peril, but also a kettlebell strapped to my neck, pulling me down, down, down, away from myself.

Heidi clears her throat meaningfully, as if I won't notice. Nova says, "Well—I mean, maybe. I think so. I assume so. That's between them, and of course I'd never ask him about something so personal."

My hands are in my jeans pockets now, under my ski pants, not feeling my car keys. *Fuck.* They're gone. I give myself a final pat-down, but I know the truth: my keys are lost on this mountain under ice and snow.

"Oh my god. Oh my god, *oh my god.* What have I done?" I whip off my coat and shake it, hoping keys fall out in some kind of winter miracle. "This *can't* be happening."

The women squint at me in confusion. "What is it?" Heidi asks.

"I…you're going to hate me. I…I think I've lost the car keys." I put my coat back on. "I'm…" My throat constricts. "I'm so sorry. I've screwed us. They're *gone*. They're not here."

"We haven't hiked that far, believe it or not." Seychelle shrugs. "They won't be that hard to find."

"Hey…it's ok." Heidi stuffs her hands deep in her coat pockets and strolls down the mountain. "Let's move until we get cell service. Everyone keep looking and kicking the snow."

I'm recalling the long, winding, desolate drive to get to the parking lot for this little hike. "How can you all be so calm? There's no one around, and even when we make it to the car, it's miles to the main road."

Everyone is moseying along, searching as they go. Ten more minutes of purposeful walking and Heidi gets cell reception. She makes a call and chatters in rapid German.

"Ja. Genau, genau. Danke schön." Heidi concludes the call, slips her phone in her pocket, and blows on her exposed hands, scarlet with the cold. "They'll meet us at the lot within the hour."

I don't say it, but if she's just called the Swiss version of AAA, I don't know how that can help. Can they start a car without keys? Can they resurrect my entire key ring, including the keys to the house, Wesley's office and the garage?

The women are no more than slightly put out. They chat and pace, warm their hands, talk about what we're eating for lunch. I'm staring at the ground, kicking snow, getting on my hands and knees to feel around.

We make it to the car in fifteen more minutes, just in time to greet a police van and a car rolling up with lights on, sound off.

"The police!" What a coincidence. "Do you think they'd jimmy the car open?"

And then what? Hotwire it?

Three uniformed officers pour out of the vehicles. Heidi waves, strolls over to them, and begins speaking in German.

The two cops from the van open the back doors. Out jump two gigantic, barking German Shepherds. The scene is surreal. They walk toward me.

"What is going on?" I ask the others.

"Do as they say," Seychelle advises.

I flinch, but stand my ground.

"Bitte. Stand still. No sudden moves," a uniformed officer orders.

I do as instructed, and the beasts sniff me like I'm their next meal, and I am certain they can smell my fear, and I remember how much I love dogs. *Cute doggie. Nice doggie. Good girl.*

The handler finally calls them off. One officer heads up the trail with a metal detector, and the other two take the straining dogs as they bark and dart about in a frenzy.

Ten minutes later, the entire pack comes walking back down the mountain. An officer is dangling my car keys in the air. The man doesn't so much as break his stride as he hands them to me, then paces back to his car. Another officer turns back and says curtly, "Please be more careful in the future."

And they are gone, key-finding superheroes off to their next key-related mission.

"Did that really just happen?" My mouth hangs open as I watch them go. I turn to my friends.

"This is the Alpine equivalent of the cat up a tree," Heidi shrugs. "They have units for this kind of thing. In the Alps, it's a part of life. If they can send in the troops, they will. With so few murders and kidnappings around here, they're often available."

"Well," Seychelle says brightly. "Shall we go get pissed? I need a bottle of wine immediately, if not sooner."

I drive us to the restaurant in Meggen, a storybook town across the lake from Lucerne. Heidi orders raclette for the table. Thick squares of cheese as big as playing cards come fanned out on a platter next to a cast-iron contraption with six mini-pans in six slots. Each holds a slab of melting cheese.

I watch as Heidi selects two boiled potatoes, two pearl onions and a gherkin from another platter, drapes the square of melted raclette over them, and digs in with a knife and fork. I follow suit, stifling so many questions.

That's it—that's the meal. Cheese sheets on pickles. It's pungent, one of the stinkier cheeses I've had here, and it's delicious.

Seychelle picks up the bottle of Chablis and tops us all up.

"How's your neighbor, by the way? Any more runes? Maybe some eye of newt?"

"Ha. Nothing to report," I lie.

I look past her at the lake, so quiet this time of year save for whitecaps as the surface kicks up with the snow now coming down.

"Well. You'll *really* get to see the Swiss in their natural habitat next week," Seychelle replies.

"Oh, yes," Nova says. "TIG employees get the afternoon off. Everyone dresses up. It's a gas."

"What are you wearing?" I ask them all.

"It's a surprise," Heidi says.

"What should *I* wear?" I ask.

"That's the beauty of Fasnacht. Go wild. Be as much yourself as you've ever been. More," Heidi replies.

Myself. Who is myself? She's touched on a bigger question than I can answer with a simple costume.

"I'm still nervous about going," I say, half-joking, to see what they do.

"About what?" Heidi narrows her eyes. She knows exactly what I mean.

"You all told us at the gala how wild and scary it is. How we need to watch out. And then there were those expats who disappeared…" I sip my wine.

"Oh, stop it. We were kidding around. That other stuff…that's all just coincidence," Seychelle glugs some wine.

"It's still weird, you have to admit." I'm not going to pretend with them anymore. Not as much as I have been, anyway. "There was Lars and Lara, Fitz, and that other one…what's her name…I feel like Seychelle told me a while ago and I forgot?"

"Kiki?" Nova pipes up.

Kiki. Cici, with a C? Could this be CM?

"None of this matters," Heidi says. "She was another expat stopping by here on a journey to discover where she belongs. It wasn't Lucerne. There's no big mystery."

She slides another square of cheese onto her plate.

"Forget all that. Fasnacht is a *blast*," Nova assures me. "If anything, it bonds us expats even tighter. You're not allowed to miss it."

CHAPTER

THIRTY NINE

I stuck to one glass of wine at lunch so I'd be alert for the meeting Violet set up for me. I make it to my office with ten minutes to spare and wait as the laptop flickers to life.

Right on time, three faces are splashed across the screen.

Vi kicks things off. "Rose Stone, meet Professor Flor Diaz. Flor is a doctor of theology and religious studies on the faculty here at Columbia."

Flor, their mass of flaming red hair pulled up into a heavy topknot, leans in. "First things first: I'm a witch, but I'm also a Christian. All Wiccans are witches, but not all witches are Wiccan. I'm not a TikTok witch. I don't sell spells or create bullshit fortune-cookie formulas for making a boy like you. We clear?"

"Crystal," I reply.

"Good." Flor's face relaxes and they smile in the warm way Grandma Mixie used to, with the corners of her eyes crinkling. "Now. Let's see if we can't make some sense of what's happening to you."

I try to form a simple question in my mind, but there is too much information vying for attention, so I serve it up as it comes to me.

"I'm freaked out that my new friends burned effigies of my husband and me and danced around yelling BURN, BURN, BURN," I blurt, hearing my own voice rise as I recall the unease of that day. "Are these people witches, or Satanists, or something else? It feels like there's some occult undertone or symbolism to so much of what's happening…it's like the answer is staring me in the face but I'm not seeing it."

Flor nods as if this is a totally regular problem to have.

"Violet filled me in on everything. First of all, that event doesn't sound like a magical space to connect with the divine," they say. "More like a pagan version of a church picnic with bits of folklore thrown in like amusement-park characters."

I exhale with a long breath I didn't know I was holding.

"There *is* a belief in many cultures that you can put a curse on someone by burning in effigy, with the aim to maim or kill a target," Flor continues. "But since you're still alive, that seems unlikely.

"Off the top of my head, there's also an ancient Czech ritual of burning witches in effigy. They believed the power of witches would diminish in the warmth. So, if we wanted to take the bonfire literally, it would follow that they think *you're* the witch. As that is, once again, unlikely, you're probably dealing with a clumsy attempt to mimic local folklore. It's hard to say without knowing the people or their true intentions."

"So you don't think they mean us harm?" I stop myself from biting my thumbnail. "It's just…when I told my friends about the runes that showed up on my doorstep, they immediately thought it was connected to witchcraft. Switzerland has a shameful history with witches, just as America does, as I'm sure you know, and my friends seemed nervous talking about them. Like they thought someone was trying to get to me somehow."

"I can't say if your new friends are out to get you or not," Flor replies. "But if they are, and that's a big *if,* they're not doing it with spells or summoning spirits or demons. All the different kinds of pagan practices are very personal. One practitioner might favor runes and *not* be a witch, one might be a witch and never touch a rune. Your friends are off base to jump to witchcraft."

I take that in, and decide that while it makes sense, it doesn't explain everything.

"Unless they know something I don't."

Flor blinks, then nods. "True. Based on what you and Violet have told me, though, if there *is* malice afoot, they're using imagery from local folklore to scare you. That's not witchcraft. There's another name for people who do that."

I have my pen ready. "Oh?"

"Assholes," Flor deadpans.

Vi snickers.

"Look," Flor says, "I can see why you're concerned. When Vi came to me about your experiences I was intrigued. I stayed up half the night reading about Swiss folklore. They have one of the richest histories in the world because of the variety of cultures, the Germanic influence...you've got the French, German, Romansh...the point of folklore in any culture is to keep a shared history alive. It's an oral record of sorts that can bring people together across generations."

"It's certainly been an education," I say wryly, recalling the Christmas Eve child snatcher.

"I'm sure it has," Flor says. "And you've got Fasnacht coming up. How lucky you are to be able to experience something so vivid!"

If they only knew.

"Anyway," they say, "if a bunch of privileged expatriates—no offense—try to appropriate that culture, there's every chance it won't ring true. Their displays will be off in little ways that, to the Swiss, would render them unrecognizable."

And there it is. Those are the words and the educated perspective I needed to gel my disparate thoughts. I get it now: My new friends are cosplaying Swiss people and Swiss traditions, and whether or not someone or something harmed Jacqueline and has now targeted me, the danger will not come from a chanting circle in a wood with screaming children and hot cider. It's something else. Something smaller yet more damaging, perhaps.

"Thank you so much, professor," I say. "You have no idea how much this has helped."

Flor's expertise and perspective has calmed me. Standard, earthly aggression I can handle; it's the untouchable, amorphous, invisible mess of belief systems and good versus evil I find tough to battle.

I ask, "Did Violet show you the photos of my neighbor's plates on the hill?"

Flor nods. "Oh, yes. I studied them closely. Unlike your friends, I'd say your neighbor very well might be a witch."

I keep my game face on, though I'm surprised by this take. I'd all but decided my neighbor was simply eccentric.

"The symbols on the plates are all signs of wisdom, enlightenment, justice, protection, and luck," Flor says. "It's all connected to the earth. What is it about your neighbor that makes you uneasy?"

I tread carefully. "It was the talking board, for one thing. I felt like I was in a trance for at least part of it. She seemed to believe we were communicating with a spirit."

Flor checks their watch, then tells me, "A spirit board, or Ouija board, whatever you want to call it, can be part of a witch's practice and have nothing to do with summoning spirits. Many are drawn to it because there *are* no structures or parameters. No restrictions or prejudices. There is a lot of knowledge we can pull from within ourselves using these boards."

They wait for me to nod my understanding before going on.

"Was there any chanting? Any emblems or offerings?"

I shake my head.

"And the session gave you some insight?"

"It did," I admit. "That's why I'm confused. How could I tell if she *was* trying to hurt my husband and me? If she was using some sort of spell against us?"

Flor appears confused. "I'm still unclear as to what would make you think she's trying to harm you."

Nothing. "My husband thinks we should be wary of her."

"But you don't?"

"I don't know."

"It sounds like your husband's heard too many fairytales promoting the ugly old witch trope," Flor says.

I have a strange need to defend Wesley. "She doesn't seem malicious, but some things *are* a little off-putting," I reply. "My husband's sudden rash. The bizarre behavior in a storm. And the symbols everywhere around the house are not…usual."

"That can all be explained away," Flor replies crisply. "You're in a new country. You're skating on *their* rink. It's their culture, their ice. People in other parts of the world aren't going to act the way Americans are used to. The cultural norms that might seem like witchcraft to you might be entirely usual in Lucerne. Maybe your husband is allergic to Swiss soap."

I know she's right, but her bluntness stings.

"It's been a huge adjustment for both of us," I say. "Maybe we're not doing it so well. Still, I can't dismiss the runes, and to think of her creeping outside my house in the middle of the night…"

Flor crosses their arms and tilts their head.

"*Now* we're getting somewhere. I highly doubt she left those runes. She seems happy to deal with you directly. More to the point, I'd expect her to leave protective and uplifting symbols—the Norse rune *algiz*, or witch's foot, for example. The ones you've received are negative. They're bald-faced warnings."

I reach down into my collar and pull out the heavy silver amulet. "She gave me this after the talking board session."

Flor squints at it and leans in so I can see up their nostrils. I hold the piece up to my camera and they examine it.

"Whether your neighbor is Wiccan or pagan or Christian or agnostic, I assure you she means you no harm," Flor says. "Quite the opposite. She's clearly worried someone *else* is going to harm you. I would look for more signs of protection from her, frankly. The runes…well. I'd proceed as if those are another thing entirely. Someone else entirely."

They shake their head slowly. I can tell they believe me. "Which means," Flor adds, "that you're approaching the question backwards. Ask not what her magic is or what it means. Ask what her magic is in response to."

I pause for a beat. Even in my tired state I know what she's getting at.

"She's seen something I haven't. She knows something I don't."

"BINGO. I think it's safe to say she thinks you're in danger," Flor says in a hushed tone that makes my blood run cold.

I rub my eyes and try to think. I look up to see Vi getting antsy, and on cue my friend opens her mouth to say goodbye, so I jump in.

"There's a bird following me."

Vi blinks and frowns at me. Flor is still listening.

"Ravens, crows, blackbirds, whatever you want to call them. They're always around," I go on. "But when I notice them— really *listen*—I'm sure I hear one particular bird. I know it sounds preposterous, but I swear he knows me. I feel like a gothic fiction cliché or over-the-top sitcom character even talking about it, but it doesn't help that a group of them is called a *murder* of crows. I mean, if they were called a...a...*bouquet* of crows, no one would be afraid of them, right?"

I'm babbling, but Flor is generous, and kind, and speaks to me as they gather up papers as if they're late for something.

"Ravens are talking birds. They're clever," Flor says. "The recurring cultural references you speak of are a nod to the very validity of such symbolism. There absolutely could be a bird following you—and that's a good thing."

Flor stands, binder in hand. "Contrary to what many people think, ravens are symbols of protection. Sometimes they're spirits crossing between worlds. That bird could be there to watch out for you, Rose. Be grateful. Thank the bird. If you get close enough to connect with it, it might speak to you."

I am triggered.

The bird is Jacqueline.

The bird is my dad.

The bird is Grandma Mixie.

I'm not imagining it. I blink back tears. I'm so, so tired.

"Then again," Flor says, "sometimes a bird is just a bird."

CHAPTER

FORTY

When Wesley and I are reading in bed later that night, I ask him, "What are we doing for Fasnacht? Heidi says it's a huge deal for your company."

He doesn't look up from his tablet. "That carnival thing? I guess we get the afternoon off or something. Drinks in town and all that."

"But what do we *wear*? It's not like we have old troll costumes hanging around."

His eyes flit away from his screen.

"Wear? I have no idea. Pete mumbled something about getting ready at work beforehand. I'll do whatever the guys do. I'm sure they'll sort me out."

I search the internet for the best carnival costume shops and find a funky one up in the hills toward Liechtenstein, then peruse some Fasnacht pictures and videos. It looks like anything goes—*anything*.

I read about its history. It's a tradition from the 15th century that has its roots in religion. Fasnacht is a symbolic letting down of the hair before Lent, and the Swiss go wild and use the carnival as a time for expressing joy and happiness.

I'm forced awake in the middle of the night by noises that penetrate our walls and the static of the white noise machine.

Slamming. Heavy footsteps. I'm not going out alone this time.

"Wesley. Wesley!" I rock him by the shoulder.

"Wha—what? What's happening?"

He sits up and rubs his eyes.

"There's someone in the house!" I whisper.

"*What?*" He swings his legs out of the bed and grabs the golf club he keeps in the corner.

We tiptoe across the warm tiles in our bare feet, Wesley wielding the club like a sword, open the door as quietly as we can, and peek out. The house is silent. Outside, there is no wind.

"Wait here," he whispers when we get to the end of the hallway at the mouth of the living room.

He clears the house room by room, like on a cop show. I have my finger poised to dial 911 before I remember it's all different here. I remember a 103, I think, and maybe a 112? They have at least five emergency numbers.

I step into the living room, then pad to the kitchen and find nothing out of place. I hear Wesley open and shut the laundry room door, then the storage room door, then I hear him rattle the locked front-door handle.

I check around the kitchen and living room. What was the *bang*? Was something taken? The TV is here, my laptop, Wesley's tablet.

My laptop. I double back and take a good look at it on the dining-room table.

There's a white piece of paper sticking out of the closed cover like a thin, dry tongue. I hear Wesley ascending the stairs.

"Everything's in order," he says. "I can't see any sign someone broke in. Are you *sure* you heard something? You must have been having a nightmare."

I pull the paper out. Even before I unfold it, I can tell it was written on paper ripped from my reporter's notebook, which I keep in a drawer in my office.

Two words are written in thick block letters with a Sharpie from that same drawer:

GET OUT.

I turn to see Wesley at the top of the stairs.

"Look at this." My hand shakes as I show him the paper.

He tucks the golf club under his armpit and takes the note, frowning as he processes it.

"Someone stuck it in my laptop. It doesn't look like anything was taken, but someone wanted me to see this. This was left for *me.*"

I can see the wheels moving behind his eyes as he tries to make sense of it.

"I've had it with all of this, Wesley. I'm calling the police."

"*No,*" he barks. "Please." He swiftly softens his tone. "We can't. They told me at TIG orientation *never* to call the police unless you're in the middle of a life-threatening emergency. It's not like back home. We're immigrants now, Rose."

"I think a home invasion qualifies as an emergency! There's no way I can go back to sleep. I feel unsafe."

He takes me by the shoulders. "I'll talk to the legal department tomorrow. We'll get some help. I promise. If someone wanted to hurt us, they would have. This is nothing but a prank. I think we both know who it was—that nosy neighbor again."

"She doesn't break into houses," I say. "But you know who doesn't have to break in? Anyone who works for TIG. They own this house, and we have no idea how many other people have keys."

"I'll take care of it," he says. "Trust me."

I wake up on the first day of Fasnacht and decide to throw myself into this local tradition. I drive Wesley to work, and as I pull onto the road along the lake, I ask him the question neither of us has broached since the home invasion two days before.

"Is TIG going to do anything about someone breaking into our house?"

He closes his eyes for a long moment as if to say, *I was hoping to avoid this.*

"Do you trust me, Rose?" he asks. "Do you believe I'd never let anything happen to you?"

"Let's say I do," I reply. "You're not always around, though. What about when I'm home alone?"

"OK." He can't look me in the eye. "I talked to my boss—"

"Brett."

"I talked to Brett and TIG's in-house counsel and…well, don't shoot the messenger. Please? But they…"

Oh, I see. I get it without him having to say another word. "They didn't believe me. They said I made the note up, planted it myself, imagined the noises? That's unacceptable, Wesley. What have we gotten ourselves into?"

He sighs, flits his eyes up at me then back out toward the lake.

"I never heard anything…I didn't wake up until you poked me," he says. "The note is on your paper, with your pen. Maybe you did it in your sleep?"

"Have I sleepwalked since you've known me?" I grip the wheel so hard I feel the seam of the pleather wrap imprinting on my palms.

"I don't know," he shrugs. "I haven't known you that long."

"Ouch."

"Rosie." He turns to me as I pull into his parking space. "I love you. You know that. But I'm asking you not to make a big deal of this. I can't afford to draw attention to myself at work while I'm still trying to impress everyone."

I say nothing.

"We'll put cans in front of the door downstairs to make some noise, and we'll add an extra layer of security on the balcony doors, OK? I'll keep a knife and a whole set of clubs in our room. We'll lock our bedroom door at night."

I shrug, and he kisses me goodbye.

"Good," he says, hopping out of the car. "We've got a big social event coming up. I want us all to be one big happy family at our first Fasnacht."

"Have a good day, dear." I say it without feeling. He doesn't appear to notice.

I drive away fast, make it out of town, and drive up, up, up toward Liechtenstein, and it occurs to me it would be the perfect time to visit this tiny country, but I don't have a passport.

I find the store, and a smoking shopkeeper shows me a hanging mess that appears to be part bodysuit, part chainmail, part superhero costume with a cape, plus a Venice-style mask. For fifteen francs I look like a medieval serial killer who's the child of a goblin and a werewolf. I pay the man and race out of the store to get ready for the big night.

CHAPTER

FORTY ONE

I park in Wesley's spot at TIG and hop out, don my feather/crown headpiece and my mask, and set off to find the gang at Mr. Pickwick.

I feel utterly self-conscious in my costume as I cruise through the edges of town on foot. I'm making good time until I pass the Bahnhof and hit a roadblock before the bridge to Old Town.

The sidewalk is lined with ogres, snakes, cat-headed serpents, trolls, witches and lurid, giant-headed creatures from your worst nightmares. Suddenly my costume isn't so weird.

There's a distant hum, a vibration felt in the soles of my feet. It's starting.

I don't know when I'll be able to cross the bridge, but I have no choice but to wait.

In another minute the drumbeats, horns, trumpets and flutes flood the air so no other sound exists. The first line of the parade brings the weight of a thousand drums down on the crowd. It is the sheer size—of the sound and the monstrous, costumed frontline beating their bass drums—that rocks me.

It is an invasion. My entire body vibrates with the music; I'm spackled with goosebumps and overcome with a mix of excitement and fear.

Their steps are fast and sure, far from the relaxed lope, grins and waves at an Independence Day parade. The instruments rattle my ears and boom through the town, heralding in something you can't fight. It can only be signaling doom. The vibration feels like the end of the world, the size of the army like a takeover no mortal can stop. It's like nothing I've ever seen.

Before long, the parade and the crowd begin to blend, filling the streets and spilling into alleys like water rushing into a maze. I think of what I could tell Vi about it, but this scene, this chaotic temporary societal breakdown, is indescribable.

Now I know what they meant at the gala. This is a life-changing experience. You can't fake this, or recreate it. By the time you understand that, you have no exit. You're part of it.

Figures in owl heads big as full-sized garbage cans banging a bass drum. Bloodied shark heads the size of a dorm-room fridge. Huge heads of mustachioed men made of industrial-grade *papier-mâché*, misshapen, vacant-eyed, looming over the crowd. Revelers in sinister old-fashioned dive masks or gas masks, monstrous, unidentifiable, anonymous, unleashed.

A fringe group of figures, shorter, robed and disguised, breaks away. They appear to be homing in on me. Their yellow eyes under their black hoods are focused on me.

Or am I being profoundly paranoid? No one else seems to notice them. No one notices, me, alone, swallowed up, anonymous. There are three. They are dressed like Druids, and resemble oversized Jawas from *Star Wars*.

They remind me of the *Schmutzli,* but slightly different. Not the same kind of creature that touched me on Christmas Eve.

Now I understand. Now I see how a person goes missing during Fasnacht, how they can disappear. There is no amount of planning, care, keen awareness, strength, weaponry or smartphone panic button that can save you when someone wants to pull you out of the melee.

Any writhing or screaming will be lost in the noise. It will be seen as part of the show.

The earth-shaking part of the parade passes, and a quieter crowd, sans instruments, follows it, and I manage to dart in front of them to get to the bridge. On the other side, it's just as chaotic. A figure is one of the only still ones, and I feel their eyes on me.

It's hard to know in this place who's watching *me* and who's simply passing the time watching everything that moves. But here, I know. He is watching me. Or am I in a sleep-deprived fever dream?

No one is following you.

In this throng of thousands, no one is singling out Rose Stone Blackwood. I am not someone's obsession or target. I'm permanently jetlagged. I'm imagining things.

I need an anchor. My husband, our friends, even the sketchy ones. I crave familiar faces, albeit ones who will be dressed like monsters. I make it to Pickwick's and blow through the door. I see them right away, even through the wall of bodies packing the pub, and their appearance shocks me more than any of the monsters have.

My friends all look like fashion models.

They're in our usual back booth with an extra table shoved up to it to make room for the guys.

I see them before they see me. Seychelle in a minidress, Heidi in an LBD with a hint of cleavage on display, Nova in sky-high heels. The men in fashionable going-to-the-fancy-club outfits. Wesley in a crisp, fitted periwinkle top that takes my breath away.

And makes me furious.

Heidi instantly knows it's me even in my carnival garb. "Rose! Over here."

"Oh. My. God." Seychelle catches sight of me and lets out a shocked laugh. "What did you *do?*"

Nova is snickering behind her hand.

Wesley is bent over with laughter. "What the…what are you supposed to *be?*" He shouts it, because it's bedlam.

He holds out his arms as if to behold me, then leans in for a forehead kiss, because my weird mask is in the way of my mouth.

I turn to Heidi. "You said to go wild! You told me about the scary and weird costumes. Why didn't you *tell* me none of you were dressing up?"

"What?" She cups her ear.

I repeat myself, louder this time, with feeling.

"Like *this*," she says through laughter, pointing two thumbs at her breasts. "Go wild and look *hot.*"

Brett, smirking like his wife, checks me out. "The fun of Fasnacht is sitting back and watching these dorks act like freaks for one night while we have a sublime boozing session and pick them apart like frogs in a high school biology class," he says.

"We never said *costume*," Nova laughs.

Are they fucking with me? Is there another plausible explanation? Or am I too tired to comprehend basic language these days, and made a knee-jerk decision about a costume based on my assumptions after researching the carnival?

"Aw," Wesley says, noticing my expression, an amalgam of hatred and humiliation.

It was him. It occurs to me Wesley was the one who knew I was talking about a troll costume ripped out of the pages of Grimm's fairytales, and Wesley who let me believe he and his TIG colleagues were doing that, too.

He lays a gentle arm around my chainmail-clad shoulder. "Let's get you some drinks. You're already behind—you'll feel better once you catch up to us. Brett! Drinks over here for my girl."

Nope. When I was waiting in the crowd by the bridge, I made the decision to keep my wits about me tonight. I'll hold a drink, I'll nurse it for hours, but I'm staying sober.

I listen to their running commentary on the crowds and the costumes, and no one expects much from me, so I get to stay quiet.

When it's time to move on, I welcome the fresh air. The crowds continue to be both a shield and a hazard. I'm tensed, alert, always making sure my feet are anchored to the ground.

If someone wants to take me, they're going to have their work cut out for them.

The next morning, Wesley doesn't stir when I rise at nine, and after coffee and eggs on toast, I text the number Teresa put in my phone in the Zurich nightclub, asking her to meet up.

She responds within minutes.

Have you visited the Löwendenkmal yet?

I don't know what that is, but I text back, *I keep meaning to...*
I have a few minutes free before work on Monday. Meet me there
at seven.

The streets around the monument and its gardens are deserted.
Even the touristy Old Town is quiet at this hour, and every
clomp of my boot echoes sharply as I traverse the stones.

I am surprised to find the Löwendenkmal, or the Lion of
Lucerne in English—a famous tourist attraction—so far off the
beaten path and so quiet and empty. Apparently it is low season
for the wounded lion.

The Löwendenkmal is carved deep into a towering stone wall. I
stare at it, rooted in place; I can't look away. The soapstone relief of
a fallen beast in agony brings out emotions in me I didn't expect.

"You and Mark Twain."

I flinch as I hear a voice next to me. I whirl and see Teresa
with a headband holding back her lilac hair, leg warmers over
yoga pants, and a thin jacket.

"Sorry?" I clear my throat. I wipe away a tear with my coat
sleeve.

"Twain called our lion 'The most mournful and moving piece
of stone in the world,'" Teresa says. "It's as if the artist captured
the cries of the Swiss Guards killed during the French Revolution
and packed them into one square of rock in one little park. It's a
time capsule of pain."

I stuff my hands into my parka pocket, wishing I'd brought a
hat. It's suddenly snowing, with flakes meandering through the
sky, in no hurry to make it to the ground. We start walking
around the pond.

"I'm surprised it took you this long to contact me," Teresa says.

"What did you mean that night at the gala?" I blurt. "When you said they'd never let me out."

"What do you think I meant?" She asks.

"I haven't a clue." Oversized flakes are tickling my nose. "I assumed you were being hyperbolic and probably metaphorical. But I do believe you were trying to tell me something."

"Well…maybe not totally metaphorical," she replies. "I wanted you to know you have another friend here. That everything isn't always as it seems. You'll see. The more time you spend with the TWAGS, the more you'll get it. I saw them working you that night, and anyone would've been drawn in by their charms, but I had a feeling you were different."

Different from what?

"Sometimes I feel like I'm lost here," I say. "And I don't know who the big bad wolf is."

Teresa stops at a bench, brushes off the newly fallen snow, and takes a seat. I plop down next to her.

"Let me tell you a few things about your new friends," she says. "They're not as put-together as you think. Every one of them has been searching for stability their entire lives. They're damaged in ways that might surprise you."

"Oh? They've never mentioned anything to me…"

"There's nothing in their past that you or I would clutch our pearls over," Teresa says. "Take Heidi. She grew up poor—I'm talking rural, dirt poor—and while no one here would judge her for it, it bothers her. She doesn't like people to know she had to pee in an outhouse for half her childhood."

As the daughter of a seasonal worker and an emotionally absent mother, I can relate. It's too easy to carry your parents' childhood mistakes and misfortunes into your adult life.

"Nova's a stay-at-home alcoholic who lives in abject terror people will find out about her past as a high-class escort. Which, OK, no big deal," Teresa goes on. I'm uneasy because I'm not sure I have the right to hear their secrets. "But she was arrested for it at a fancy London hotel and she has a record. She can't have people knowing Sweden's surfing darling shagged men for money. Selling your body for sex is legal in Sweden, but that doesn't mean it's not frowned upon in some corners of society.

"And Seychelle…well, you know her story. She has this amazing, cool life, but no one back home will let her forget she's illegitimate, and that bugs her more than she'd ever let on."

"That attitude is so gross," I say. "Not to mention outdated."

"Of course it is," Teresa says. Her nose is bright red now, and her lips are turning blue. "You've just described the royals. Legitimacy is everything to them, and we've seen how welcoming they are to mixed-race people joining the family."

"And Kristoff?"

"What about him?" Her pitch rises.

"He's royalty, too, right?" I Googled the couple, and reading between the lines of the society magazines, it seems theirs was some sort of arranged marriage to keep royal blood in the family.

"Kristoff is like a fourth cousin of a prince or something," Teresa shrugs, clearly unimpressed. "He's a nice enough guy, but he isn't a one-woman man and everyone knows it. Hell, Seychelle knows. Heidi and Raj are the only ones whose marriage seems to be on solid footing."

"What about Jacqueline and Peter?" I reach up and shake some snow out of my hair.

"Ah, the beautiful Jacqueline. She grew up wealthy in Hong Kong, and by all appearances she had—has—a charmed life. When she met Peter on a business trip to Switzerland, it was love at first sight. But then…then she found out what Peter is really like. How he, shall we say, views monogamy as more of a suggestion than a promise. We all knew they hit a rocky patch recently, but I think a lot of us thought they'd go the distance, maybe come to an understanding. I guess you never really know what goes on in someone else's relationship."

Teresa throws her hands up. "Do you see? These women are all wounded souls. This life is utopia for many who come to Switzerland, and especially for those who are lucky enough to work for TIG. If they think their idyllic life is under threat, they'll react accordingly."

I'm afraid to ask what she means by "react accordingly."

"How do you know all this?" I ask instead.

"I oversee the employee background checks for The Group," Teresa says. "It's my job to know everything about everyone we hire, *and* their families. We find that people with more challenging backgrounds tend to stay put. They know a good life when they find it. And, well…they're discreet. Discretion is an absolute requirement and they have that in spades."

I'm rocked by the revelation she's more than the "glorified secretary" label Heidi slapped on her. This also means Teresa knows my life, too. *My* wounds. *My* damage.

I find it odd the way she's painted the TWAGS as harmless, yet still doesn't seem to respect them or believe I should get close to them. I decide to ask the big question, consequences be damned. She knows everything about all of us, anyway, so it shouldn't matter.

"Have you heard from Jacqueline? I know they say she's gone back home, but…I guess, well, where I'm from, you don't wake up one day and find your friend gone, write her off, and then never search for her."

"Look," she says, twisting on her seat to face me head on. "Peter's a typical upper-class English bloke. I'm not going to pretend he's not a douchebag sometimes. But he's no murderer. Trust me, Rose, Jacqueline took off. You *really* don't have to worry about her."

There's that phrase again: *Trust me.*

"I know this is a lot to take in," she says. "But once you live here for a full cycle you'll see what everyone's talking about. You'll instinctively understand the natural order of things. The leaving. The cleaving. The goodbyes. Or no goodbyes at all, and those… *whew*…those can be hardest of all."

She lowers her voice. "Can I be honest? I'm more concerned about you."

She removes a glove, reaches into her fanny pack, and pulls out an orange pill-bottle with the label scraped off and puts it in my hand.

"Benzos. They're not for long-term use, but they'll break the cycle. Sleep a few nights straight through and it's all gravy after that. Take two around dinnertime and I *promise* you you'll sleep like a baby from here on out."

I take the bottle. I know better than to ask her how she knows about my ongoing jetlag.

She hops off the bench. "I've gotta get to work. This has been fun. You should come running with me one morning. Those endorphins *really* kick in when you're out in the elements!"

Just like every other time we've met, Teresa makes an abrupt, show-stopping exit.

CHAPTER

FORTY TWO

More sounds, more noises in the night. I am beginning to make friends with the ruckus. I rise each time I hear it every few nights now, and have a listen, but as always, whatever is causing it is gone before I get there.

A few days after I meet Teresa, I find the noise has left me something.

Another note, on a COOP receipt this time, the only scrap of paper available in the house since I started locking my office door from the outside:

YOU'RE NEXT

I am alone in the silence, no moonlight penetrating the thick clouds, and this is, of course, jarring and frightening to read. But the fear fades, because I am growing impervious to these odd happenings now; my reality has begun to blend with my sleep, with my imagination, with my nightmares.

It's too late to call Violet for a hit of reality. I know what she'd say, anyway: *This damn fool is trying to scare you with bad horror movie titles. I say leave THEM a note: FUCK OFF.*

I'm beginning to think Wesley could be right: I'm dreaming it all, or the jetlag is making me hallucinate, or I'm sleepwalking. I pad back to the bedroom, lock us inside, and snooze for four good, uninterrupted hours.

When I jolt awake the next night, I lay with the comforter up to my chin because I've heard something very different to the usual thumping and bumping.

I check the clock, and am thrilled to see I slept all the way to five-thirty, which has happened about three times since we moved here. Could it be I'm finally breaking the cycle?

There it goes again. Everyone in the valley will be subjected to the sing-song tone of European sirens, of emergency services blaring their horns in our bucolic neighborhood.

"Wesley," I whisper. "Do you hear that? Something's going on." I throw off the covers, stand up, and feel for my flannel PJ bottoms.

"What the hell?" He groans and turns over. "It's always something with you. Can't you just sleep through the night *one* time?"

"Don't you hear the sirens? I'm going to see what's the matter."

I wrap myself up and put my ear to the front door. I hear voices, men speaking in loud, alarmed tones, now the sirens have died down. I crack open the front door and my stomach shoots acid up my esophagus and burns the back of my throat.

There is stretcher with no one on it across the way. I hear a loud German conversation, but no real urgency. I step outside and see two police officers—the now-familiar *Polizei* embroidered on their backs—and two EMTs on the stone landing. There is no sign of Astrid.

An officer catches sight of me, holds up a hand, and barks orders at me in Swiss German.

"Entschuldigung," I say, standing stock-still as if confronted by a wild dog. "Sprechen sie Englisch?"

"Let the man do his job."

I whip around. Wesley is behind me.

"What happened?" I ask the officer.

"A resident of this home has died. Give us room." He holds up two hands, pushes the air, as if he can push me, too.

"Frau…" I realize I never knew her last name. "*Astrid* was killed?"

"Killed? No one spoke of killed! She had a fall. A *fall.*"

"I assumed because the police are here—"

"It is customary for Polizei to attend an unexpected death. Now, *please* move away. *Bitte.*"

I can't look away. I can hear distressed voices coming from inside Astrid's home, low talking, quiet tears.

"Rose. He said we need to go inside. Have some respect." My husband grabs my arm—hard.

I yank it away. His grasp triggers a memory of advice Grandma Mixie gave me before I knew I'd need it: *The first time a man lays his hands on you in anger, get out. There is always a second time. Always.*

The lights of Polizei cars and an ambulance flash red and blue so the hill looks like an outdoor disco, round and round they go, and with every rotation Wesley's face lights up like a devil, and then a member of Blue Man Group, and then darkness, and then a devil again.

I can't comprehend Astrid is gone. She cared enough to spend time with me at my lowest point, to do her best to console me through a language barrier. I'll never forget that. As when Mixie died, and my father disappeared, I am again wrecked by the inconceivable impermanence of a living soul, of flesh and blood and bone all existing one minute, walking and vital and alive, and then not, and now there is another person gone from this earth forever.

The selfishness overcomes me quickly, unbidden. I feel the loss of her protection as a seeping, sinister unease.

Wesley has gone inside. I wait another minute, scanning the landing and the hill for any clues, but there is no fresh snow to find footprints in or blood to identify a murderer. A fall is quiet, lonely. It is an end with a million possible causes.

I have been warned enough times not to go to the police in this town about anything, so this is my only chance to question whether someone might've harmed Astrid.

"Bitte," I say to the officer. He turns.

"I ordered you to go!" He shouts.

"I—I wanted to let you know I'm here if you need a witness." I stand my ground. "If there are questions about what happened to Astrid. She was so fit and healthy…"

He sighs. "Fit and healthy people fall all the time. We see it in all ages," he replies in a slightly less angry fashion. "There is no reason to believe this was anything other than an accident. If we need you, we know where to find you." His walkie crackles and he responds, turning away from me, dismissing me.

I step to our doorway and glance down for any runes or other items, then up at the doorjamb. On the five-inch surface above the door someone has etched a shaky symbol.

Six petals, perfectly drawn, inside a circle.

I snap a picture, then walk back into the house and sit on the sofa to learn what it is. Wesley, I presume, has stormed back to bed to catch a few more hours of sleep before work.

Professor Diaz told me to expect more symbols of protection, and she was right. I discover the new one above my door is a ritual protection symbol, also known as an apotropaic mark, more colloquially known as a daisy wheel, though most research in this field describes these symbols as hexafoils.

Astrid did everything she knew how to warn and protect me. In then end, it might've killed her. I curl up under the throw blanket, alone on the sofa, and cry for her.

Wesley is in a foul mood when he emerges, showered and smelling of aftershave, at eight a.m. I hear sighing, heavy footfall, and an expletive as he fumbles around in the kitchen. I pretend to be asleep.

As soon as he's gone, I brew an espresso and take it to my office. It's time to look for CM. Jacqueline gave me the clue and Astrid dragged its importance out of me, and it means something, so I'm going to do this for her. Astrid tried to help me then, so I decide the least I can do is help myself now.

I've poked around half-heartedly before, but TIG people are tough nuts to crack because they have only the faintest social media footprints. Most have faceless LinkedIn profiles or Facebook pages like ghost towns, ramshackle and outdated, disused, often set to private with no pictures.

Now I have a new place to search. When we became official club members, we were given access to the Expat Social Club website. I log on, find the membership directory, and scroll down to M.

It takes seconds to find CM. Two of them, actually: Charles Meier and Celine Moreau. Of course, these finds only highlight the fact I have no idea what I'm looking for. How will I know which CM is the right CM, or if they're even a human being's initials? CM could be a company or a lost dog.

I find Charles and Celine's Facebook pages. Both are set to private, but each has a profile photo of them posing with their families. Now I know I'm barking up the wrong tree, because I recognize the people in the pictures from the gala, so there would be no need to "find" either of these CMs.

I shift gears and work backwards. I know more people from TIG now thanks to the holiday events and our German lessons at their offices, so I add new names to the mix. I travel down a rabbit hole of social media accounts and endless pages with identical names and wrong cities and countries, wrong ages, wrong spellings.

I click and scroll for hours, plowing through multiple platforms. It's all about cross-checking. Who's hitting *like* on which posts, who's replying, who's friends with whom.

Nothing strikes me as relevant until I search for Wesley's assistant, Pieter Buhler. When I do, the algorithm is on my side.

His face pops up on Facebook after a few pages of clicking.

I scroll through the few public posts on his page. Something always seeps through the cracks no matter how private you try to be. Someone tags you or adds you to a public post, or you leave comments on a public post, or…

BINGO.

Her name is grayed out, but it's there, in the comments section under a profile pic Pieter added two years ago: The correct CM. I *know* it's her.

Her name is Carrie McFitzhugh.

Carrie McFitzhugh is CM, but she goes by another nickname, too. The answer hits me like a cartoon anvil to the head. My new friends mentioned her several times: the "Fitz" who disappeared at Fasnacht is Carrie McFitzhugh, aka CM.

She is connected to the younger, junior TIG employees on social media, she's no longer in Lucerne, and her initials match Jacqueline's hidden note.

My whole skin is tingling as I consider what this means. *Is Fitz alive?* I don't know what to think anymore. I pound my keyboard, punching her name into Google, and I find her quickly because she's not hiding.

Carrie McFitzhugh is on QuickChat, where she reposts information about voting rights and intersectional feminism and shares the occasional selfie while hiking in desert-like conditions.

She's active right now; I watch her feed refresh before my eyes. I DM her in a gush of speed typing, telling this stranger everything that's been going on. A few minutes later, three tantalizing dots appear.

Someone is typing.

I wait, my heart pounding. After another minute, a response pops up: *How did you find me? How do I know this isn't a trap?*

I write back as fast as I can, lest I lose her: *Ask me anything.*

I'll show you my ID, whatever it takes. I have to know what happened to Jacqueline. Please. I need your help.

She takes her time responding. I wait, watching the three dots like they're a living thing, throbbing then disappearing, appearing and throbbing, then gone again.

Finally, the dots turn to words: *I understand. I can meet you in Milan tomorrow. Bring identification.*

I immediately confirm I'll be there. I hope she accepts an American driver's license, because my passport is nowhere to be found.

CHAPTER

FORTY THREE

The next morning, I drive Wesley to work, kiss him goodbye, and set a course for Milan. Three hours, a couple claustrophobic Alpine tunnels and one nerve-wracking border crossing later, I am sitting at a Milan café with Carrie McFitzhugh.

"Who knows you're here?" she asks when we're both settled, hands wrapped around cups of hot chocolate topped with clouds of Chantilly cream.

I lick cream off my top lip. I ordered it because Fitz did, and I don't regret it. It's so thick I can stand the spoon up in it.

"No one," I lie. I had to tell Wesley I was coming to Italy because he tracks our car, so I claimed I heard about a shop that sells a particular rare wine I wanted to buy him. "You said you wanted identification?"

I pull out my driver's license and Fitz examines it. "I looked you up," she says, handing it back. "You're good. Don't worry about getting back into Switzerland without a passport, by the way. They have open borders."

I was nervous as a drug runner when I pulled up to the Switzerland/Italy line, but no one was there so I cruised through, making sure to go the exact speed limit. Now she tells me it was a waste of adrenaline.

"This place is stunning," I say, staring up at the ceiling the packed and grand Galleria Vittorio Emanuele II.

"A beautiful piece of art infested with tourists," Fitz shrugs, stirring her chocolate, folding in the rich cream. "I needed a busy place in case you weren't who you said you were. I don't have long, so…"

She's not here for chit-chat, that much is clear. She's around 5' 5," buxom, and looks like she works out. She has auburn hair cut in a pixie and freckles sprinkled across her nose and cheeks.

"Why did you leave Lucerne so abruptly?"

"The million-dollar question," she smiles bitterly. "I left because The Group is shady as hell and I wanted to pretend I never crossed its cursed threshold."

Vague. I'll keep pressing. Carefully.

"How did you end up there in the first place?"

"I have dual citizenship because my mother was born in Geneva," she replies, glancing around as if someone might be listening. "I wanted to work abroad, so before I graduated from college, I applied for every job I could find in Switzerland. A professor in the economics department at Berkeley caught wind of my search and recommended me to TIG. It happened so fast…TIG hired me in the marketing department after graduation. At first it was amazing. I got a Christmas bonus, I was learning German, I was seeing new places…"

"Sounds idyllic," I say. "What went wrong?"

She sets down her cup and dabs her upper lip with a cocktail napkin.

"My bosses assigned me to assist on one of Peter Pewter-Browne's new accounts. My job was to keep the client happy, get them tickets to Eurovision and football matches, that kind of thing. But I figured out pretty quickly this particular client was a cousin of a despot who'd had every dissident in his country disappeared. Peter knew. Werner Fiat, TIG's CEO, knew. They *all* knew the cousin was laundering assets through TIG on behalf of a warlord. It wasn't hard to figure out. But in Switzerland, as long as an AG can check all the boxes on the money laundering screenings required for new clients, it doesn't matter what the reality is. TIG didn't care. The cousin complied with all Swiss regulations and that's all that mattered."

"What did you do when you found out?" I ask her, my mind automatically going to the obvious question: *Has Wesley been inducted into this dirty business yet?*

"I told my boss about my concerns," Fitz shrugs. "I told him I was uncomfortable working on that account. Next thing I knew, I was called into Brett's office. Kristoff and Peter were there, too, staring me down. I was offered a choice to resign, sign an NDA on the spot and get a payout. Not a generous one, mind you. But it was better than a kick in the teeth.

"*Don't* sign, and—they were very careful about how they said this part—if I didn't cooperate, it was clear I was looking at a smearing of my name or even legal action. They made me feel physically unsafe. They literally talked about how sometimes people go for hikes in these treacherous mountains and never come back."

"Oh my god," I shake my head slowly. "Do you think they'd actually...I mean..."

"I don't know," she replies. "It might sound melodramatic, but it felt like they were threatening my life."

"It actually doesn't sound outlandish," I say, thinking about how Peter possibly tried to push me over a cliff.

But one thing *isn't* making sense. "Are you aware some of the women are saying you disappeared in the middle of Fasnacht without a trace?" I ask. "I'm assuming *someone* in that group knew you were leaving of your own accord and weren't abducted or thrown in the river, yet they led me to believe you vanished without a word. Surely you told someone you were going. Goodbye drinks with Pieter, maybe?"

She shakes her head. "No way. That was a condition of the settlement. I had to walk out of that meeting and get out of Dodge, do not pass *Go*, do not speak to anyone. Goodbye drinks are far too risky because they breed uncomfortable questions and drunken confessions. Yeah, I was at Fasnacht that day—I had to walk through it to get to my flat. Maybe someone from TIG gave me a drink. Maybe I made some small talk. Then I got the hell out of there."

That explains a lot, but not everything. It's time to pose the big question. If I get the tone wrong, I'm afraid Fitz will shut down, and the rickety tower of clues I've built will collapse.

"If you left Lucerne for work reasons," I begin carefully, "do you have any idea why Jacqueline might think you hold the answers to what happened to her?"

Her eyes go wide. "What? No," she shakes her head. "I don't. Why would you ask that?"

I explain about the Swiss book and the hidden note, and for the first time, her bravado wavers.

"I don't know what happened to Jacqueline," she says, then swallows hard. "But I wonder…"

"*What*? Tell me. I'm so close, Fitz. I need to figure out what I'm missing."

She looks down as she fiddles with a paper napkin. "We did have an unusual conversation shortly before I left," she says, "though I didn't think much of it at the time. Jacqueline and I were ahead of everyone on a Club hike, and she talked to me out of the blue about Peter's kids and how attached she was to them, as much as any mother could be. 'I'll be in this town as long as they are,' she said. And then, out of nowhere, she asked if I ever felt trapped there. I lied and said no, because it's my boss's wife, right? So she says, 'The scenery is so stunning, but nothing is ever as perfect as it seems.' I chalked it up to an expat bad day. Sometimes everything feels wrong and you just want to go back home."

"Did she say anything else?" I push, though she's already told me one important thing: Jacqueline clearly believed CM could testify that the stepmom would never leave the children behind voluntarily. "Like maybe…was she afraid of Peter, or Brett or even Kristoff? Did Peter ever get aggressive with her?"

Fitz shakes her head as if to loosen stuck memories. "I'm trying to think, but…no. The odd thing about it was that she was confiding in me at all. I didn't run in TWAG circles. Now that I think about it—" she stops, closes her eyes for a moment. "Stupid me. Of *course*."

Of course, *what*? I wait, though every wasted second pains me.

"Maybe she *was* trying to tell me something," Fitz says, wincing.

"It's possible she viewed me as the only one she could trust at that point, because—and I'm making assumptions here—Peter mentioned me around the house, and Jacqueline could have overheard him talking about my questioning the company's ethics and she assumed I'd never betray her to him. Maybe that chat was a cry for help. Maybe I missed—"

"Hey, hey," I stop her. "Believe me, I've been beating myself up for weeks. Jacqueline came to my house and flat-out said she needed help, and I didn't rush to get involved either. But whatever happened to Jacqueline is not our fault."

She exhales. I don't think I've convinced her.

"I'm not sure where this leaves us," I say. "If I could ask you one last thing…do you think any of the TWAGs are capable of being involved in her disappearance? Sometimes I think we're friends…other times I don't have a clue who they really are."

Fitz half-smiles. "That's pretty much their M.O. I don't have the answers, but I don't believe for a second Jacqueline voluntarily dropped off the face of the earth. I *do* believe that if someone did something to her, TIG executives and their wives would help cover it up."

I shiver thinking about how you can't really know anyone. Not really.

"I still don't get *why*. There are other nice places to live," I say. "There are other high-paying jobs with perks. Why would they sell their souls to stay in Lucerne—"

"Oh, my dear, there aren't a lot of other places like this," Fitz shakes her head. "Switzerland has the skiing, the resorts, the culture, the safety, the quality of life, health care, the natural beauty, the money. Their kids are equestrians, soccer stars, scientists. They'll speak a minimum of three languages. They're as healthy as it gets. They meet all the right people. They're a stone's throw from a zillion travel destinations. Call it groupthink, mass delusion, peer pressure, a cult. Whatever helps you understand how serious these expats are at protecting their cozy, privileged lives. If you stay in line, you never have to leave."

"But if you don't…"

She raises her eyebrows. "That's what I'm telling you. These people make the mafia look like Fraggle Rock. The Expat Social Club is part of it, too. They help keep everyone in line. TIG lays on the professional and financial pressure, and the club adds tremendous social pressure to new expats. No one wants to be an outcast. It's a cozy place to be, and it's not easy to give up, especially when your family is fully enmeshed with it. Think of TIG as the stick and the social club as the carrot."

I take a sip of water, then ask her, "Are you saying they're connected? Does TIG secretly own the club or something?"

"Nah," she shakes her head. "But the same families run both of them, so you can see how the line would get blurred over the years."

"Speaking of those families, did you know Jacqueline was having an affair with Kristoff before she disappeared?" She doesn't mince words, and neither will I.

Fitz pauses, checks me for honesty. "Seriously? *Whew.* Poor Seychelle. I wonder if she knew."

"So do I."

The server drops by. I want to order an aperol spritz, but Fitz isn't drinking and I'm driving, so I order another sparkling water. She orders nothing.

"Do you think either Kristoff or Seychelle are capable of murder?"

"Isn't anyone?" Fitz replies. "If Jacqueline overheard or saw something she shouldn't, or if Kristoff or Peter physically hurt her in some way and the TIG Board thought she was going to report it to canton police...well, who knows. Anything's possible."

I think about Jacqueline flinching at the gala, obviously bruised by someone or something.

"It's starting to seem like TIG would rather see their execs dead than divorced," I say.

Fitz doesn't argue. "Divorce is messy, and angry spouses have big mouths. Married couples reduce the number of randos coming in and out of their executives' lives, which is why TIG doesn't like single staffers at senior levels. Keeping the company in good standing, staying under the radar and protecting their cash cows is everything. The banality of evil on display, as they say. I'm not saying these guys come to Switzerland to kill their wives, but it's a damn a good place to do it if you decide you want to."

Pieces are starting to slot in for me, one by one.

"Fitz..."

"I go by Carrie now."

"Sorry. Carrie. I know you were in Lucerne before their time, but do you know what happened to the Rawlings family? I can't find any information on them."

Carrie pauses, sighs. "I was hiding like that my first year out of TIG, too," she says. "Then I got tired of being afraid, thus why you were able to find me. I've heard rumors. Apparently they went to live with in-laws in Wales. Lars saw something he shouldn't, some papers or bank accounts, and TIG shut him down fast, like they did with me."

It brings me some comfort to think the Rawlings family might be safe back in their home country after all.

"If I could just get a handle on those missing six hours between poker night and when Peter says he went looking for Jacqueline, I could figure it out and get the Polizei on the case anonymously," I say. "Why were her car and her passport left behind, how did the staff and the kids not hear anything, did she make it back home at all that night...Peter stayed at home, I'm almost certain of it. Did he have someone else take her? What about Kristoff? Is Brett someone who would—"

"Whoa," Carrie says, shaking her head. "Forget all that. You're not going to get them on your own. You're not Interpol. You're a TWAG with a B permit. They'll squash you like a bug. Your best shot is to take your investigation closer to home, where you have access to private things that you don't have at Peter's or Kristoff's houses."

"I'm babbling. I'm sorry," I say, yawning. "I haven't been myself since we got here. I *cannot* beat this jetlag."

"Jetlag?" She makes a face. "You've been in Lucerne for over three months. That's not jetlag."

"Wesley says I screwed up on day one and got into a bad cycle," I yawn again. It's addictive. "He went for a run when we got off the night flight. I took a nap. I haven't had a good night's sleep since."

Carrie looks at me the way my mother used to when I fucked up, and I feel the same dread.

"Forgive me for being blunt, but from everything you've told me," Carrie says, "it sounds like you might want to get to know your husband better. How was he introduced into TIG? That's a key question. Think about how many upper-crust stars are working at the JP Morgans and the Goldman Sachs and Blackrocks and all the ones who pay ridiculous money for guys like Wesley. One in a million gets hired as an executive at TIG. When you're recruited by them, it's for a very specific reason."

Funny, Wesley said that to me back in New York. I thought it was a Liam Neeson joke: *They need my particular set of skills.* I wonder now if it was a particular set of morals they were looking for.

"I have to get back to work," Carrie says. "Do you have any other questions?"

"Why did you agree to meet with me?"

A slideshow of expressions crosses her face, and she eventually settles on defiance.

"Because, fuck them. Because I don't want to be afraid of them anymore. Because I don't want this shit to happen to anyone else."

"Those are the best reasons," I say. I reach out for the bill, but she yanks it away.

"So he doesn't see it on the credit card statement," she says. "And wonder who you were meeting."

We part ways, promising to keep in touch.

I make the three-hour drive back to Lucerne with no trouble at the border. Wesley is asleep when I return, so I set the wine I bought to support my cover story in the fridge, and tiptoe off to sleep in the office.

CHAPTER

FORTY FOUR

I manage to sleep until nine the next morning, not even waking with the sounds of Wesley getting ready for work.

I drag myself out of bed and brew a macchiato, then open my laptop in the bright, sunny living room and get straight down to business. Carrie's words ring in my ear: *Start closer to home.*

First I check Jacqueline's alleged new Insta account from her rebooted life in Hong Kong. There is, all of the sudden, a new photo.

It's taken on a busy street and tagged #HongKongLife.

But the location of the person who posted it is *Lucerne, Switzerland.*

Either Jacqueline's doing fine and came back to town, or someone pretending to be her accidentally kept the location tag on. I study this account's posts again one by one. I examine the length of Jacqueline's hair, the whiteness of her teeth, her crow's feet or lack thereof. Anything to signal these photos are not current, not in chronological order.

But there are no tells for someone who hardly knew her; if they are not genuine, they are carefully curated and filtered. I didn't know her well enough to find red flags in her wardrobe, her shoes, her hairstyle.

What am I missing? What other details do the pictures provide? *Be a journalist. Don't be distracted by what they want you to see. Look beyond Jacqueline.*

I study the airport photo but find nothing to identify its location. It's brilliantly generic.

I pace. I throw open the French doors, let in some fresh air, stand alone on the freezing balcony. Two crows sit on the edge, and I do as Flor recommended. I speak to them. I ask them how they are, if they need anything. They scream at me and fly off in a huff.

I pad back into the office in my fluffy socks, staring down at my phone as I go.

And then…

Why didn't I think of this before? I was too mired in distractions. I was too tired.

I race to my desk and revive my laptop. I note every detail in Jacqueline's photos, starting with the three Hong Kong storefronts in the picture with her friend, and I plug them into the search engine. Street names, business names. It doesn't take long.

The restaurant directly behind Jacqueline does not exist. It went out of business four years ago, replaced by a furniture store. These pictures are old. Every last one of them. Jacqueline didn't go back to Hong Kong, which I knew in my blood the day my new friends called me into Pickwick's and were more worried about Peter than his missing wife.

The finality of proof in my hands brings a frisson of relief. I can break free of the doubt, see the gaslight bobbing in front of me and *know* the flame is real. Now I have to find out who's carrying the lamp.

I don't know if the Expat Social Club board is pure evil or not, or if they're deranged, or if they're simply protecting people who are evil. It has occurred to me they believe they have a "good" reason for rallying around Peter and believing his weak explanation about Jacqueline's disappearance.

Was there an accident? Was the TIG board served up a believable story, like Jacqueline threatened to take the kids and hit Peter in a moment of anger, and Peter accidentally knocked her back and she hit her head on the edge of a table and died? And then, did his friends and colleagues cover it up to avoid an international incident, to spare Peter a life sentence, and to keep his children from losing their father?

I carry my laptop to the couch and think about photographs, and about how images can seem like incontrovertible evidence but can also be used to support epic lies and create an alternate reality. Images can fool us. Photographs can be manipulated.

I dig out the virtual file Vi sent me the day we were having drinks with the Dead Newspaper gang, and key in the password. I immediately see why Wesley "passed" Violet's background check.

The most damning information is a highlighted comment under a Yale fraternity reunion Facebook post with a picture of all the brothers who attended the event. A poster named Chloe Barnes wrote, *Everyone looks great. Wesley looks like a robot. Knock, knock, Wes. Anyone in there? Ha ha.*

Embedded in the file is a notation in red type:

Note: This was the only negative-leaning comment found in all available social media posts.

I use my sock-puppet Facebook account to friend Chloe, and then send her an enticingly vague private message that'll probably go to her spam folder. Next, I scan the group photo to see if the three fraternity brothers who were in Wesley's wedding party are in it. The guys do not have visible accounts on social media, but their names are in the caption under the reunion picture.

They're all there: Jonny Hwang, Theodore Marsden III, Colin Vanek. I'm oddly relieved to know these people, who made the trip to our little placeholder wedding, who shared fond memories and nice stories about Wesley over lunch, who seemed genuinely happy for him, actually exist.

I check the caption and start matching the names to the young men's faces in the photograph, and within a minute I endure another gut punch. The Jonny, Theodore and Colin in the picture do not remotely resemble the three men who stood up in my wedding.

I rise and do the only thing I can think of: I breathe.

I face Pilatus for a moment until the jolt of panic abates, then pad to the kitchen. I fling open the fridge door and grab a bottle of wine, my hand shaking as I pour half of it into an oversized glass.

I need Vi. This situation is so abjectly, impossibly absurd it can't be real, though I know it is. Nothing can be ruled out now. I text her: *911. Call as soon as you can.*

I shoot another text to Marty begging for two favors and promising to buy him fried food for life when I'm back in town.

Marty responds first. He sends me scans of Bertie and Harold Blackwood's drivers' license photos along with a note:

Wesley's parents live in Jupiter Island, Fl. They still own the Westport house. BUT. Did you know it's listed on Airbnb??

No, I didn't.

I don't have to take but a glance at Bertie's and Harold's license photos to know those aren't the people I met. That's not the woman who came to city hall and bought me a post-wedding salad at Houston's; that's not the man who hugged me and said, *Welcome to the family. You'll be like the daughter I never had.*

It is so absurd to think my fiancé rented out fake parents that I laugh out loud.

What kind of person am I sleeping with? How did I not see it?

I race to the bathroom and throw up an acidic brew of coffee and wine.

After I'm sick, I spend long minutes staring into space, as if in a trance. I wonder for a moment if I'm even alive, if maybe I died crossing the street in Brooklyn and this is purgatory.

My laptop dings, and I scoot back to my seat. "Chloe" has accepted my friend sock-puppet Facebook account's request and messaged me back:

OK, "Mary Finkle." I'm not surprised he's messing with your head, whoever you are. What do you want to know? I've got three minutes before I have to pick up the kids at daycare.

I write, What do I need to know about him that no one else sees?

Now I know you're real, ha ha. I always thought he was like a nuclear silo. Sitting all innocent in a field until someone sets him off. Then the explosion would be apocalyptic.

There was a girlfriend (Doreen??I think??) who was obsessed. She came to the frat house one night and literally tackled a girl who was talking to Wesley. The girl was a stunner. Brunette, legs for days, daughter of a diplomat. But there was no sign they ever hooked up.

I write, Was her name possibly Darlene?

Yes!!! Right. A townie. Very intense. She would've killed the hot girl if the frat brothers hadn't pulled her off. Wesley stood there smirking. He loved it. It was fricking scary.

I ask, But he didn't dump her?

He had a princess, a model and a president's daughter after him. He wanted Darlene from Hamden. He's one of those rare guys who needs to be the pretty one in the relationship.

I write, But everyone else liked him? He never got in real trouble?

No!! I always thought he would. He was on every guest list for every yacht party and ski trip b/c of his looks & pedigree. I always thought he was "off" but he fooled everyone. Gotta go. Good luck.

I'd forgotten about old Darlene, especially since there was no mention of her after college in the background file. I check the file again and examine the one blurry picture of her they were able to find.

She really does resemble me. Five-six to five-seven, brown stringy hair like I used to have before my London highlights, nothing anyone would remember. I find a Facebook page for a Darlene DeWitt in Hamden, Connecticut. It's set to private and has a cat as the profile pic.

Vi calls back when she gets my text at eight a.m. her time. "Tell me everything," she orders.

I start with how I think someone in Lucerne is posting old photos of Jacqueline because they screwed up and left the location tag on.

"Whoever posted that probably has Jacqueline's phone," Vi says. "Do you think it's possible they're *all* in on it? Then again, how could that many people keep the same secret?"

"It's hard to fathom," I agree. "I've had my doubts since the Pickwick's bartender swore he remembered the exact moment he saw Jacqueline ordering a pint *after* Nova said she saw Jacqueline get safely in her car and drive toward home."

My phone beeps and I pull it away from my ear.

"Hang on," I say.

There is a message blazing across my screen punctuated by two red exclamation points: *Your Listen & Know app is full! Please clear your files and update the app to the latest version to continue recording!*

I have no such app. I installed no such tool.

Someone did, though.

I'm surprised at how quickly and effectively I'm able to act with a brain like hot stew: melted, lumpy, thick. I cough and splutter and run a thumb over the microphone.

"*What*? I didn't hear that. Vi—Violet? I'm losing you. There's some terrible static on the line. Shit, I've lost you. I'll—"

I end the call, turn my phone off, and race to the kitchen. I grab a paring knife and pry out the battery. I don't have a car today, so I grab a wad of cash from the sock drawer, strap on a backpack, and head out for the two-mile trek to town.

I'm shaken by the mysterious app on my phone. The violation hits me harder than I want it to, probably because the culprit could be a selection of people who claim to care about me. Is it my husband? Is it one of the other people in this town who've had access to my phone when I was drinking, not paying attention, or sleeping?

I make it to town and buy two burner phones, charge them at an Irish pub called Shamrock, a place I've never known the TWAGs to visit, and calm my nerves over an Irish coffee.

When one of the burners powers up, I call Violet back and explain everything. We formulate a plan, and I pray it's enough to end this once and for all, and that I can stay safe for one more night.

CHAPTER
FORTY FIVE

You have to stir fondue constantly or the cheese will stick to the bottom, the sides, and the seam of the pot, and it will harden like cement.

I watch the gruyere and emmental swirl like thickened eggnog. I'll keep stirring it until Wesley gets home, as long as it takes to prepare perfect molten cheese for my husband.

The table is set with a ceramic pot, a sterno flame ready to set afire, and a bottle of white wine in a silver ice bucket. Proper fondue takes work to eat; it's a balance between stirring and controlling the flame to stop the cheese from hardening before you can finish.

The ritual of it will be the perfect buffer during this evening's dinner, and will keep me busy enough that I won't have to *act*, a skill that comes and goes depending on my level of anxiety. Fondue is filling, too, so no one will feel a twinge of desire while weighted down with globs of cheese. I don't want Wesley touching me.

My husband has some deviant wants and needs, but he also has his kryptonite, and it is menstrual blood. I could put on the best act of my life tonight, treat him like the king he thinks he is, but if I hint that I'm bleeding, he'll be repelled like a vampire to the sun. He's also terrified of tampons, even the fresh ones, even the box itself.

He's home. I hear the scrape of the key, the jerking of the impossible *L* handle, the whoosh of the wide door opening.

"Something smells incredible," my husband calls as he traipses up, shoes clacking on the tiles.

I greet him at the top with an apron and a kiss. "Get comfortable," I purr. "I've got a gorgeous dinner for us. *And* a surprise after-dinner treat."

His face relaxes. "Sounds like heaven. Let me get changed—I'll be ready in five."

He takes off down the hall carrying his soft briefcase, jacket hanging off his arm. I set out two side salads, fretting over the lack of fresh avocado—they've been hard to come by in this town—then pour the wine in deep crystal goblets.

"Oh, shit!" I yell as loud as I can. He hears me.

"What is it?" It is a faint echo five rooms away.

"Shit, shit, *shit*. I forgot how to do the final flourish on the after-dinner surprise." I slide in my socked feet toward the bedroom. "*And* my phone is out of power. Died while I was cooking and I didn't even notice. Can I borrow yours? Have to look up the instructions *now*. Hurry—the cheese is gonna harden…"

I'm at the bedroom door.

"I dropped it at that table thingy at the top of the stairs," he yells back. "Where we keep the mail. Hang on."

"Just give me your code!"

He pauses. The silence says everything. When I'm about to yell louder, he barks out the six-digit code, and I run back to the kitchen before I forget it.

Two minutes later he emerges in jeans and a sweatshirt. He makes a beeline for his phone, which I already put back on the mail table.

"Just in time," I say. "Have a seat."

He shoves the phone in his pocket and sits at the table. I light the steno, dash back to the kitchen to grab the pot with two gloved hands, then carefully pour the hot cheese into the ceramic cauldron.

We sit across from each other, the steaming fondue like an active volcano between us. "Dig in," I smile, spreading a white cloth napkin on my lap, tugging at the corners to straighten it.

I take a sip of wine. Wesley spears a cube of bread, dips it halfway, and brings it to his mouth, chews, swallows.

"Is that truffle I'm tasting?" he asks. "Truffle fondue is is the only fondue I want to eat from now on."

I dive into the fondue twirl some molten cheese into my mouth. It really is delicious. It came in a plastic bag from the mini mart in the Bahnhof.

"Rose," Wesley says, playing with the stem of his wineglass, "I know things have been hard since we arrived here. I can tell you're freaked out about Fasnacht, and Zermatt, and…"

This rare appearance from Serious Wesley comes out of nowhere. I hold another square of bread dripping with boiling cheese.

"I'm over it," I lie. "Life happens." I take a bite and chase with some wine.

"No, you're not, nor should you be," he replies. His eyes meet mine. "You were right to be freaked out. I just…you can see my position, can't you?"

No.

"Of course." I realize my spear is pointed directly at his face. I stab at a chunk of bread instead of his eye.

"This is the best job I've ever had. The introductions alone are priceless. If I stick it out, I'll have a chance at my dream of starting my own business. I'd have contacts beyond anything my friends have back in the New York firms."

Great. You can be friends with the oligarchs and despots and billionaires who fly to space while children starve five miles below them.

"I want to make it up to you. I want to take you away this weekend. What do you say?"

Something's happening tomorrow, then. Vi and I suspected a move was imminent, and we agreed that all my assumptions and conclusions up to this point might be flat wrong—including who's behind it and what their motive is. What if Jacqueline's disappearance and everything after it has been an extended *Cruel Intentions*-level prank at my expense?

"Love makes you do things," my husband goes on. "Make adjustments, make you forget about black and white, push you into the grey until you take a wrong turn and discover a different color entirely."

He spears a cube of bread and dunks it until it hits the ceramic bottom. "'I was never really insane except upon occasions when my heart was touched.' Do you know who said that?"

He pulls out the bread and expertly swivels it so the cheese doesn't have time to drip down his spear. He rests the hot bite on his tongue and waits for me to guess.

"I have no idea."

"Poe. Edgar Allan Poe. Believe it or not, that creeptastic master of horror who married his underage cousin had some wisdom to share about love."

"He also had some wisdom about how it was it was a good idea to plaster his friend inside a wall while he was still alive," I reply.

I am realizing my husband is, among many other things, weird.

"*Yes!*" Wesley jabs his two-pronged implement at me. "God, you're hot when you get me. Of course, I know you don't mean it literally, because that story is fiction. I know it well. *Cask of Amontillado* was a formative piece of literature for me. And people still don't get what it means. It's not about revenge, or murder, or justice. It's about *betrayal*. There is no betrayal without trust. You must choose those people you're going to trust very, very carefully. But even then, the most intense treachery can be born."

"Nevermore," I say softly, but he's past listening now, lost in his own thoughts, probably about himself.

We're nearing the bottom of the cheese. I swirl a bread around and hit the garlic clove.

"Whoever snags the garlic has to clean the pot," Wesley says. "That's the rule. No way around it. This is Switzerland, remember?" He winks at me, and I act disappointed.

As if he was ever going to clean the pot.

After we knock back a shot of kirsch, I order him to wait for his surprise on the sofa while I set the ceramic to soak.

I emerge with a cut-glass tumbler of neat Blanton's and a nip of Sauternes for me. His eyes are starting to close as he scrolls through his phone, and I catch him blinking fast as if to stay awake. I set the glass on the coffee table and sit next to him.

"You OK, honey?" I ask with a brow furrowed in concern.

"You're not so bad, you know," he says, lifting his glass and taking several long sniffs. "Fucking perfect." He knocks it back.

I sip my dessert wine and watch him. He leans back, closes his eyes, lets the glass tip in his hand.

"Oooh, watch it!" I say with a laugh. "Stay with me, sweetie."

He blinks, nods, takes another sip.

"That food made me tired, too," I say. "And you've had such a big week at work…"

His head bobs, then jerks back upright. I let him take one more sip of bourbon and then I spring up off my cushion.

"Oh! I almost forgot. Can you help me do one thing in the bedroom before we settle in for a movie? I promise it'll be quick."

"Can't it wait?" He yawns.

"Not really," I plead. "It'll only take a sec. I can't move a box. It's essential. I promised Nova I'd give her this book by tomorrow."

Wesley blinks a bit more, then stands, shaky, suddenly complying because I invoked the name of his boss's wife.

"Bring your drink," I say, holding onto his arm, leading him down the hallway. The remaining brown liquid sloshes in his glass as he clumsily moves down the hall. We make it to our room, and he sinks down on the edge of the bed and stares at the floor.

Out of habit, he tosses back the final drops of bourbon.

"Where is this box you speak of?" He's slurring. I take the glass from him and set it on the nightstand. A bit of drool dribbles out of the corner of his mouth.

He begins to fall forward, but I push him back. He's snoring before his head hits the pillow. I lift his legs for him, remove his shoes, then lean down close to his face. I listen to his breathing. It is even and not labored. He'll be fine.

I race away, shut the door, lock him in, and slide back down to the living room in my fuzzy socks to make a phone call.

CHAPTER
FORTY SIX

The text comes through a minute after I make the call: *I'm here.*

I run downstairs and throw open the front door. A whoosh of winter air blows my hair back. My best friend is standing at the threshold, trying to pretend she's not out of breath from the stairs.

"Girl," Violet grins, holding out her arms.

"*Girl.*" I squeeze the breath out of her and stifle an oncoming sob.

It's surreal to see her at my door, even though I was the one who asked her to come when I called from the Shamrock pub. When the Listen & Know app alert appeared, we both knew I was in actual, real, imminent danger, but key questions remained: Who am I in danger *from,* and how does this turn of events connect to Jacqueline? I don't know if my husband is involved in any of it, but Vi and I agreed it was time to find out. She hopped on a plane five hours later, and she's been holed up at the Grand Hotel in Old Town until now.

"Hey, hey," she gasps into my hair now. "You're going to be OK. I promise."

She pulls back and throws a nervous glance up the stairs behind me. "Is the coast clear?"

"He's knocked out."

"How'd you do it?"

"Sedatives from my new friends." I kept every pill from London, from Zermatt, from Teresa. "I dosed him a little at a time, in every drink he had tonight. By the time he got to the bourbon, I could've spiked it with ammonia and he wouldn't have noticed."

After I hide Vi's shoes in the brush outside the door, we tiptoe upstairs.

"Nice place," she says, taking in the view. "I can see why you were reluctant to leave."

The moonlight spotlights the mighty Pilatus standing guard, frosted and steadfast, across the valley.

I pour us two sparkling waters.

"What if he wakes up?" Vi whispers.

"The bedroom door is locked from the outside, I have his phone, and even if he stirs, he'll be confused enough so I can manipulate him, at least in the short term," I reply, handing her a glass.

"Good," Violet nods. "Let's tackle that list. Time to flip the narrative on this jerk. I mean, alleged jerk."

I lead her to my office and lock the door behind us. I stream a news station on my laptop to mask our voices in case Wesley wakes up, and I set his phone and my notebook on the futon between us.

"First things first: What did Marty say when you asked him about the spying app?" I ask. "Is there a chance Wesley—or whoever installed it—heard any of our conversation about the Instagram photos?"

An evil grin spreads across her face. "Nope. Marty said the Listen & Know app isn't designed for spying. The data it records stays on your phone. It's meant for personal use—reminders to yourself, to record meetings or traffic stops, things like that."

She raises a finger. "Here's the rub for the person who's trying to stalk you: Once the app's memory is full, it stops recording. *If* it's Wesley, he's probably been retrieving the files when you were in the shower or whatever, and maybe your conversations got so boring he started getting sloppy. Marty says you need the physical phone in your hand to retrieve the data. Getting around that, even attempting to access your device remotely, would require a hacker with more skill than that vanilla icicle you married."

"Thank you, Marty." I exhale. "I've been making a lot of calls from my laptop, so there will be a ton of holes in whatever Wesley thinks he knows."

"If it is him, are you *sure* he's not checking your computer, too?"

"He doesn't have my laptop password," I assure her. "Marty made me set up two-factor identification years ago. I would've known if Wesley tried to get into it."

"I feel like we're dancing around the elephant in the room," Vi says carefully. "Are we assuming Wesley installed the app? Even though it could be someone else? Your phone was out of your hands at that Zurich club..."

"I thought about Seychelle, or even Teresa," I say. "But Teresa didn't have it long, and Wesley's the one with regular access. And also…why would she?"

"Why would *he*?" Vi counters.

"I don't know." I throw my hands up. "I don't know how I got from investigating a new friend's disappearance to being under surveillance myself. I don't know how I got from infatuated newlywed to suspicious expat wife. But I'm not going to do what my father did. I'm not going to ignore signs I'm married to an abusive prick, nor am I going to get myself stuck in a shitty marriage."

I unlock my husband's phone with the code he gave me and start going through his call logs, text messages and emails.

Vi's fingering the guidebook I brought out for her visit.

"So this is the cursed tome I've heard so much about," she says, flipping through it. "Spooky."

I'm half listening as I click through my husband's phone for the first time ever. I never had a reason to spy on him before. I sift through every app, every messaging platform and all his notes.

"His Swiss phone has nothing," I say as I scroll through his work email. "Not a thing. His only contacts are me, the BMW dealership, and his TIG colleagues."

"Text chains?"

"Nothing. Not even a text from me. What kind of psychopath deletes everything from his phone as he goes? He has fewer contacts than I do. His parents aren't in here. Neither are his old New York friends."

We say it at the same time: "He has another phone."

"Which brings me to the next item on the list," I say. "I need to search his briefcase. You'll search…well, can you look literally everywhere else? *Someone* has Jacqueline's phone and if it's been my house this whole time, I'll kick myself. Oh, and I need my passport. I mean like yesterday."

I pad down the hallway, silent as a Swiffer broom in my fuzzy socks, and put my ear to our bedroom door. They warn against mixing alcohol with benzodiazepines, but I've learned my husband's tolerance for substances is robust, and I can hear him snoring like a warthog which tells me he is, indeed, alive.

I slowly turn the key but can't stop the loud click. I wince, pause, and listen out; there is no break in his snoring.

I fling clothes around my closet and then his, find nothing, then rifle around drawers looking for a second phone and/or my passport. I'm also seeking other things I can't name. A gun? A manifesto? A love letter from another woman—or man?

I go through his briefcase. The contents are stultifying, full of spreadsheets and dull memos, a comb, some vitamins.

I tiptoe back into the bedroom. *It's always the sock drawer,* I think. I start at the top of his dresser and run my hands from corner to corner, from front to back. His socks are laid out in perfect rows, so I have to be careful.

I feel something. *Yep.* Always the sock drawer. The item is stuffed in the back corner inside a sock. I reach in and pull out a box that resembles a tin of breath mints. The product's logo is one word in lurid red: WACH!

I take photos of the front and back, then tiptoe toward the door. Wesley is on his side, under the covers, snoring and grunting. I lock him in and go straight to the internet to translate the words on the label.

German: WACH

English: AWAKE

There is one active ingredient listed on the back of the tin: pseudoephedrine. I don't need an app to know what that means. Is my husband taking cut-rate meth to get through the day?

Oh. No, he isn't.

I am.

The cold realization wraps around me and squeezes, and I know it is not going to let me go.

CHAPTER

FORTY SEVEN

I find Violet sitting on the futon, nose-deep in the guidebook. I lock us in my office.

"I know why I never kicked the jetlag," I say, holding the container between my thumb and index finger. "Found it in his sock drawer."

"It's always the sock drawer," she says. "What is it?"

"Pure pseudoephedrine. Speed."

She closes the book and uses one finger as a placeholder.

"What does your husband taking stimulants have to do with *your* jetlag?"

"My husband," I say slowly so she can catch up, "sleeps like a baby and snores like a chainsaw. He's not on stimulants."

"*Ohhh*," she breathes. "But *you* are. Holy shit, Rose! You think he's been drugging you?"

"I know he has," I say, my stomach churning as grief and fear give way to a cold rage. "The only good sleeps I have are when he isn't around. Every time he brought me a glass of wine, every time I left my drink to go to the bathroom, he must have been dosing me."

My knees wobble and I sink down next to her. Violet lets out a low whistle, and seems genuinely rattled for the first time since this all started.

"I think we should quit the plan," she says. "Now that I'm here and I see the set-up, I think it's too dangerous. It would be horror-movie stupid to try to unravel this on our own. You know the girl who goes into the basement when she hears an ax murderer down there? We have to be smart enough to not go into the basement. Let's get you out of here."

"We can do this, Vi," I argue. "We can take down one guy."

"We're not up against one guy," she argues. "Everyone's a suspect right now, and this country has a zillion places to hide a body where no one will ever find you."

I put my head in my hands. The mix of emotions is impossible to manage with my exhaustion. My brain is like the world's most chaotic yard sale, sprawling and cluttered.

"You were right about him all along." It needs to be said. Just once.

"Bullshit," she replies. "I did the background check and then sent you off to Switzerland with this broken person."

"I should have dug deeper. I should have listened to you."

"Where's the romance in that?" Vi throws her hands in the air. "Who asks for ID from their fiancé's parents? Who would ever assume three groomsmen were hired actors? Nah. There's some evil you can't account for. If you live like that, you're not living. You had some bad luck running into a psychopath like this. Now. What was it you said on the phone about flipping the narrative?"

I'm quiet for a moment, knowing she's right. I'm sick of

waiting for the next message or loud noise or fake Instagram post. I'm ready to finish this.

"I skimmed the book," Vi says.

"The whole thing?"

"Pretty much," she says. "I think it's safe to say it was the note Jacqueline wanted you to see, not the book's contents. Like your friend Heidi said, she probably had it in her purse after someone returned it to her. She clearly suspected she was in danger and figured this was a safe way to send you a message."

"But why the weird claim that only pregnant women are allowed to see it?"

"I thought about that, and I have a theory," Violet says. "You had that awkward chat about kids, so she knew mentioning it would get your hackles up. It would ensure you paid attention."

"That's not a bad theory," I say. "It actually explains a lot."

"Anyway, the book is ultra creepy. These people know how to do horror. The big movie studios could learn a thing or two from the Swiss. Whew-*wee*," she whistles. "I'm not about to tempt fate. You won't catch me in some Alpine cave getting eaten by a *fluegelmeister*."

"Don't try to tell me a *fluegelmeister* exists."

"It could. Have you *read* this book?" She shakes it at me. "You're at the mercy of some wild customs and belief systems. This country has some serious Wicker Man and Midsommar vibes in their folklore playbook. We're talking serpents with human faces and lizards with multiple tails. We won't even talk about the Tatzelwurm."

"Let's not," I shudder.

"Right. So unless your new friends are going to attack you

with gnomes and a gigantic, cat-faced snake with T-Rex-style arms, I fail to believe your new friends are out to get you." She pauses. "Then again, maybe this whole thing is a performance for one person—you."

"But why?" I ask. "What's our working theory? What's the most likely scenario?" I don't want to say any of it out loud. Let her do it.

"I think the simplest explanation is that undercooked flan you married has an insurance policy on you that we don't know about," she replies. "Either that, or he's doing all this to protect someone else. Peter? Kristoff? Brett?"

"Or…"

"Or what?"

"Or Wesley is a garden-variety egomaniac and his bad-husband energy has nothing to do with Jacqueline, the runes, Astrid or any of it."

Vi sighs. "It *is* hard to imagine you arriving here and, what, days later he murders his new colleague's wife? Nah."

"None if it makes any sense. I have a feeling we're going to find out tomorrow either way," I say, then check the time. "It's late. You should go back to your hotel. Get some sleep."

We both stand, and I walk her down to the front door.

"You sure you're OK?" She grabs me in a tight hug, and I close my eyes. My friend, my family, my ally.

"I will be," I say.

I almost mean it.

CHAPTER

FORTY EIGHT

I wake with a start to see Wesley sitting at the edge of my bed staring down at me. I bolt upright.

"What—what's happening?" I rub my face to wake up faster, to become conscious, to catch up with him. "You going to work? You can take the car."

He's grinning like we've won the lottery. "Don't you remember? The big surprise is today. I've got the day off. Up you get. We've got a long trip ahead of us."

He leans down and kisses me on the cheek, and I swallow my gag reflex.

I reach over to my nightstand, but my hand swipes a clean surface.

"Where's my phone?" I mumble, rising quickly, swinging my legs out of the bed.

My husband is standing now, a foot from me, still grinning.

"I've got it. No screen time allowed today—no cheating. It's you, me, nature, and being entirely present."

He's toying with me, and I want to run, but I remind myself why I'm here. Why I stayed.

"How many nights should I pack for?" I yawn to release some tension.

"Fill your backpack," he advises, watching me from the doorway now. "Casual, warm stuff is your best bet. Pack good socks."

I rise, and he won't move, so I'm forced to brush past him to get to my office.

My computer is gone. *Don't panic.* I peek out of the room. "Wesley! Where's my laptop?"

"I told you, darling. No screen time. You get me all to yourself."

"That's sweet," I manage. "But I have admin to do before we go. I promised Vi I'd email her before we went on our trip. And I have a bill to pay that's due today."

"You told her about our trip?" He's in the office doorway.

"Of course," I reply, managing to keep my voice steady. "She's suitably jealous."

"Fine," he acquiesces. "I'll put the laptop out for you when you're dressed."

I race to dress and pack, then head back out to the dining room. He's standing over the computer.

"Give me some space," I snap. I'm irritated, and he should know me well enough to know I'm not going to hide it.

He takes two steps back, then taps his watch. "We're on a schedule."

He watches as I boot it up. I can't log in. "I need my phone for two-factor authentication."

"No can do," he holds up his hands. "It's powered down and packed away."

"Then unpack it. I promised I'd email her."

I hold out my hand. I'm not his captive. *Yet.*

"Tell ya what," Wesley says. "New York won't be awake for hours. We'll be at our destination by lunch, and I'll give it back then. Come on, now—we're running late."

"Do I at least have time to eat something?"

"I've got power bars. Let's bounce."

He grabs my hand and tugs me toward the stairs, rushing me, dragging me at his pace. I can't think. I need a moment to make a decision. He's deliberately moving fast so I have no time to react, but I defy him when we make it to the street. I pause to flip through my options.

The neighbor's house to our right is up another long stretch of stairs, the house next to them is accessible only by a locked elevator, and the children have left for school. I look left, right, down the hill. I hear nothing; not even my raven friend.

How did I become so fearful of my own husband? It's surreal.

Wesley turns, sees I'm not being pliant, and steps up to me. I feel his hot breath on my face.

"Rosie," he coos. "What's the matter?"

"I want my phone back," I say, my voice shaking despite my best efforts to remain calm. "And I want to know where we're going."

He nods, purses his lips, stares at the ground. "I get it." He gazes up at me. "This must be weird for you. I probably didn't factor in how much so. How about this: I'll tell you where we're headed, and I promise I'll give you your phone when we get there. Deal?"

He's charming me now, reminding me why I fell for him. He's *Wesley*, my first real committed relationship, the man I'm legally hitched to, the one I let inside me in every way. Who wants to hurt me.

"Have you heard of the Ice Hotel?" He asks.

"No."

"It's been all over the Swiss media," he says. "It's built every year up on Pilatus in the middle of nowhere. It's super hard to get in, but TIG books the best room in the place for a few weekends every season."

The TWAGS never said anything to me about any super-trendy Ice Hotel.

I don't have to go, but I do. Anything else is limbo. I cannot spend any more of my life in purgatory. He starts walking up toward Sonnenberg, the opposite direction from our garage.

"Whoa. We're not driving? You didn't say we'd be scaling a mountain today." *Ha, ha.*

"You're tough. You'll be fine."

I got four hours of sleep and my nerves are shot. I am far from OK. I trudge along behind him, never finding the scenery and open space as malevolent as I do right now. It's a prison with no walls. It is oblivion.

We walk up for half an hour before things level off as we get closer to Pilatus. The snow grows deeper as we go, the trail more treacherous, with more chunks of ice to fall on and steeper drop-offs.

I see a figure up ahead. He's walking slower than usual, but I'd recognize the gait and the stick anywhere.

"Grüezi," I wave. He is staring at me in a new way, his usual serious face turning downright concerned.

When we're close, he stops. "Grüezi. You are carrying this

heavy bag up in this weather?" He jabs a finger to the sky. "Snow is coming. Take care."

Take care. Same thing my neighbor said to me weeks before she died. My nausea is strengthening by the minute.

Wesley is checking his watch and won't make eye contact.

"We're going up to the Ice Hotel." If it exists.

Güggeliman shakes his head. "That is not the way. You must go around. *Around.*" He points toward central Lucerne in the distance. The other way. "The Ice Hotel is—"

"Thank you. We're fine," Wesley says. *Thank you* is said like, *Fuck you.*

He takes my arm and holds tight.

"These locals need to mind their own business," Wesley snarls as we keep walking. "Ignore him."

We walk for another hour and still there is only snow.

"I'm exhausted," I tell him. "And I have to pee."

I move off down the hill, out of his view, and pull my pants down. I call up to him, "How much farther?"

"You'll be able to see it from here when you come up."

I hike my pants up just as he peeks over to get a look at me. I zip up my coat and he offers a hand. I refuse it and scramble up on my own.

"You can see it up there, can't you?" He puts one arm around me and points with the other.

I see nothing. This is not the way to any hotel. Chicken Man was right. I follow my husband anyway, because there is no way out. Wesley covers me like stripes on a barber's pole, grabbing me every couple of minutes under the guise of offering help over an icy patch, but his message is clear: *I own you.*

A layer of translucent winter haze filters the sun so it looks like a fuzzy yellow ball, and I'm hit with the memory of the moment we met, when we began our banter, our dance of opposites attracting over those congealing canapés.

I see the deviled eggs. The party. The way he only had eyes for me. Or did he? My unconscious is working overtime. *Listen, Rose. Pull up the memory of that day. What do you see in the room? What do you hear?*

"Up there. See?"

Finally, a few meters ahead, I see the destination. A figure stands at the top of a craggy peak, their back to us. We're barely halfway to the summit of Pilatus; this is a lower peak, some distance below the summit.

"Just a few more feet, and…there. See?" Wesley drags me by the hand as we approach the figure.

I see hands on hips, wide shoulders, proud posture. The form looks familiar. When the person turns, I recognize the face, too.

CHAPTER

FORTY NINE

"You look cold, Rose. What took you so long?" Teresa smiles at me with the contempt of a high-school mean girl.

Wesley, his face flushed, squeezes my upper arm. "I thought you might've guessed. But I think you're surprised. Are you surprised?"

I'm breathing heavily and clutching my chest. I hate heights, and I hate that I didn't see this coming. I thought we'd be traveling by car, so my backup plan didn't account for a spontaneous hike.

I try to back away, but Wesley clutches me in a vice grip.

"Uh uh uh," he sings, tutting me, holding me in place. He puts his lips to my ear, and my skin crawls. "My mother told me when I was ten years old I could get anyone to follow me anywhere. I never believed her until high school. Women, men, kids. I can get anyone to do anything I want. I thought you'd be more of a challenge."

"Sorry to disappoint you," I snap, pulling my head away from his slobbering mouth.

Teresa steps forward, away from the edge of what I can see now is a sharp drop-off, though I can't tell how deep it goes. I'm going to assume it's treacherous.

There's no more maxi dress, no more rainbow hair. Teresa sports dirty blonde hair now, accented with blonde highlights that look a lot like mine. She's wearing white snow pants and a fitted white jacket to match. Fashionable. Impossible to recognize, but for the voice.

Wesley removes his arm and steps away from me, taking a spot next to Teresa near the edge.

"It's been fun," he says to me. "I'm almost sad it's ending."

He smiles fondly at Teresa. "Your performance was utterly perfect."

Teresa takes an exaggerated bow, rolling her forearm as she does. "Thank you. Thank you very much."

Wesley says to me, "You gotta have the angry misfit character to build trust. You know, the outsider with a heart of gold who gives the new girl something to run to. Otherwise, the new girl might panic and do something stupid like fly out of this place. You didn't, though, did you, Rose? Even when you knew something was terribly wrong, you stayed. They all do. Humans are odd creatures, aren't we?"

I exhale, the smoke of my breath blending into the snow that's started falling.

I feel my throat closing and my knees threatening to buckle when I need them ready to *run*. Fight or flight, my ass. It's *fight, flight* or *freeze*. Even now, as I begin to adjust to my new reality, I struggle to make sense of it, to peel away the layers.

My mind is racing to connect all I learned before with what I know now, the pieces jockeying to complete the puzzle. It feels impossible; I'm discovering evil is gelatinous, messy, and dripping out of every box I try to fit it in.

"When did you decide to kill me?" I ask Wesley.

"When do you think?" Teresa takes another long step to me.

The realization hits me as soon as her face is near mine. The iron wall in my head melts, blending the conscious and unconscious, showing me what I've missed this entire time.

I recall the blurry photo of Wesley's unhinged college girlfriend Darlene from ten years ago. Then I imagine the same woman a decade later at the Connecticut party where I met Wesley. My mind travels back to the Westport mansion; I cast my eyes around the room, try to pick out who else didn't belong in that rich environment, try to remember what I saw before I bellied up to that fateful buffet.

"You're Darlene," I say to Teresa. "Except you had different hair then…a sort of dirty dishwater color."

I saw her again, after that, too, I realize now.

"You followed Wesley and me out to dinner when we first got to Lucerne!" I knew there was something recognizable about that hooded figure. "*You* knocked me down in the square."

Teresa/Darlene crosses her arms and regards me with her mouth curled in a snarl.

"He's *my* man. I didn't appreciate another woman having her grubby hands all over him. I can't believe you didn't figure it out earlier," Teresa says. "You call yourself an investigative journalist?"

I shoot a look to Wesley, who's watching us with the kind of satisfied smirk that his Yale classmate Chloe described in our Facebook chat.

"You can't blame me," I reply. "I haven't slept in three months thanks to this prick drugging me every day. I think I'm up to speed, though I don't understand how someone like *you* got into TIG in the first place, Darlene."

"It's *Teresa*," she snaps. "But sure, honey, I'll tell you. When Wesley left New Haven after graduation, I let him go, started using my middle name, and made something of myself. I got my business degree and studied under a professor who put me forward for an assistant director role at TIG. Said they needed someone who wouldn't be so hung up on rules, who could be creative and make tough decisions, so he sponsored me. You don't get into TIG without a sponsor."

"But how did you and Wesley get back in touch?" I can't comprehend how any of this came to be.

"I flew back to Connecticut last summer to visit family," Teresa explains. "I was doing quite well for myself and I knew it was time to reconnect with Wesley. He jumped at the chance to get back together. I told him I could get him into this amazing company and land him a coveted Swiss visa. He was fascinated, but there was one problem—"

"He needed to be married to be considered," I interrupt her.

"Correct," Teresa says. "*I* couldn't be the wifey, of course, because that would raise alarm bells with the TIG board. It had to be a legitimate sponsorship, not some starry-eyed love interest pushing her boyfriend on them. I, along with the professor who got *me* into TIG, vouched for Wesley. He had the education, the pedigree, and an instinct for bending the rules when needed. He was perfect.

"The Group had to see a perfect façade," Teresa goes on,

clearly enjoying every moment of rubbing their betrayal in my face. "So we introduced a wife into the mix. Then, when you were out of the way, Wesley and I could fall madly in love as I consoled him over his loss, and all would be right in the world. We'll be TIG's golden couple. I intend to be the first woman on the board one day."

"That doesn't explain how you decided on *me*," I say, "or why either of you went to such extremes for what amounts to a nine-to-five desk job."

"It's funny," Teresa gazes at the Pilatus summit above us. "Wesley and I stayed up nights trying to think of anyone we knew who'd be a good fit. And then we went to a party thrown by Wesley's neighbor in Westport and *bam*, there you were! Alone, ill-at-ease, wrinkly, pounding champagne as if liquid courage would make you belong."

"*You* would know," I hit back. "You don't fit in with the upper crust any better than I do."

Teresa's eyes harden and her face flushes. I hope I've embarrassed her in front of her dream man. "I do now," she says, recovering quickly. "While you've been eating pastries and watching romcoms, we've been fucking and eating veal, two things you two never did much."

I let out a nervous snort. "That what he told you? Honey, we're newlyweds. Once a day and twice on weekends."

Her eyes widen and she swivels from Wesley to me and back again. Her obvious fury pleases me, even in my dire situation.

I turn to Wesley. "This entire time—on the beach, at the party, at the wedding, in bed…it was all a twisted plan to get me here and then…what?"

Wesley throws his hands up. "Hey. We had some fun, babe, don't get me wrong. But it was a means to an end."

All this information goes some way to explain the bizarre fake groomsmen and hired parents. I say, "That was a risky move, hiring actors for a real legal wedding ceremony. What did you tell them?"

Wesley blinks a few times, clearly thrown that I know about that.

"Out-of-work actors don't ask a lot of questions when you're paying triple union wages," he says. "So you figured it out, huh? Well done. I've wondered what you told yourself to allow your husband to ban photos at your own wedding. You must have twisted your idea of what's normal into a pretzel. But you complied, thank god. There couldn't be any photographic evidence of that wedding, and god knows my actual parents would have a heart attack if I married someone like you."

Asshole.

"What I still don't get is *why*," I say. "You have everything already. A high-paying job and a family trust, houses, a Manhattan apartment..."

"I didn't have *this*," he says, again, spreading his arms around as if this craggy peak is worth killing for. "I didn't want to rely on my parents anymore. They use money to control me. This way, I'll have my own pile of wealth...*and* theirs, eventually."

"But why the convoluted act for these past months?" I ask them. "Breaking into the house? Leaving runes at my door? For what?"

"It worked so well on Jacqueline that I knew you'd be easy," Teresa says, smiling proudly. "And I didn't have to break in.

Wesley gave me a key to your place on day one. It was important that you leave a well-documented trail of obsessing about fairytales and serial killers and paranormal bullshit. Witchcraft. Runes. You told everyone you got messages that no one else saw. Fake home invasions? People following you? You're not *well*, Rose."

"People *were* following me."

"Not people. Person. Me." Teresa jabs her own chest with two gloved fingers. "You needed to get away. You were losing your mind, and you unwisely ventured up into the Alps on a frigid winter day. Your frantic husband called me for help, and we followed you, but it was too late. The Swiss only look so hard when there are witnesses to an unfortunate fall."

Wesley is nodding along. "Mountain rescue doesn't search bottomless crevasses," he says. "Especially when the missing woman has no family to make an uproar, go to the press, or even look for her."

I'm starting to freeze. I wiggle my toes to stop them from going numb. I need this to go on for as long as necessary. *Stall, stall, stall.*

"Why kill Jacqueline? What did she ever do to either of you?"

"Ugh, that busybody. She came to my apartment to get that stupid book," Teresa, apparently still angry, says. "She caught your husband and me in flagrante delicto, and she knew it was more than an affair. She knew something big was going down, and since she always hated me, I knew she'd fuck everything up. We had no choice."

"Keep telling yourself that," I say. "How did the two of you pull it off?"

I race to cobble together a timeline. If they were scaring Jacqueline for days by the time she visited me, and Wesley and I had been in town less than two weeks, then they must have been sleeping together since virtually the day we arrived. I think about Wesley going on a long "run" while I napped after we got off our night flight. There's every chance he was with Teresa, and now I want to throw up.

"Wesley told Peter he was too drunk to drive home from poker night and pretended to pass out on the sofa, and when everyone was asleep, he packed Jacqueline's things and left that note on the computer." Teresa taps Wesley on his upper arm. "But this dope left one of her passports behind. Americans have trouble grasping the concept of dual citizenship."

It's not hard to figure out what happened next. "Meanwhile," I say, "you were in Zurich drugging my drink and planting spyware on my phone. You must have raced back."

"Did the trip in forty minutes flat," she says. "I wanted an unimpeachable alibi. Clubbing in Zurich with you and Seychelle? No way I had anything to do with Jacqueline disappearing that night."

"But you did, though," I point out, because I'm starting to understand the plan now. "You texted her to meet you at Pickwick's for an urgent matter."

"Yes!" Teresa smiles as if this is genuinely fun for her. "I told Jacqueline that Peter was at the hospital with one of the kids, and I insisted I drive *her* SUV because I was sober and she was upset. It was so easy. I took her to your place, Wesley brought your car home to meet me there when he was done, and we drove Jacqueline's Porsche back to the house."

"*You* killed her?" I say to Teresa. I glance at Wesley, who's watching the incoming storm like it's an IMAX movie rather than a dangerous, real-life weather event.

"I did," Teresa nods. "It was a simple strangling. I got in the back seat and used her silk scarf, and as much as she flailed, her hands couldn't reach me. It was quick. She wasn't strong."

The words from Jacqueline's tiny note speak to me like an echo from the past: *Find me.*

"I assume her phone and my passport are at your place," I say. "But where is Jacqueline? Where did you put her body?"

"You don't get to know everything. This isn't where we reveal every detail on your command," Teresa says. "I'm sure you're aware there are a million gorges and crevasses and rushing rivers in the general area."

I'm recalling what Carrie said about how the expats in this town might not kill, but were likely to stand by and let it happen.

"You both knew Peter was likely to join in on the narrative about Jacqueline leaving him, because he was banging the nanny and he'd told a bunch of people the romance was gone from his marriage. You were pretty sure he wouldn't make waves for TIG—or make himself any more of a suspect than he already was."

I turn to my husband. "Big man," I say. "Having your girlfriend do your dirty work."

"Oh, those hands aren't clean," Teresa sings.

It takes me but a moment.

"Oh, my god," I cry. "Of course. You killed Astrid. You absolute psychopath!" I resist running up and punching him, because it will make it easier for him to toss me off the cliff. "How *could* you, Wesley? What's wrong with you people? All this for a big house? A Porsche? To feel important?"

That's when everything falls into place. The details don't matter, I realize now. It's the *why* that got us here, the *why* that caused so much damage. The evil is bottomless. Wesley Blackwood is a psychopath, and the game and the killing and the manipulation have always been a way for him to feel alive. He's been toying with Darlene since college, and, boiled down, this expat drama is the same frat party game, just with higher stakes.

Darlene entered his life again last summer and he saw a chance to play again, to feel something. Anything.

Vi nailed it when she said, *There's some evil you can't account for.* Suspecting my husband might've killed Astrid and *knowing* he murdered a good-hearted woman peels away the last thin skin of hope protecting me.

I finger the pentacle around my neck. Astrid died for these megalomaniacs. I want to turn and run down the hill, but then what?

"Why?" I scream it. "Why are you two doing this?"

Wesley sighs in exasperation. "You haven't been paying attention, Rose. TIG is everything. They're everywhere. They're invested in all the richest sectors and businesses. But joining The Group at this level requires sacrifices. You have to follow their rules. Thanks to you and the social club, I'm set for life."

"Congratulations," I say to my husband. "You sold your soul for a desk job at a marketing company."

He purses his lips. "I suppose I shouldn't be surprised you don't get it," he says. "Who would want more than this? What else is there? Don't say fame; fame is gauche and invasive.

Notoriety stops you from doing the things you really want to do, because everyone's watching. This place is the essence of everything the human species ever sought. Beauty, comfort, fine food, fine wine, friends and eventually, Swiss citizenship."

"You don't really think you'll get away with this," I say.

I'm not sure where the bravado comes from, but it bubbles up and I go with it.

Teresa offers the sympathetic head tilt you'd give a young child. "We *have* gotten away with it. That's the beauty of the expat community. We're transients and movers. Expat life is about sudden departures, new people, saying goodbye, never really staying long enough to create strong bonds or truly know a person."

Teresa smiles. "Now, if you don't mind, I'll take that rock on your finger. The Blackwood family diamond is mine. Always has been."

I ignore her demand. "You two are in serious denial. All psychopaths eventually turn on each other."

As if on cue, Wesley turns to Teresa. "Darlene, honey, there's something I've wanted to say for awhile now."

She reaches up, smiling shyly, touching his cheek with one gloved hand. "Tell me, baby."

She truly believes she has him.

"That Ivy League professor you call a mentor? The one who sponsored you with TIG?"

Teresa/Darlene's face wobbles. She's starting to get it now.

"He was using you," Wesley smiles. "You know that, right? Wealthy, powerful people need lower-class folks like you to do their dirty work, and more important, to take the fall for them."

He turns to me. "You're both trash. And I'm going to stumble back down this mountain after trying to save two dumb American girls who got too close to the edge for a selfie, and, as often happens these days, things went horribly wrong."

I can see Teresa is in shock, and she isn't pivoting as quickly as Wesley and I have. She truly thought he was hers, that she was the one person who could change him and control him. Except you can't trust a narcissist and a psychopath. Their special skill is to make you think you can. I know that now, far too late.

"You couldn't possibly have thought I'd ever *marry* you, Darlene. You should know better than that."

Darlene opens her mouth, manages to get out a few words, "Wait, but Wes—"

While she is mid-word, Wesley shoots one arm out to deliver a powerful sucker punch. The force of it pushes Teresa so hard she can't hold her footing, and she tumbles over the edge, screaming *Wessss-leyyyy* with a guttural terror that echoes through the gorge and burrows into my skull until it stops, suddenly and completely.

Wesley peeks over the edge and shakes his head as if it is a shame his longtime love is gone, as if someone else has done this, as if he had no hand in it.

I again consider rushing him, but one false move and a swift hit from his fit body and I'll go over, too. I'll have no chance to get out of this.

He reaches out one long arm and wiggles his gloved fingers to beckon me to the edge. "Your turn," he says.

It takes everything in me, every acting skill I can muster, every bit of will, but I do it; I start laughing out loud, mocking, cackling, and doubling over for effect. Ten-year-old Violet speaks to me from the past, from that playground in Seagrass Cove: *Men are afraid women will laugh at them.*

"Fuck you," I scream through forced belly laughs, and because of a nervous reflex, I think, the laughter becomes real and therefore more convincing. My husband's bravado wavers; I see it in his trembling lips.

The thing is, through all the lecturing and Teresa's screaming, Wesley didn't hear a crunching sound coming from a sparse wood about thirty yards to my right. It's the crisp, fast, determined sound of boots on packed snow.

"You're going to have to fight me," I stall, catching my breath. "You're going to have bloody scratches and bruises and a fat lip. You won't get away with this."

Wesley runs through the snow right at me, and before I can react, he grabs me in a bear hug and drags me toward the edge.

"Bullshit," he grunts. "Both of your parents are MIA. No siblings, a dead grandmother. No one's going to file a report. Who's coming for you, Rosie?"

"You're right about the family," I say, going limp, hoping my dead weight will stop him in his tracks because struggling isn't working. "But you're wrong about the other thing."

"Oh?" He stops as I slip out of his arms and manage to scramble to my feet.

"You didn't account for the Best Friend Factor," I say, pointing toward the wood.

CHAPTER
FIFTY

"**O**h, hey, y'all," Violet calls as she stomps toward us like she's meeting us for happy hour. I'm in awe of her cockiness. It's a calculated move to show this asshole he doesn't scare her, and it's an epic performance.

Wesley rushes me so fast I can't get away and locks me in a choke hold.

"What took you so long?" I gasp.

"I was supposed to follow your *car*," Vi replies. "I didn't plan for a foot expedition across the Arctic tundra."

She gestures down to her jeans, which are coated with a layer of ice, not to mention boots that are more suited to a stroll down Fifth Avenue than an Alpine trail.

"Thankfully, I had this to track you." Vi holds up her phone, then swivels when she hears a noise behind her, and I see a thin man emerging. "*And* I bumped into a brilliant guide along the way. I asked him if he'd seen the adorable newlyweds today, and whaddaya know, he had—and he was suspicious."

"What the hell is going on?" Wesley is spitting with rage.

"Here he is now," Vi says as Chicken Man/Karl/Güggeliman strides up to us.

"Karl!" I smile through my shock. "*How?*"

"Hello again, Rose." He shoots a withering look to Wesley, who has dragged me until we're steps from the edge. "Like I said, you must go *around*."

"What the hell is going on?" My husband is slow to understand.

"We're flipping the narrative," I say. "No more jetlagged, helpless wife dependent on you for everything. Welcome to your comeuppance."

I turn to Violet. "Did you get any of that?"

She holds up her phone. "I did. Still recording. Some of it might be muffled, but you got it too, right?"

"Yep," I gurgle, glancing down at my coat pocket, where the microphone end of my burner phone has been poking out the whole time. I hid it in the crotch of my pants before we left the house, then stashed it in my coat pocket during my "toilet" break.

"Let her go," Chicken Man orders.

"Not a chance," Wesley replies. "I'm walking out of here with her and you're going to get out of my way. You can't prove anything. The police will take The Group's word for it. They don't care about foreigners. TIG will take care of me. A muffled recording that could easily be faked means nothing."

"You can't fake those screams." I tell him.

"*What?*" Vi asks me.

"It was Darlene the whole time. Teresa is Darlene. She went over the cliff. Wesley pushed her."

"Wait, who's Teresa again?" Vi knits her brow.

"I'll explain everything when I can talk again." My husband's forearm is pressing into my windpipe.

"Maybe they do not care much about you foreigners," Karl says to Wesley. "But they care very much about Luzern's Güggeliman and his beloved murdered sister, who spent two days a week at the old folks' home reading to the residents."

"What the hell is a Güggeliman?" Wesley loosens his grip, probably unconsciously, and I use the chance to go limp again. I slip through his arms, fall to the ground, and roll away.

Karl pulls a gun from inside of his coat, cocks it, and shoots Wesley in the shoulder. The guy has to be the quickest draw on the German side. "That's for my sister."

Wesley cries out and crumples, holding his chest as he hits the snow. I'm triple shocked right now, because I didn't have a clue Karl was Astrid's brother. I scramble to my feet once again and run to my friends.

"Whoa," Violet cries. "I thought Switzerland didn't allow guns?"

"Non-citizens can't have them," Karl replies. "But all Swiss homes do. We are the porcupine army. Everyone is armed, and when there is a threat to our nation, every home will rise up and fight."

I'm watching Wesley, who is incandescent with rage and, I hope, in extreme agony. His eyes are the most honest I believe I've ever seen them: reflections of pure hatred and a loss of control. I smile at him.

"How the *fuck*," he says through gritted teeth. He wants to murder me in front of everyone.

"We saw your half-baked kidnapping plot coming a mile away," Violet says.

"We've been recording everything since we found your spyware," I add. "You're our first podcast. You're going to be famous whether you like it or not."

There is a new sound: the feral staccato of dogs barking down the mountain, followed by the roar of a helicopter flying over the trees. A blast of snow envelops us until we are invisible.

"What is this?" I shout over the blades.

Vi shades her eyes and watches them come. Three cantonal police officers and two German Shepherds are approaching us from below, and a high-tech, fancy red helicopter is landing between us and the woods.

"I called the cops and told them I lost my keys up here," Vi shouts. "I figured they'd send the dogs like that time you lost yours."

Wesley appears to be bleeding out, with claret blossoming in the snow around him. Two people in red jumpsuits spill out of the helicopter as the pilot cuts the engines.

"Mountain rescue." Karl turns to me. "My son is a pilot and guide for Air-Alpine, the most elite rescue team in Switzerland. I called them after I met your friend."

A strapping man of about thirty-five jogs up to us. "Grüezi, Gérald," Karl greets his son.

Karl speaks to him in German, and they both rush over to the edge of the gorge, presumably looking for Darlene. Vi and I follow and peek over, and I'm thrilled I didn't know earlier how deadly the drop is. It's unfathomably deep and covered in jagged rocks all the way down.

Gérald shakes his head as if to say there's no hope. No one could survive that drop.

Karl turns to Vi and me. "You should go with the rescue team. You'll be safe," Karl says. "I'll hike back down with the police."

"I'm terrified of flying," Violet says, hugging herself. "I don't know if I can get on that thing."

Gérald is next to her in an instant.

"Do not be afraid," he says, then catches her as she loses her footing. She takes a suspiciously long moment before she manages to right herself.

Gérald holds her for as long as it takes. I watch this instant chemistry and I think, *Here we go again.* Karl is talking to the police, gesturing to Wesley and then to me. Wesley is now trying to stagger down the mountain, but a German Shepherd is on him in a few brisk bounds.

When Violet is steady, the helicopter kicks into gear and Gérald shouts to us, "We must get going. The weather is closing in. This is a recovery mission now. They will come back tomorrow to search."

He heads off with his partner to talk to the cantonal police, who seem utterly baffled about the scene, as Karl returns to check on Vi and me.

"I'm so sorry about Astrid," I tell Karl. "She was kind to me and she tried so hard to warn me. I had no idea she was your sister. Was she…was she a witch, or a wiccan, or…?"

"A *witch? Nein.*" He tilts his head and scrunches up his face.

"She was Swiss. This is our way."

I bite my lip, unsure if I should bring this delicate question up, knowing I had a hand in it by not seeing Wesley for who he is.

"How did you know Astrid was murdered?" I ask.

"The police said she fell carrying laundry down the stairs. Astrid did not do laundry," he replies. "Ever. I visited her every week to do it for her. I found her at the bottom of the stairs in the early morning before I went to work that day. The laundry was strewn everywhere, like it was tossed there, and there wasn't much of it."

"She tried to warn me, but I didn't understand," I say, my voice cracking. "I'm so sorry, Karl."

He shakes his head and meets my eyes in that unnerving way the Swiss do, though I have to admit it's growing on me.

"Do not blame yourself," he says. "That man did this, not you. Astrid asked me to translate between her and her neighbor so she could talk to you about your husband, and of course I did not know the neighbor was you. But then we agreed she should not do that, because if she did, it could make things worse for you. She wanted to get you away from him but not put you in danger.

"She wanted to get to know you better before she made trouble. It all started when she saw your husband with a smaller woman. They were carrying a dark-haired lady into your car. When my sister stared after them, they told her the woman was too drunk and needed to be taken home. But it didn't look right to Astrid. She pressed them, but the sober woman shouted at her in German. Astrid had no recourse. All she could do was try to learn more, to comfort you when she could."

"She was a wonderful woman," I say. "And Karl…your English is perfect. You never needed practice."

"Eh." He shrugs. "You seemed like you could use a friend."

With Chicken Man's statements and our recordings, I hold onto hope that Wesley will be charged and prosecuted. The BMW is fitted with the tracking device he was so excited about, so I'm hopeful it will lead authorities to Jacqueline's body. I'll do everything I can to make it happen.

"I need a drink," Violet says. "We can get something to eat and start sketching out the storyline for our podcast."

"I'll take you to town when this all blows over. I mean, as soon as the police let us," I reply.

"I want to see this famous Pickwick's where it all went down. I want a cider and black," Vi says.

"Sure. And I still haven't been to the *Kunstmuseum*," I say, but I barely hear myself. I am floating. The exhaustion. The unconscious pouring out of my emotions, the unknowable finally revealed, bringing with it pain and catharsis.

My knees buckle and I sink into the snow.

Violet cries out, "Oh!" and she reaches down, crouches, holds me as I collapse.

I hear my own voice, wobbly but determined.

"Violet?"

"Yes, sweetie."

"Thank you."

With that, the dam bursts, the tears come, and Violet holds me and rocks me in the snow as all the buried knowledge and grief and loss overflows at once, banging down that iron door until I can't ignore it a moment longer.

I hear the familiar murder of crows, its wings flapping in unison, its calls growing distant as they fly away from me.

Notes & Acknowledgements

This book is a work of fiction, though naturally there are moments and settings inspired by real expat life, and those are a nod and a wink to my expatriate friends, my Swiss neighbors and friends, and the Canton of Lucerne. Dark and unnerving as this book is in parts, it is a love letter to Switzerland. My years as an expatriate provided some of the most exciting, dramatic, and valuable experiences of my life.

I am forever thankful to our next-door neighbors, whose kindness in our last months in the country can never be repaid. Thank you to Güggeliman, who practiced German with me in real life and let me cut the line when (legitimately!) necessary.

I can never forget our beloved SASL (Swiss American Society of Lucerne), whose members welcomed us and eased our way into a new world with kindness, understanding and friendship. Thank you to Helen Houseman for a mean artichoke dip and for being there for one of the toughest times of my life, to our good friends the Smiths, to fellow expat and author Carris Kane for being an emergency beta reader, and all the other expats who were briefly in my life during that time.

For this novel I took that wonderful experience and those lovely people and let my imagination run wild, turning the most dramatic elements of expat life into a twisty mystery, my favorite kind of story to read *and* write. I hope readers one day get to visit the locations I've written about here, because Lucerne is a wonderful place to explore.

xoCourtney

Real-life view from the balcony at the home of "Rose" and "Wesley"
© *Courtney Hargrove*

Other Titles by Courtney Hargrove

"Just a great read. Prepare to be amazed. Be careful of [the] wow factor in this book."—*Amazon reviewer*

"I couldn't put this book down. I fell asleep to it."— *Goodreads reviewer*

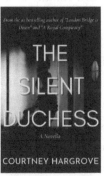

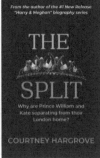

Content Warning

This book is a psychological mystery/thriller and contains the expected dark moments and betrayals referenced in the description, plus:

Gaslighting
Spousal emotional abuse
Motherhood
Drug use/addiction
Brief, over-the-clothes nonconsensual groping and mention of sexual assault
Fertility issues
Discussion of dark folklore and witchcraft
Some swearing
Death of a character's father in flashback
Some flashbacks to playground bullying
Murder, attempted murder, and discussion of human trafficking
Hostage-taking
Infidelity
Mention of depression

I truly hope I covered all points likely to upset a reader, as I don't want anyone to encounter unexpected triggers in my work. I'm sure reviewers and readers will let me know if I have, so in later editions I can add anything I might've missed.

Thank you for reading.
xoCourtney

Made in United States
Troutdale, OR
08/15/2024

22069620R00235